RAISING THE ROOF

RAISING THE ROOF
Children's Stories and Activities on Houses

JAN IRVING
and
ROBIN CURRIE

Illustrated by
Marijean Trew

1991
TEACHER IDEAS PRESS
A Division of
Libraries Unlimited, Inc.
Englewood, Colorado

TEACHER IDEAS PRESS
A Division of Libraries Unlimited, Inc.
P.O. Box 6633
Englewood, CO 80155-6633

Library of Congress Cataloging-in-Publication Data

Irving, Jan, 1942-
    Raising the roof : children's stories and activities on houses /
Jan Irving and Robin Currie ; illustrated by Marijean Trew.
        xiv, 244 p. 22x28 cm.
        Includes bibliographical references and index.
        ISBN 0-87287-786-8
        1. Libraries, Children's--Activity programs. 2. Dwellings--Study
and teaching (Primary) 3. Children--Books and reading. I. Currie,
Robin, 1948-   . II. Trew, Marijean. III. Title.
Z718.3.I785 1991
372.64-2--dc20   90-27475
                                                          CIP

To all our homes on this good earth
May we share them in peace and understanding

Contents

Introduction

Raising the Roof: Children's Stories and Activities on Houses is a source book for program and classroom planning. It is similar in purpose and structure to *Mudluscious: Stories and Activities Featuring Food for Preschool Children* (Libraries Unlimited, 1986); *Glad Rags: Stories and Activities Featuring Clothes for Children* (Libraries Unlimited, 1987); and *Full Speed Ahead!: Stories and Activities for Children on Transportation* (Libraries Unlimited, 1988). These books introduce children to quality literature and provide enrichment activities in which children can actively participate. The stories and activities are appropriate for children preschool age through third grade.

Raising the Roof uses homes and houses as the focus for learning to appreciate language just as *Mudluscious* used a food theme, *Glad Rags* used clothing, and *Full Speed Ahead!* used transportation. Children will learn such expressions as "no place like home," "roll out the red carpet," "home is where the heart is," and "living in the dog house." Traditional folk literature frequently features homes as the beginning and end of an adventure. Here we offer new versions of "The Three Little Pigs," "Goldilocks and the Three Bears," and "The Gingerbread Man" to heighten children's appreciation of these tales. The more than 250 picture books annotated in the eight chapters of *Raising the Roof* provide a wide variety of stories. They range from simple board books and the comforting texts of modern classics such as *Good Night, Moon* for the youngest child, to the sophisticated humor of Jon Scieszka's *The True Story of the Three Little Pigs* for older children (and even adults!).

Schools, childcare centers, and libraries are developing literature based programs that extend interests beyond basal readers and workbook exercises. The stories and activities in *Raising the Roof* will encourage reading readiness and promote the enjoyment of stories so that young readers stay interested in books beyond decoding skills and classroom assignments. A special focus on whole language activities appears in each chapter under the heading "Floor Plans" and the skills index, a feature of our other books, includes even more emphasis on language skills.

Homes and shelter are a basic necessity for all people, and the topic of homes is emotionally related to families and family life. Although our definition of *family* has changed to accommodate many different living arrangements, the word still suggests comfort, security, and belonging. Beyond the family unit, children will learn about different kinds of homes people live in, both in this country and around the world. Through the annotated book lists and activities we have created, we introduce homes in different cultures to sensitize children to the cultural diversity in our larger world home. We have made an effort to dispel sex-role stereotypes so both boys and girls will be encouraged to care for the home, decorate it, and even build it.

The scope of the chapters ranges from parts of a house to different kinds of homes, house construction, and remodeling. The first chapter, "Upstairs, Downstairs, and In My Lady's Chamber," looks at what rooms and objects make up a house. Chapter 2, "Highrise to Hillside," explores different kinds of homes in the city and country and homes away from home. (The divided family that maintains two homes is an important topic, but outside the scope of this book.) "Pyramids and Pagodas" traces homes from the beginning of humanity's need for shelter to the present and looks at homes in different cultures, celebrating our uniqueness rather than reinforcing stereotypes. Chapters 4 and 5, "All Spruced Up" and "More Room! More Room!," deal with the building, tearing down, remodeling, and cleaning of homes of all kinds. That special territory of children, "Hidey Holes," is the theme of chapter 6. It shows us little places and private spaces that children can enjoy without grown-ups. Animal homes are the focus of chapter 7, "Caves, Coops, and Cages," both homes animals build themselves and those provided by humans. The final chapter is for the dreamer. "Castles in the Air" will lift children's imaginations to the world of fantasy and fairy tale dwellings.

Each chapter is structured in parallel form. The chapter introduction presents the overall theme and purpose of the subject. The literature section of each chapter provides annotations of picture books on a subtheme and then includes related literature activities from fingerplays and action rhymes to a wide variety of storytelling methods such as flannel-board and participatory stories told with masks. There are also many cut-and-tell or draw-and-tell stories. Games follow the quieter literature activities to provide a change of pace. A craft section follows.

An addition to this book is the final section of each chapter entitled "Floor Plans." Featured in this section is a noteworthy book that captures the essence of the theme. This focus book lays the groundwork for suggested reading, speaking, and writing activities. Because of the current curricular interest in developing whole language skills, our floor plans can inspire teachers to discover even more ways for children to interact with language in the classroom. Whether you use a whole language approach in your school or use these activities with children in a public library setting, we have designed these plans for you so that children become so actively involved with language that it becomes a part of their lives.

The two-part skills index will guide you in selecting activities that teach cognitive and social interaction skills. The skill areas have been modified from skills we identified in our previous books and include fourteen skills: self-awareness, gross motor, color recognition, counting, size and shape relationships, following directions, group cooperation, role playing/creative dramatics, sequencing, classification, musical, artistic, language play/rhythm, and word recognition. In addition to this core list are the new areas of cause and effect and predictable language/predictable outcome. These last two skill areas are included as thinking skills in most language arts programs.

We thank the many people who have continued their interest and support of our books, especially Paula Brandt, Carol Elbert, Pat Franzen, and Phyllis Hilston.

Setting Up the Program

We suggest books and activities so you can create your own program. Your final selection of the type and length of activities and stories should be based on your own situation. To give you some ideas, here are two sample programs the way we might set them up. The programs are derived from chapters 6 and 8.

HIDEY HOLES

Sample Program*

Initiating Activities:	Begin with "Hidey Hole Hello" (p. 136) as the children arrive. Repeat this until all the children have introduced themselves.
First Story:	Start the program with *Maebelle's Suitcase* (p. 138). In this treehouse story Maebelle joins the birds.
Related Activities:	Follow up the treehouse book with "This Place Is for the Birds" (p. 148), a participatory story with bird masks.
Second Story:	Continue with the book *There's a Nightmare in My Closet* (p. 138). This popular closet story might encourage children to talk about their own nighttime fears. You might like to have a sock puppet around to listen to each child's brief account.
Related Activities:	Sing "Secret Places I Like to Hide" (p. 143) with children adding actions and sounds as appropriate. Then share the cut-and-tell story "Inside Penelope's Closet" (p. 150) and discover another creepy, crawly closet creature.
Third Story:	Read *A Little House of Your Own* (pp. 137 and 155) as a culmination.
Related Activities:	Invite children to act out the rhyme "Secret Hiding Places" (p. 152).
Final Activities:	Use "Home in a Trunk" (p. 153) as an action rhyme and then make "Trunk Collage Craft" (p. 154).
	Use the writing activity from "Floor Plans," having children write about things they would like to do in a hiding place all their own.

---

*Based on chapter 6.

CASTLES IN THE AIR

Sample Program*

Initiating Activities:	Light a candle to set the magical mood of this fantasy and fairy tale house program as you read the poem "Magic Door" (p. 185).
First Story:	Read *The Fisherman and His Wife* (p. 191), the folk tale about a woman who overstepped the bounds in wishing for ever grander houses.
Related Activities:	Sing the song "Only in Fairyland" (p. 193), and then share another version of the fisherman and his wife story, "The Fisherman and His Wife Retold" (p. 201).
Second Story:	Read *The Three Little Pigs* by Marshall or select one of the other versions listed in the bibliography (p. 192).
Related Activities:	Engage children in the interactive story "Three Pigs in a Blanket" (p. 199).
Third Story:	Read *Hansel and Gretel* with illustrations by Susan Jeffers (p. 192).
Final Activities:	Change the quiet, slow pace by engaging children in the "Gingerbread House Made to Order" (p. 195) chant and playing the "Track the Treats Game" (p. 211).

---

*Based on chapter 8.

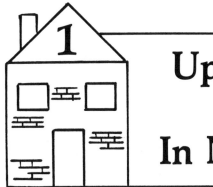

Upstairs, Downstairs, and In My Lady's Chamber

INTRODUCTION

Welcome to our book! Come and explore the rooms of a house, upstairs, downstairs, and, in the words of the Mother Goose rhyme, "in my lady's chamber." We begin with experiences that are close to home and common to most children's environments. The picture books in this chapter include beginning board books that simply identify rooms of the house as well as stories about children's favorite rooms and a prized piece of furniture. Here are poems and songs about the whole house, specific rooms of the house, and furniture and other items in those rooms.

The first subtheme of this chapter, "All around the House," includes books that take you on a tour through all the rooms of a house rather than focus on one room in particular. These are fascinating books for young children who are learning to identify places and things in their environment. But they are also excellent books for children beginning to read. The activities in this section include welcome chants and songs, stories, and activities that explore the full scope of a house.

The second subtheme, "Bedrooms, Bathrooms, and Breakfast Nooks," takes us to the specific rooms you find inside a house. The picture books focus on the three rooms of the subtheme—bedrooms, bathrooms, and kitchens. Our activities include stories about things a child keeps in his or her bedroom, songs about things children put in the bathtub, and songs about sounds we hear in the kitchen.

The third subtheme, "Beds, Chairs, and Stairs," takes a look at furniture and furnishings in the rooms of a house. The books include Ezra Jack Keats's classic *Peter's Chair* and the newer title *A Chair for My Mother*, by Vera Williams. Both books are about children who gain maturity as they pass on an outgrown chair to a younger sibling or help the family save for a much wanted chair. Many of the books in this section tell about the people who own the furniture as much as about the objects themselves. Our activities will teach classification, rhyme, and rhythm, as well as provide opportunities for creative dramatics.

Continue the language learning in the final section of the chapter, "Floor Plans." The focus book, *Ten, Nine, Eight*, will provide the springboard for reading, writing, and speaking activities you can develop with children in your classroom or library.

INITIATING ACTIVITY

ANYWHERE YOU HANG YOUR HAT IS HOME!

Greet each child with this cheery welcome. If the weather is too warm for them to be wearing hats, you might leave a pile of hats at the door for the children to put on and then hang up as they come in. Those already seated can do the motions with you.

One and two and three and four,	*(Hold up one finger at a time.)*
Who's that standing at the door?	*(Shade eyes with hand.)*
(Child's name)'s waiting on the mat.	*(Point to child.)*
Come on in and hang your hat!	*(Beckon with arm; touch head as if taking off hat.)*

LITERATURE-SHARING EXPERIENCES

Books for All around the House

Balian, Lorna. **Where in the World Is Henry?** Abingdon, 1972.
    A little boy's search for his dog, Henry, takes him from his own house and town out into his country, his continent, on to the farthest point in the universe and back. The boy finally finds Henry under the quilt at home.

Blocksma, Mary. **Did You Hear That?** Illustrated by Sandra Cox Kalthoff. Children's Press, 1983.
    Mysterious sounds lead a child to discover more and more creatures under the bed.

Coontz, Otto. **The Quiet House**. Little, Brown, 1978.
    A lonely dog finds three new friends in a surprising place.

Gretz, Suzanna. **Teddy Bears Stay Indoors**. Four Winds Press, 1970.
    The five fuzzy, colorful Teddy Bears amuse themselves on a rainy day by pretending that they explore outer space and go on other adventures.

Gridley, Sally. **Knock, Knock. Who's There?** Illustrated by Anthony Browne. Knopf, 1985.
    All sorts of creepy creatures knock on the door and ask to be let in, but the door only opens for Daddy, who brings hot chocolate and a bedtime story.

Hitte, Kathryn. **What Can You Do without a Place to Play?** Illustrated by Cyndy Szekeres. Parents' Magazine Press, 1971.
    A city boy describes some of the things he and his friends do for fun because they have no place to play.

Hooker, Ruth. **At Grandma and Grandpa's House**. Illustrated by Ruth Tosner. Whitman, 1986.
    Some of the pleasures at Grandma's and Grandpa's house include a long hall for running, a "staying overnight" room with bunk beds, and a yard with a tree to climb.

Kilroy, Sally. **Noisy Homes**. Four Winds Press, 1983.
    Sounds often heard around the house are represented in pictures and words, including the ring of the telephone and the splash of a baby in the bath.

LeSeig, Theo. **In a People House**. Illustrated by Roy McKie. Random House, 1972.
    A bird and a mouse discover all the things in a house, from chairs and stairs to keys and bureau drawers.

Let's Look All around the House. Photographs by Harold Roth. Grosset and Dunlap, 1988.
Clear color photographs picture rooms around the house, but the real fun is lifting the flaps and peeking into a coat closet, the refrigerator, the oven, and other places inside and outside.

Lobel, Arnold. **Owl at Home**. Harper & Row, 1975.
Owl has visitors and adventures right at home.

Lynn, Sara. **Home**. Macmillan, 1986.
Bold red, blue, yellow, and green illustrations and brief text show furnishings in a home.

Rockwell, Anne. **In Our House**. Crowell, 1985.
Each room of the house is identified along with things we do there and objects in that room. Rooms include the living room, the kitchen, the basement, the garage, the bathroom, and "my very own room."

Watson, Carol. **The House**. Illustrated by Colin King. Usborne, 1980.
Objects in each room of the house are illustrated and clearly labeled in this book for youngest readers or for new English speakers.

Related Activities for All around the House

WELCOME SONG
(Tune: "London Bridge")

Act out this song with two children forming a roof of a house in the traditional London Bridge fashion. Lower the roof on the words "Step right in!" As each child says his or her name, give out party hats and invite each child to sit down. After all children have been welcomed, you are ready for the next activity.

> Welcome to our open house,
> Open house, open house
> Welcome to our open house
> Step right in!
>
> Won't you tell us, what's your name
> What's your name, what's your name
> Won't you tell us what's your name
> (*Pause for child to say name, then—*)
> Welcome (Name)!

A PLACE FOR MY FACE
(Fingerplay)

Peek-a-boo	(*Hands to face.*)
Where are you?	
See the door	(*Move one hand back like door.*)
I'm peeking through	
Behind my fingers	(*Both hands up to face.*)
Is a place	
I can hide	
My smiling face.	(*Remove hands and smile.*)

AT MY HOUSE
(Counting Fingerplay)

There is one tree tall and green	(*Hold up one finger; reach arms overhead.*)
At my house	(*Touch straight fingertips overhead.*)
There are two doors in and out	(*Hold up two fingers; point fingers of each hand in opposite directions.*)
There is one tree tall and green	(*Hold up one finger; reach arms overhead.*)
At my house	(*Touch straight fingertips overhead.*)
There are three beds for sleepy heads	(*Hold up three fingers; rest head on hands.*)
There are two doors in and out	(*Hold up two fingers; point fingers of each hand in opposite directions.*)
There is one tree tall and green	(*Hold up one finger; reach arms overhead.*)
At my house	(*Touch straight fingertips overhead.*)
There are four flowers in a row	(*Hold up four fingers; frame face with hands to become flower.*)
There are three beds for sleepy heads	(*Hold up three fingers; rest head on hands.*)
There are two doors in and out	(*Hold up two fingers; point fingers of each hand in opposite directions.*)
There is one tree tall and green	(*Hold up one finger; reach arms overhead.*)
At my house	(*Touch straight fingertips overhead.*)
There are five sidewalk cracks to hop	(*Hold up five fingers; hop.*)
There are four flowers in a row	(*Hold up four fingers; frame face with hands to become flower.*)
There are three beds for sleepy heads	(*Hold up three fingers; rest head on hands.*)
There are two doors in and out	(*Hold up two fingers; point fingers of each hand in opposite directions.*)
There is one tree tall and green	(*Hold up one finger; reach arms overhead.*)
At my house	(*Touch straight fingertips overhead.*)
And I live there too!	(*Point to self.*)

ROOMS OF THE HOUSE CHANT

Clap out the rhythm of this little verse, then at the end try to come up with as many names or different rooms of the house as you can. This should increase children's vocabularies as they discover such words as "conservatory" and "ballroom."

Upstairs, downstairs
Let's take a look
Name some room
Any little nook

Bathroom
Bedroom
Family Room
Den
Living Room

Parlor
Basement
Kitch-en
Playroom
Attic
Porch
Hall
Tell me
Have we
Named
Them all?

BREAKFAST SYMPHONY
(Action Rhyme)

Coffee perks	*(Open and close palms at shoulder height.)*
Clock rings	*(Wiggle wrists with hands flopping.)*
Yawn awake	*(Yawn.)*
Birds sing	*(Flap arms.)*
Paper lands	*(Clap.)*
Shower drips	*(Drop hands loosely to sides.)*
Snapping cereal	*(Snap fingers.)*
Smacking lips	*(Smack lips.)*
Bark, dog.	*(Bark.)*
Buzz, bee.	*(Wiggle fingers by ear.)*

(Say all together:)

Our house in the morning

Is a breakfast symphony!

WHAT'S THAT NOISE?
(A Participatory Chant)

Teach the children the lines they have in the chant. You may wish to have an assistant lead the children in their parts.

Leader: Creak, creak, creak.
Children: What's that noise?
Leader: That creaking noise,
That creaky, squeaky, eek-y noise?
Children: What's that noise?

Leader: It's just the hinges on the door
Or the aging wooden floor
Children: Well, I wasn't scared, anyway!

Leader: Squeak, squeak, squeak.
Children: What's that noise?
Leader: That squeaking noise,
That creaky, squeaky, eek-y noise?
Children: What's that noise?

Leader: It's just a tiny mouse
In the basement of this house
Children: Well, I wasn't scared, anyway!

Leader:	Eek, eek, eek.
Children:	What's that noise?
Leader:	That eek-ing noise,
	That creaky, squeaky, eek-y noise?
Children:	What's that noise?
Leader:	It's just a silly bat
	And the attic's where he's at
Children:	Well, I wasn't scared, anyway!
Leader:	Just an ordinary house
	With ordinary noise,
	So don't be scared at all ...
	(*Get softer and softer on this line.*)
	BOO! (*Loud.*)

WHAT IS MAKING THE NOISE AND WHY?
(Draw-and-Tell Story)

Teach the children to make the eerie sound (E-e-e-eo-o-o-ow) with you. Then tell the story while you draw the figure as shown.

One day when Danny was in his room, he heard a strange sound. It was not the garbage disposal grinding up garbage. It was not the radio playing a funny song. It was not the washing machine in the spin cycle. It sounded like this: E-e-e-eo-o-o-ow.

Danny was a little afraid, but he went to look for the sound. E-e-e-eo-o-o-ow. Danny heard the noise again. What was making that noise and why?

First Danny looked in the kitchen in the sugar bowl. (*Draw small circle.*)

O

No noise there.

Then he looked in the dining room in a teacup. (*Draw another small circle next to the first.*)

OO

No noise there.

E-e-e-eo-o-o-ow. Danny heard the noise again. What was making that noise and why?

Danny looked in the dog's water bowl. (*Draw medium circle around first two.*)

No noise there.

So he looked all around the outdoor swimming pool. (*Draw large oval below medium circle.*)

No noise there.

E-e-e-eo-o-o-ow. Danny heard the noise again. What was making that noise and why?

Quickly Danny looked all the way up in the attic and all the way down into the basement. (*Add long curved line at bottom of large oval.*)

No noise there.

He looked through one-two-three-four-five-six slats on the window shades. (*Draw three short, straight lines below each of the first two circles.*)

No noise there.

E-e-e-eo-o-o-ow. Danny heard the noise again. What was making that noise and why?

Then he lifted the lid on the piano and put it down. (*Add triangle to one side of the top of the medium circle.*)

No noise there.

And he lifted the garage door and put it down. (*Add triangle to other side of the top of the medium circle.*)

No noise there.

E-e-e-eo-o-o-ow. Danny heard the noise again. What was making that noise and why? Finally he lifted the lid on the clothes hamper. (*Draw inverted "v" below first two circles.*)

There was the noise. What do you suppose was making that noise? (*Cat.*) (*Add eyes to first circles drawn.*)

And why? (*She wanted out of the hamper.*)

Danny took the cat out of the hamper and put her down in a sunny spot in the living room. After that the only noise he heard was purrrrrr.

WHERE DOES IT GO?

Fold a piece of cardboard in half. Cut four doors in one side. Tape the edges together. Number the doors 1, 2, 3, 4. Behind door 1 draw or paste a cutout picture of a table and chairs. Behind door 2 draw or paste a cutout picture of a bathtub and sink. Behind door 3 draw or paste a cutout picture of a TV and sofa. Behind door 4 draw or paste a cutout picture of a bed and night light. (*If you use other objects, adjust the story and pictures accordingly.*)

Mark and his family were moving to a new house. Mark was not sure about this new house. In his old house he knew just where everything belonged.

When they got to the new house, Mark's mother said, "Please put the placemats in the dining room. Do you want me to show you where they belong?"

"I can do it," said Mark. "I know where everything belongs."

So Mark put the placemats in a room that had a white tub and a shiny sink. (*Open door 2.*) Was that right for placemats? (*No.*) Mark's mother didn't think so either, so she helped Mark put them in the room with the big round table and the six chairs. (*Open door 1.*)

Then Mark's mother said, "Please put the bars of soap in the bathroom. Do you want me to show you where they belong?"

"I can do it," said Mark. "I know where everything belongs."

So Mark put the bars of soap in a room that had a TV and a long sofa. (*Open door 3.*) Was that right for bars of soap? (*No.*) Mark's mother didn't think so either, so she helped Mark put them in a room that had a white tub and a shiny sink. (*Open door 2.*)

Then Mark's mother said, "Please put the remote control in the family room. Do you want me to show you where it belongs?"

"I can do it," said Mark. "I know where everything belongs."

So Mark put the remote control in a room that had a soft bed and a night light. (*Open door 4.*) Was that right for a remote control? (*No.*) Mark's mother didn't think so either, so she helped Mark put it in a room that had a TV and a long sofa. (*Open door 3.*)

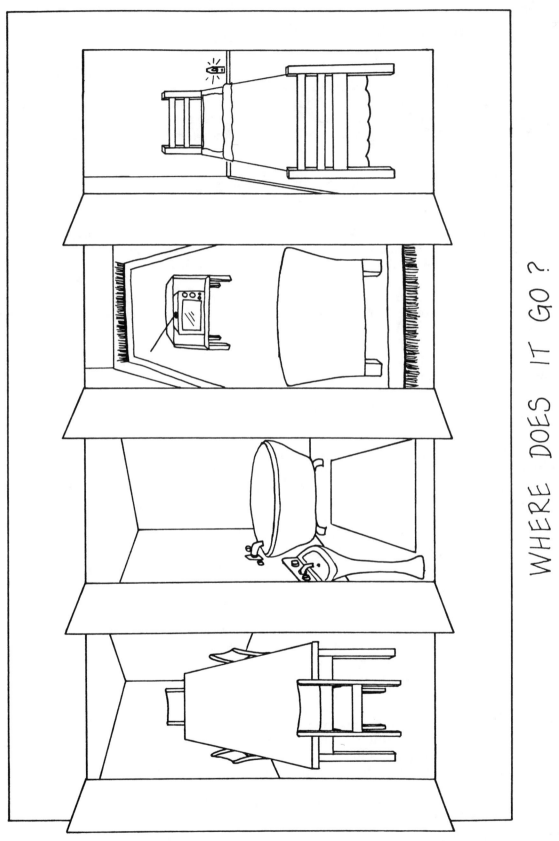

WHERE DOES IT GO?

("Where Does It Go?" continues on page 10.)

Finally it was time for bed. Mark's mother said, "Please put your teddy bear in your room. Do you want me to show you where it belongs?"

"I can do it," said Mark. "I know where everything belongs."

So Mark put his teddy bear in a room that had a big round table and six chairs. (*Open door 1.*) Was that right for a teddy bear? (*No.*) Mark's mother didn't think so either, so she helped Mark put it in a room that had a soft bed and a night light. (*Open door 4.*)

As Mark's mother tucked him in, she said, "Thank you for all your help today. You put away the placemats and the bars of soap and the remote control and your teddy bear."

"Yes," said Mark in a sleepy voice. "And NOW I know where everything belongs."

JUST THE RIGHT PLACE
(Object Story)

Use the following objects (or pictures of them) to tell this story: toaster, hat, rug, tennis racket, lamp, and two toy rocking chairs. You may wish to place the objects around the room as you tell the story and have the children help you remember where they are.

Mr. Murphy had an old toaster. It was too good to throw out and too old to use every day. So he took his old toaster and put it in the closet. "Now," said Mr. Murphy, "I found the right place for the toaster." And he did.

Mr. Murphy had an old hat. It was too good to throw out and too old to use every day. So he took his old hat to the closet, but the toaster was there. So he put his old hat in the attic. "Now," said Mr. Murphy, "I found the right place for the hat." And he did.

Mr. Murphy had an old rug. It was too good to throw out and too old to use every day. So he took his old rug to the closet, but the toaster was there. He took his old rug to the attic, but the hat was there. So he put his old rug in the basement. "Now," said Mr. Murphy, "I found the right place for the rug." And he did.

Mr. Murphy had an old tennis racket. It was too good to throw out and too old to use every day. So he took his old tennis racket to the closet, but the toaster was there. He took his old tennis racket to the attic, but the hat was there. He took his old tennis racket to the basement, but the rug was there. Finally he put his old tennis racket under the bed. "Now," said Mr. Murphy, "I found the right place for the tennis racket." And he did.

Mr. Murphy had an old lamp. It was too good to throw out and too old to use every day. So he took his old lamp to the closet, but the toaster was there. He took his old lamp to the attic, but the hat was there. He took his old lamp to the basement, but the rug was there. He took his old lamp under the bed, but the tennis racket was there. Finally he put his old lamp in the garage. "Now," said Mr. Murphy, "I found the right place for the lamp." And he did.

Mr. Murphy had an old rocking chair. It was too good to throw out and too old to use every day. So he took his old rocking chair to the closet, but the toaster was there. He took his old rocking chair to the attic, but the hat was there. He took his old rocking chair to the basement, but the rug was there. He took his old rocking chair under the bed, but the tennis racket was there. He took his old rocking chair to the garage, but the lamp was there. Finally Mr. Murphy put his old rocking chair on the front porch.

And then a funny thing happened. His neighbor came over and said, "Are you having a porch sale? I'll give you $10 for that old rocking chair." Mr. Murphy sold the rocking chair to his neighbor. And he got a wonderful idea. He went and got the old toaster from the closet and the old hat from the attic. He got the old rug from the basement, the old tennis racket from under the bed, and the old lamp from the garage. Then he put them all on the porch. In no time at all they were sold (some people will buy anything at a porch sale!).

Mr. Murphy took the money and bought a new rocking chair. He put it on the porch, but before anyone could buy it he sat in it and rocked and rocked and rocked. He liked his new rocking chair on the porch. "Now," said Mr. Murphy, "I found the right place for everything." And he did.

HERE IS THE HOUSE
(Fingerplay)

This fingerplay may remind you of "The Church and the Steeple," but it is a different version about the home.

Here is the house	(*Fists together.*)
With the roof on top	(*Touch index fingers.*)
Open the doors	(*Separate thumbs.*)
See Mom and Pop	(*Hold up middle fingers.*)
Open them more	(*Hold up all fingers.*)
The kids are inside	(*Wiggle fingers.*)
They're playing a game	
Of run and hide	(*Clap hands and hide them behind your back.*)
Here comes Grandpa	(*Hold up one little finger.*)
Here comes Gram	(*Hold up other little finger.*)
Here comes Susie	(*Add one ring finger.*)
Here comes Sam	(*Add other ring finger.*)
Here comes Mom	(*Add one middle finger.*)
Pop is last	(*Add other middle finger.*)
Into the house	(*Closed fists together.*)
The doors shut fast!	(*Thumbs together.*)

Books for Bedrooms, Bathrooms, and Breakfast Nooks

Bang, Molly. **Ten, Nine, Eight**. Greenwillow, 1983.
Numbers from ten to one are part of this lullaby about the things in a little girl's room as she goes to bed.

Blocksma, Mary. **What's in the Tub?** Illustrated by Sandra Cox Kalthoff. Children's Press, 1984.
Thor, the pet dog, throws many toys in the bathtub with the boy, and they both try to keep water off the floor. They are successful until Thor tries to jump into the tub, too.

Brown, Margaret Wise. **Good Night, Moon**. Illustrated by Clement Hurd. Harper, 1947.
This is a classic story about saying goodnight to each object in the bedroom, from the chairs to the pictures to the moon.

Emberley, Ed. **Home**. Little, Brown, 1987.
Part of the *First Words* series, this little board book identifies objects in the house such as the rug, mop, and bed—and people, too.

Our House. Illustrated by Roser Capdevila. Annick Press, 1985.
This wordless board book pictures hundreds of objects and things going on in the rooms of a house. The bidet pictured in the bathroom may need an explanation for American children.

Rockwell, Harlow. **My Kitchen**. Greenwillow, 1980.
Big colorful pictures enhance a child explaining how his lunch is prepared by looking at different parts of the kitchen.

Sendak, Maurice. **In the Night Kitchen**. Harper & Row, 1970.
   Humorous pictures enliven this story of a little boy's dream fantasy in which he helps three fat bakers get milk for the cake batter.

Titherington, Jeanne. **A Place for Ben**. Greenwillow, 1987.
   When baby Ezra's crib is moved into Ben's room, Ben feels as if he doesn't have a place of his own anymore. Ben adopts the back of the garage as his private place, but soon discovers it isn't much fun without a visitor.

Related Activities for Bedrooms, Bathrooms, and Breakfast Nooks

MUD ROOM
(Tune: "Pop! Goes the Weasel")

All around the rest of the house
We must be clean and tidy,
But when we come with messy boots
Go to the mud room.

Footprints, puddles, sloppy mess
It really doesn't matter
When we come with messy boots
Go to the mud room.

KEEP IT IN MY ROOM
(Poem with Objects)

If kids like to do one thing more than they like to collect things, they like to trade their things with their friends. Pass out the following objects to the children in your room: a microscope, a baseball bat, a puzzle, toy soldiers, a teddy bear, a rock collection, comic books, and a large stuffed horse. If you can't find some of these items, just substitute others and change the words in the poem. The last item should be something ridiculously large! Now, read the poem and ask the children to trade items with you as the items are named. You might end up having a discussion about things each child keeps in his or her room.

I have a microscope to trade,
One that's nearly new.
I want to trade for a baseball bat.
Is that okay with you?

I traded my microscope for a baseball bat,
Is that okay with you?
I know just where to put it.
I'll put it in my room.

I traded my baseball bat for a puzzle.
Is that okay with you?
I know just where to put it.
I'll put it in my room.

I traded my puzzle for a toy soldier.
Is that okay with you?
I know just where to put it.
I'll put it in my room.

I traded my toy soldier for a teddy bear.
Is that okay with you?
I know just where to put it.
I'll put it in my room.

I traded my teddy bear for a rock collection.
Is that okay with you?
I know just where to put it.
I'll put it in my room.

I traded my rock collection for a comic book.
Is that okay with you?
I know just where to put it.
I'll put it in my room.

I traded my comic book for a horse.
Is that okay with you?
But I don't know where to put it—
It's too big for my room!

I don't really want to trade my horse,
But I need room for two.
Come visit me in the garage—
Is that okay with you?

BEDROOM PETS
(Flannel-board Story)

Use flannel-board shapes of a gnat, crow, sow, bear, and dog to tell this funny story about some unlikely bedroom pets. Place pets on the board as they are mentioned in the story.

Stanley's mother said he could have any pet he wanted as long as he kept it in his room. So Stanley decided to get a pet gnat.

> The buzzing gnat said, "Fancy that!"
> "I'll move in to Stanley's room."

Stanley liked the gnat so much he decided to get a pet crow. A loudly squawking crow went into Stanley's room.

> The buzzing gnat said, "Fancy that!"
> The squawking crow said, "Do you know?"
> "I'll move in to Stanley's room."

Stanley liked the crow so much he decided to get a pet sow.

> The buzzing gnat said, "Fancy that!"
> The squawking crow said, "Do you know?"
> The squealing sow said, "See me now."
> "I'll move in to Stanley's room."

BEDROOM PETS

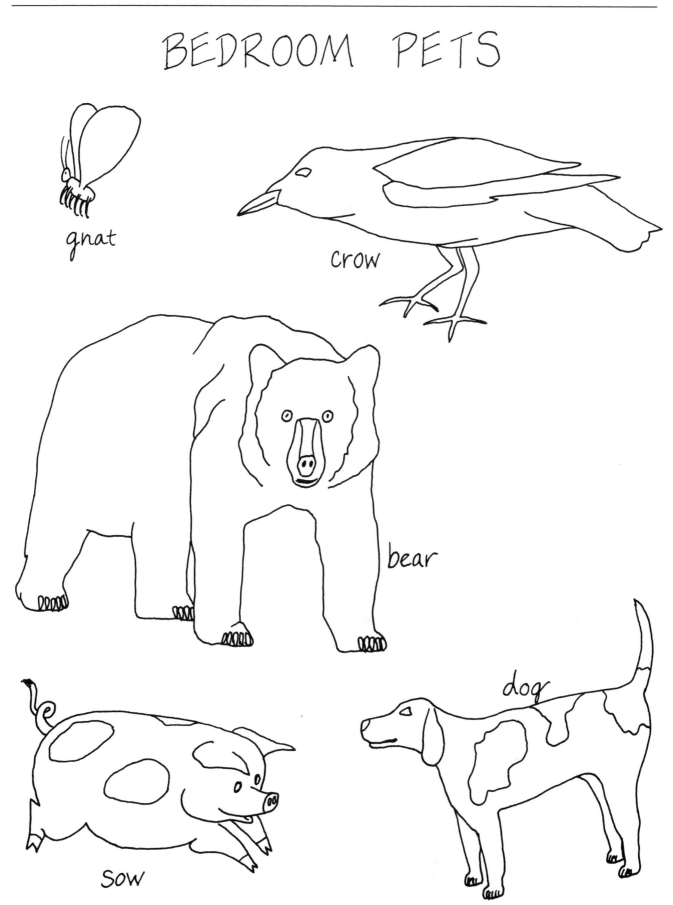

gnat

crow

bear

dog

sow

Stanley liked the sow so much he decided to get a pet bear.

> The buzzing gnat said, "Fancy that!"
> The squawking crow said, "Do you know?"
> The squealing sow said, "See me now."
> The lumbering bear said, "What a lair!"
> "I'll move in to Stanley's room."

One day Stanley's mother went into Stanley's room.

> The buzzing gnat said, "Fancy that!"
> The squawking crow said, "Do you know?"
> The squealing sow said, "See me now."
> The lumbering bear said, "What a lair!"
> But Mother, tough, said, "That's enough!"
> "Move out of Stanley's room."

And once all the bedroom pets were gone, Stanley's mother bought him a dog. But the dog had to live out in the doghouse!

KITCHEN SOUNDS SONGS
(Add-a-Verse, Tune: "Mary Had a Little Lamb")

> Soup is boiling on the stove
> On the stove, on the stove
> Soup is boiling on the stove
> Hear our kitchen sounds song!

> Bzz! The kitchen timer rings
> Timer rings, timer rings
> Bzz! The kitchen timer rings
> Hear our kitchen sounds song!

Make up your own verses with the children.

HOME COOKING
(Tune: "Home on the Range")

Oh, give me a dish
Whether beef, rice, or fish
That's been cooked up by someone at home.
If it smells good and hot,
Well, just look in the pot!
For good cooking there's no place like home!

Home-cooked on the range,
In the micro or top of the stove.
Pick up or dine out—
But you know there's no doubt
For good cooking there's no place like home!

SCRUBBY TUB BUBBLES
(Tune: "Goodnight, Ladies")

Counting bubbles,
Counting bubbles,
Counting bubbles
In my bubbly tub.

(Point to imaginary bubbles in the air.)

One-two-three-four.
One-two-three-four.
One-two-three-four
In my bubbly tub.

(Hold up one-two-three-four fingers.)

There's a thousand.
There's a thousand.
There's a thousand
In my bubbly tub.

(Spread arms wide.)

That's too many.
That's too many.
That's too many
In my bubbly tub.

(Shake head.)

Stop the water.
Stop the water.
Stop the water
In my bubbly tub.

(Clap on the word "stop.")

Mop the bathroom.
Mop the bathroom.
Mop the bathroom
Too much bubbly tub!
Now scrub!

(Pretend to mop.)

A SIMPLE BATH
(Tune: "Twelve Days of Christmas")

In my bathtub of bubbles I need lots of things
One yellow rubber ducky

In my bathtub of bubbles I need lots of things
Two sailing boats
And one yellow rubber ducky

In my bathtub of bubbles I need lots of things
Three jellyfish
Two sailing boats
And one yellow rubber ducky

In my bathtub of bubbles I need lots of things
Four bars of soap
Three jellyfish
Two sailing boats
And one yellow rubber ducky

In my bathtub of bubbles I need lots of things
Five floating frogs
Four bars of soap
Three jellyfish
Two sailing boats
And one yellow rubber ducky

In my bathtub of bubbles I need lots of things
Six soggy sponges
Five floating frogs
Four bars of soap
Three jellyfish
Two sailing boats
And one yellow rubber ducky

In my bathtub of bubbles I need lots of things
Seven painted turtles
Six soggy sponges
Five floating frogs
Four bars of soap
Three jellyfish
Two sailing boats
And one yellow rubber ducky

In my bathtub of bubbles I need lots of things
Eight motor boats
Seven painted turtles
Six soggy sponges
Five floating frogs
Four bars of soap
Three jellyfish
Two sailing boats
And one yellow rubber ducky

In my bathtub of bubbles I need lots of things
Nine octopuses
Eight motor boats
Seven painted turtles
Six soggy sponges
Five floating frogs
Four bars of soap
Three jellyfish
Two sailing boats
And one yellow rubber ducky

In my bathtub of bubbles I need lots of things
Ten blue whales spouting
Nine octopuses
Eight motor boats
Seven painted turtles
Six soggy sponges
Five floating frogs
Four bars of soap
Three jellyfish
Two sailing boats
And one yellow rubber ducky

In my bathtub of bubbles I need lots of things
Eleven wind-up shark toys
Ten blue whales spouting
Nine octopuses
Eight motor boats
Seven painted turtles
Six soggy sponges
Five floating frogs
Four bars of soap
Three jellyfish
Two sailing boats
And one yellow rubber ducky

In my bathtub of bubbles I need lots of things
Twelve clothes a-washing
Eleven wind-up shark toys
Ten blue whales spouting
Nine octopuses
Eight motor boats
Seven painted turtles
Six soggy sponges
Five floating frogs
Four bars of soap
Three jellyfish
Two sailing boats
And one yellow rubber ducky

And now there's no room for me!

Books for Beds, Chairs, and Stairs

Allen, Linda. **Mrs. Simkin's Bed**. Illustrated by Loretta Lustig. Morrow, 1976.
   Funny pink pigs keep appearing under the Simkin's bed until it appears there is only one thing to be done.

Allen, Pamela. **Mr. Archimedes' Bath**. Lothrop, 1980.
   Mr. Archimedes and his bathtub companions—a kangaroo, a goat, and a wombat—have a hard time figuring out why the water gets deeper when they all get in. Much measurement is required to see it is all of them together that make a mess—but it is such fun they go on doing it anyway.

Arnold, Ted. **No Jumping on the Bed**. Dial, 1987.
   Young Walter's habit of jumping on his bed has far-reaching consequences when he crashes through his bed and the floor into the apartment below, which begins a chain reaction of adventures that may or may not be imagined.

Blocksma, Mary. **What's in the Tub?** Illustrated by Sandra Cox Kalthoff. Children's Press, 1984.
   Thor, the pet dog, throws many toys into the bathtub with a boy and all the while they both try to keep water off the floor. They are successful until Thor tries to jump into the tub, too!

Bradman, Tony, and Eileen Browne. **Through My Window**. Silver Burdett, 1986.
   When Jo is sick at home, she watches the changing world of people and animals through her window.

Christelow, Eileen. **Five Little Monkeys Jumping on the Bed**. Clarion, 1989.
   In this version five little monkeys are getting ready for bed, but when Mama leaves the room, five little monkeys jump on the bed. The jaunty traditional verse tells how each monkey in turn falls off the bed and bumps his head and Mama calls the doctor. In the end they are all bandaged, put back in bed, and finally fall asleep so Mama can go to bed, too.

Fair, Sylvia. **The Bedspread**. Morrow, 1982.
   Two elderly sisters embroider the house of their childhood at either end of a white bedspread, each as she remembers it, with surprising results.

Freedman, Sally. **Devin's New Bed**. Illustrated by Robin Oz. Whitman, 1985.
   Devin is reluctant to give up his crib and accept his new grown-up bed until he discovers how much fun the new bed can be.

Hoff, Syd. **The Horse in Harry's Room**. Harper & Row, 1970.
   Although no one else can see it, Harry is very pleased to have a horse in his room.

Howell, Lynn. **Winifred's New Bed**. Knopf, 1985.
   Even though Winifred's big, new, grown-up bed has room for all her stuffed animals, she thinks it may be a bit too big, until her cat joins her.

Hurd, Thacher. **The Old Chair**. Greenwillow, 1978.
   An old but comfortable chair destined for the garbage dump finds a new home.

Johnson, Crockett. **A Picture for Harold's Room**. Harper, 1960.
   Stepping into the picture he has drawn with his purple crayon, Harold continues to draw his way through various adventures.

Keats, Ezra Jack. **Peter's Chair**. Harper & Row, 1967.
   Jealous of his new baby sister and worried that his parents will take his chair for her, Peter starts to run away. But when he realizes he has outgrown the chair, Peter decides they should paint it pink for the new baby.

McPhail, David. **Andrew's Bath**. Little, Brown, 1984.
   Andrew complains about his bath when his parents help, so they decide he can do it by himself. When he does, the bath-time routine turns into a ruckus with a bunch of animals in the tub.

Mayer, Mercer. **There's a Nightmare in My Closet**. Dial, 1968.
   Monsters in the closet turn out to be big funny creatures when the boy confronts them bravely.

Williams, Vera B. **A Chair for My Mother**. Greenwillow, 1982.
   A little girl, her waitress mother, and her grandmother all save their change, keeping it in a big jar to buy a beautiful stuffed chair after their furniture and belongings have burned in a fire.

Winthrop, Elizabeth. **Bunk Beds**. Illustrated by Ronald Himler. Harper & Row, 1972.
   Bunk beds provide more fun than sleep for Molly and Willie.

Related Activities for Beds, Chairs, and Stairs

HAPPY BIRTHDAY, ROBERTA RHINO
(Cut-and-tell Story)

To tell this story, fold a sheet of 8½″ × 11″ paper in half. Cut as indicated and open to reveal the birthday cake at the end.

Roberta Rhino was feeling very sad. It was her birthday and no one remembered. Not a card. Not a present. Not a cake. How sad.

Roberta waited all day, but no one remembered. Finally it was bedtime and she started up to bed.

(*Cut the first step.*) On the first step she thought about Paula Peacock. Why didn't Paula remember her birthday? Paula was such a good artist. She made lovely birthday cards for all her other friends. Why didn't she make one for Roberta Rhino? How sad.

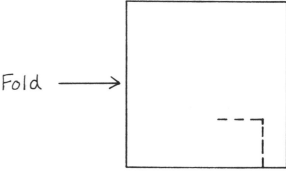

(*Cut the second step.*) On the second step, Roberta thought about Karen Cat. Why didn't Karen remember her birthday? Karen was such a knitter. She made lovely sweaters for all her other friends. Why didn't she make one for Roberta Rhino? How sad.

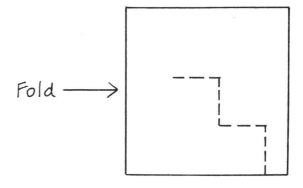

(*Cut the third step.*) On the third step, Roberta thought about Julia Jaguar. Why didn't Julia remember her birthday? Julia was such a baker. She made lovely angelfood cakes for all her other friends. Why didn't she make one for Roberta Rhino? How sad.

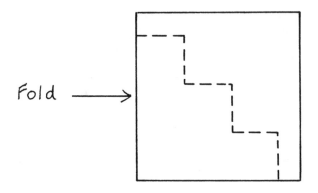

Suddenly, when Roberta was at the top of the stairs, she heard a strange noise at the bottom of the stairs. (*Open cutout shape.*)

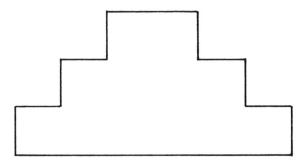

She ran down, down, down the stairs as fast as she could. And there at the door was Paula Peacock with a wonderful birthday card that had a rainbow on it. There was Karen Cat with a striped sweater just Roberta's size. And there was Julia Jaguar with a birthday cake with one-two-three layers and just the right number of candles for Roberta's birthday. (*You may wish to tape "candles" cut out of paper to the cake shape.*)

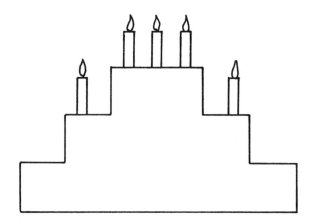

How happy!

WET TOWEL MONSTER YOUR MOTHER TOLD YOU ABOUT
(Tune: "London Bridge")

Wet towels on the bathroom floor,
Bathroom floor, bathroom floor.
Wet towels on the bathroom floor.
What will happen?

Wet towel monster yowls for more,
Yowls for more, yowls for more.
Wet towel monster yowls for more.
What will happen?

Monster squirts out toothpaste goo,
Toothpaste goo, toothpaste goo.
Monster squirts out toothpaste goo.
What will happen?

Monster drinks up green shampoo,
Green shampoo, green shampoo.
Monster drinks up green shampoo.
What will happen?

Stuff the monster with the towels,
With the towels, with the towels.
Stuff the monster with the towels
In the hamper!

(*spoken*) And slam the lid down tight!

BUNK FULL OF MONKEYS
(Story with Masks)

For this story make six masks of monkeys (p. 22): Mrs. Monkey, Milton, Marvin, Grandma Monkey, salesperson, and a delivery person. Teach the children the repeated refrain so they can all jump as they join in one chorus at the end.

Mrs. Monkey had two little monkeys, Milton and Marvin. When Milton and Marvin outgrew their cribs, Mrs. Monkey went to the store to buy them a bed. She didn't want just any bed. She wanted bunk beds. Bunk beds for Milton and Marvin Monkey.
At the store the bed salesperson said, "You know, Mrs. Monkey,

Monkeys on a bunk bed
Monkeys on a jump bed
All little monkeys
gonna jump on a bunk bed."

But Mrs. Monkey wouldn't listen. She wanted a bunk bed for Milton and Marvin Monkey.

Mrs. Monkey

Grandma Monkey

Salesperson

Marvin

BUNK FULL OF MONKEYS

Milton

Delivery person

When the delivery person drove the truck up to the Monkey house he said, "Where do you want this thing? You better put it outside, Mrs. Monkey, because

> Monkeys on a bunk bed
> Monkeys on a jump bed
> All little monkeys
> gonna jump on a bunk bed."

But Mrs. Monkey wouldn't listen. She wanted a bunk bed for Milton and Marvin Monkey. When Grandma Monkey came over and saw the bunk bed, she told Mrs. Monkey,

> "Monkeys on a bunk bed
> Monkeys on a jump bed
> All little monkeys
> gonna jump on a bunk bed."

But Mrs. Monkey wouldn't listen. She wanted a bunk bed for Milton and Marvin Monkey.

Marvin and Milton loved the new bunk bed. Marvin jumped on the top bunk. "I'll sleep here!" Milton said, "I want to sleep on top." So Marvin jumped down and Milton jumped up. Up and down. Up and down. Pretty soon the monkeys were jumping on the bunk bed.

Mrs. Monkey said, "Wait! Here is something the delivery man forgot." And she put a nice new ladder next to the bunk bed. Marvin climbed up. Milton climbed up. They did not jump on the bunk bed. Mrs. Monkey smiled, and she left the room.

As soon as Mrs. Monkey left, Marvin looked at Milton. Milton looked at Marvin, and just like everyone had said,

> "Monkeys on a bunk bed
> Monkeys on a jump bed
> All little monkeys
> gonna jump on a bunk bed."

And they did!

A CHAIR FOR ME
(Action Rhyme)

Rocking chair	(*Rock back and forth.*)
Stuffed chair	(*Curve arms to form circle.*)
Folding chair	(*Squat.*)
Puffed chair	(*Puff cheeks.*)
Tall chair	(*Stretch arms above head.*)
Small chair	(*Reach arms down low.*)
Turn all around chair	(*Turn around.*)
Papa Bear	(*Arms high.*)
Mama Bear	(*Arms shoulder high.*)
Baby Bear	(*Hand near floor.*)
Three—	(*Hold up three fingers.*)
Where is the chair	(*Palms up, shoulder high.*)
That's just for me?	(*Point to self.*)

HOUSEHOLD BALLET
(Action Rhyme)

Rocking chair rock.	*(Rock body back and forth.)*
Toaster pop.	*(Jump.)*
Piano roll play.	*(Roll one hand over other.)*
Beanbag flop.	*(Drop to ground.)*

ROCK AROUND THE ROOM
(Action Rhyme)

Dining table,	*(Feet together, arms extended at shoulder height.)*
Card table,	*(Fold arms to sides.)*
Bookcase,	*(Hand over hand, palms flat.)*
Broom.	*(Step to one side, dragging feet.)*
Floor lamp	*(Touch fingertips overhead, elbows bent.)*
Throw pillow	*(Throw.)*
Window shade—	
Zoom!	*(Roll hands quickly up.)*

GAMES FOR UPSTAIRS, DOWNSTAIRS, AND IN MY LADY'S CHAMBER

ANIMAL HOUSE

Sharpen children's listening skills and train their ears to hear similar consonant sounds with this little game. You, as keeper of the animal house, begin with this little verse with a few examples, then invite children to add other animals to different rooms of the house.

> Come to my animal house
> See the animals there
> There's a cat caught in the kitchen
> What else do you see there?

Now ask children to name an animal, an action, and the room of the house—all beginning with the same sound. Younger children may just name the animal and the room. Here are some suggestions if you're stuck: a baboon babbling in the bathroom; a dog dreaming in the den; a penguin poking on the porch; a hippopotamus hiccuping in the hall; a bear belching in the bedroom; a porcupine pouting in the parlor.

WHERE DOES THIS GO?

Use cutout pictures of rooms of the house and furniture from catalogs or magazines to play a matching game with children. Paste the room pictures on the fronts of cereal boxes that have the tops cut off. Mount the furniture pictures on construction paper. Play the game together at first, holding up a piece of furniture and placing it in the right room box at the children's directions. Leave the boxes out for individuals or small groups to work on matching skills later.

PERFECT MATCH

Make eight locks and keys out of construction paper in eight different colors. Seat the children in a circle and choose one to be It in the center. Have It hide eyes. Give eight children the colored locks to hold behind their backs. Children without locks should also hide hands. Give It a colored key. Say the following chant:

> Locks and keys, locks and keys.
> Locks open with ease
> When you find the right keys.

The child in the center points to children in the circle to show what is in their hands until the correctly matching lock is found. Give another child a chance to be It with a different colored key.

CRAFTS FOR UPSTAIRS, DOWNSTAIRS, AND IN MY LADY'S CHAMBER

ROLL OUT THE RED CARPET

Trace and cut out the house pattern on page 26. Mount on a craft stick. Insert paper strip into slit cut below the door. Roll red paper strip on pencil to curl. Attach yarn or string to end of roll so it can be rolled back and forth. (Check to make sure this works.)

MY OWN HOUSE

Cut a house shape from a file folder as shown on page 27. Draw windows and door on the outside. Divide the inside into three rooms. Label these living room, bedroom, and kitchen. Cut out furniture or objects that would belong in these rooms. Paste into correct area.

Turn this into a language activity by writing a label beside each object.

OPEN HOUSE PLACE CARD

Cut a house shape from a folded piece of paper as shown on page 27. Be sure not to cut the peak of the roof. The house will open at the bottom so it can stand. Cut out windows and door from contrasting construction paper; paste to the house. Add trim such as scalloped edges for a Swiss chalet effect, cotton-ball smoke coming out of the chimney, or rickrack trim. To use as a place card, write the name of the person on the door. This might also be used as an open house invitation. For a language arts activity, children may write a message inside the open house.

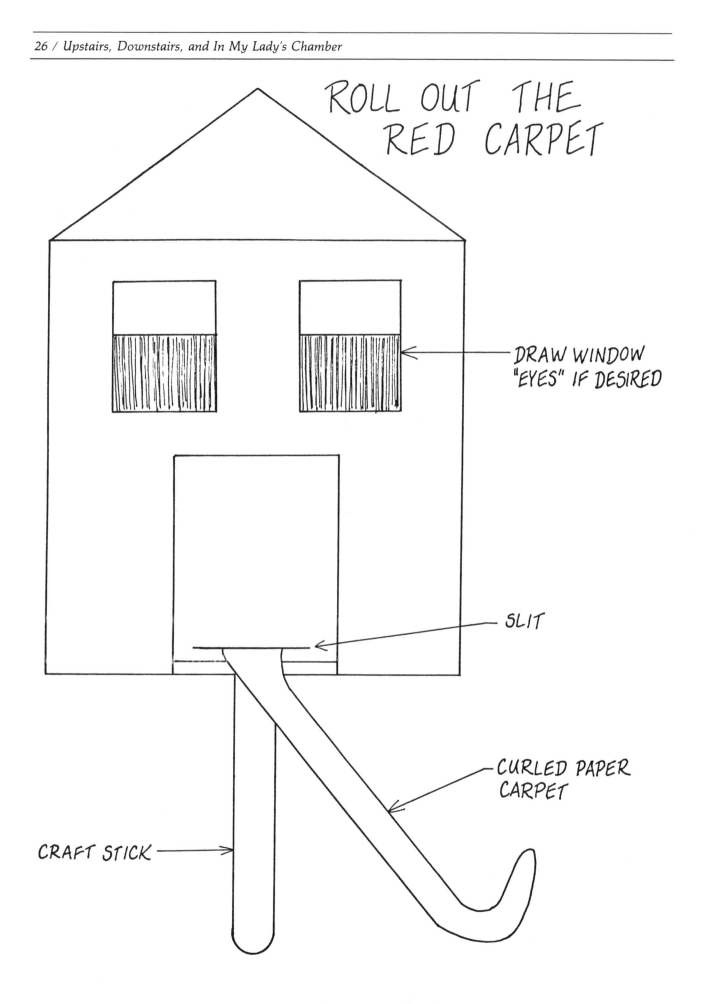

ROLL OUT THE
RED CARPET

DRAW WINDOW
"EYES" IF DESIRED

SLIT

CURLED PAPER
CARPET

CRAFT STICK

MY OWN HOUSE

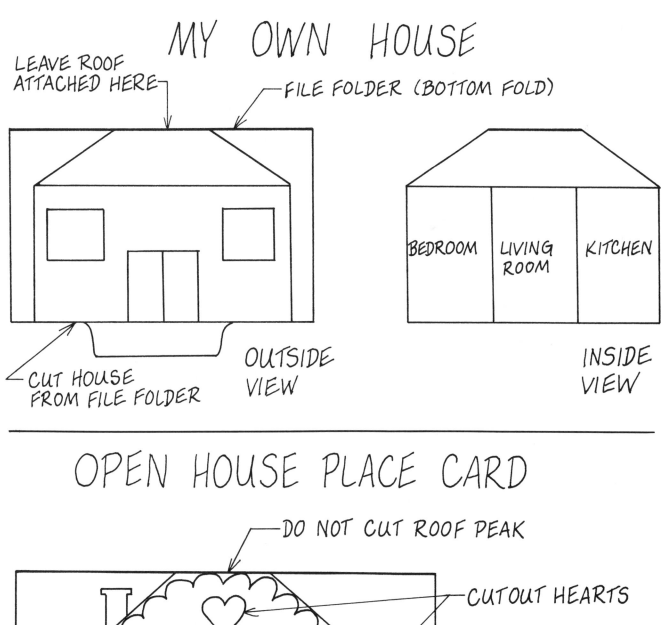

LEAVE ROOF ATTACHED HERE

FILE FOLDER (BOTTOM FOLD)

CUT HOUSE FROM FILE FOLDER

OUTSIDE VIEW

BEDROOM LIVING ROOM KITCHEN

INSIDE VIEW

OPEN HOUSE PLACE CARD

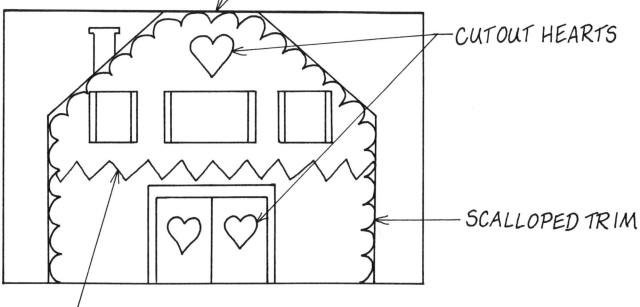

DO NOT CUT ROOF PEAK

CUTOUT HEARTS

SCALLOPED TRIM

RICKRACK TRIM

FLOOR PLANS FOR UPSTAIRS, DOWNSTAIRS, AND IN MY LADY'S CHAMBER

Focus Book: *Ten, Nine, Eight* by Molly Bang

Reading Activities

When you read this book aloud, emphasize the bedtime mood of the story by using a slow pace and quiet tone. Point to objects in the pictures that may need clarification. For example, the illustration accompanying the line "square window panes with falling snow" needs your guidance of pointing to each window pane within the windows.

Speaking Activities

Show the page with seven empty shoes. Count the shoes with the children. One shoe is missing. Ask where they suppose the other shoe went. Turn to the page with nine animals. Then show the page with two strong arms. The child only takes one animal to bed. What soft toys do the children like to have in bed with them?

Writing Activities

This book is a countdown of bedtime activities. As a group, begin with ten items, perhaps ten things to put away or do before going to bed, such as putting dirty clothes in the hamper, putting books back on the shelf, and brushing teeth. Make a list of these activities on a board. Perhaps the children will use the group list to begin one with the ten things they do at home.

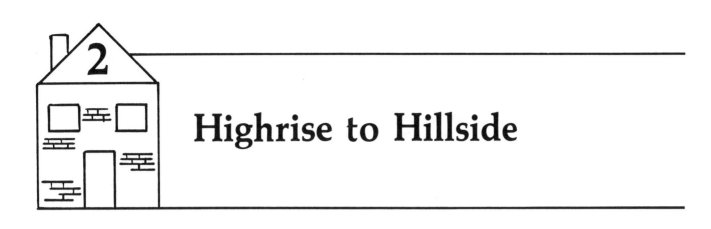

Highrise to Hillside

INTRODUCTION

This chapter shows a bird's-eye overview of the kinds of houses people live in. A chunk of the chapter is devoted to the city-country or urban-rural dichotomy, but homes away from home are also discussed. Use the books and activities in this chapter to flesh out social studies units in schools on city and country life. Programs in schools and public libraries can help children become aware of the distinctions even though city and country houses may not be as different as they once were. Children in the city may look nostalgically at rural life and dream idealistically about sleeping in the haystack or playing in a barnyard full of animals. They might assume that farm children all live in Victorian-style farmhouses with ginger-bread trim and big front porches. Children in rural areas may have the misconception that everyone in the city lives in a highrise apartment building. These distinctions may show up in some of the activities we have created simply because we use examples to show differences. But let these serve as springboards for teachable moments in which you can explore the varieties of places that people live.

The first subtheme, "Bird's-Eye View of Homes," includes books that cover different kinds of houses and those that provide both city and country dwellings. These books and the activities we have created may be used as an introduction to the topic or as a summary program.

The second subtheme, "City Sights," has an abundance of picture books about apartment houses even though people also live in bungalows, townhouses, mansions, and split-levels in the city. It is hard to find separate books about these kinds of dwellings or books that discuss houses in the suburbs or houses other than apartment buildings in the inner city. Teachers and librarians can flesh out the type of city life after reading aloud some of the books and using the cut-and-tell story "Finding the Right House," in which a family looks at an apartment, a townhouse, and a duplex until they decide on moving into a single-family dwelling.

The third subtheme, "Country Life," takes us to barns and farmhouses that people inhabit. Most of the barn books are located in the subtheme "Barns and Birdhouses" of chapter 7, which covers animals' houses. Many of the picture books listed in the bibliography reflect what is happening in society, or at least our perceptions of what is happening—grandmas and grandpas and Old MacDonald live on farms but not many real people do anymore. This perception, of course, is not necessarily the case. *Joel Growing Up a Farm Boy*, by Patricia Demuth (Dodd, 1982); *The American Family Farm*, a photo essay by George Ancona with text by Joan Anderson (Harcourt Brace Jovanovich, 1989); and *Jamie's Turn*, a real-life farm experience story by Jamie DeWitt (Raintree, 1984) provide more realistic pictures of farm life today. These books do not feature farmhouses other than in the background illustrations, so they have not been included in the bibliography section of this chapter. But the teacher or librarian may wish to use them along with some of the farmhouse books that are annotated.

The fourth subtheme, "Homes Away from Home," takes us to camp, beach houses, hotels, and even a sleepover at a friend's house. With our ever increasing mobility these kinds of houses, however temporary, are becoming familiar to most children. We have not included books about children who live in more than one house due to changing family patterns, because that is a subject beyond the intended scope of this book. Our original activities include a motel fun song and a room service story—topics children enjoy but that are not often the subjects of picture books.

The focus book, *The Town Mouse and the Country Mouse*, retold and illustrated by Lorinda Bryan Cauley, is an appropriate choice for the theme of this chapter. The story is based on an old fable but the idea continues to capture our interest and be retold with every new generation.

INITIATING ACTIVITY

ARE WE HOME YET

As children arrive, greet them with this chant that allows them to each tell a little about homes and families.

> House, home, condo, tent
> Farmhouse, townhouse, apartment
> Campsite, motel, hotel, inn
> What kind of house do you live in?

Each child can name a type of house, give an address, or tell who lives at the house (people and animals).

LITERATURE-SHARING EXPERIENCES

Books for Bird's-eye View of Homes

Adler, Irving. **Houses**. Day, 1964.
    The story of dwellings, from the caves of early man to the modern apartment buildings of today, for middle gradeschool children.

Binzen, Bill. **Alfred Goes House Hunting**. Doubleday, 1974.
    Tired of living in the playroom, a teddy bear goes in search of a home outdoors.

Burton, Virginia Lee. **The Little House**. Houghton Mifflin, 1942.
    A country house is unhappy when the city, with all its buildings and traffic, grows up around her.

Cauley, Lorinda Bryan. **The Town Mouse and the Country Mouse**. Putnam's, 1984.
    A town mouse and a country mouse exchange visits and discover "there's no place like home."

Chwast, Seymour. **Tall City, Wide Country**. Viking, 1983.
    Wide places in the country are shown, with the illustrations stretching horizontally through half of the book. In the other half of the book, tall buildings expand vertically, with elevators going up and down in the tall city.

Feder, Paula Kurzband. **Where Does the Teacher Live?** Illustrated by Lillian Hoban. Dutton, 1979.
    Three children try to discover where their teacher lives and are surprised by the answer.

Galdone, Paul. **The Town Mouse and Country Mouse**. McGraw-Hill, 1971.
The Aesop fable retold by Galdone places the country mouse in the elegance and danger of life with his cousin who lives at His Majesty's court.

Gerstein, Mordicai. **The Room**. Harper & Row, 1984.
A series of people live in and redecorate a one-room apartment in very different ways. Artists, a magician, and musicians all make unique contributions to the room's history.

Green, Mary McBurney. **Everybody Has a House and Everybody Eats**. Young Scott Books, 1961.
Two books in one describe simply the housing and food of various familiar animals.

Harper, Anita. **How We Live**. Illustrated by Christine Roche. Harper & Row, 1977.
Whimsical illustrations and brief text explore the ways people live—alone or with families, in houses or boats or apartments, and even how people feel about where they live.

Henkes, Kevin. **Once around the Block**. Illustrated by Victoria Chess. Greenwillow, 1987.
Annie is bored until a walk around the block to visit her neighbors brings several pleasant diversions.

Pienkowski, Jan. **Homes**. Julian Messner, 1979.
Brief text for the youngest reader shows such homes as a cave, castle, doghouse, fishbowl, nest, and shell.

Provensen, Alice, and Martin Provensen. **Town and Country**. Crown, 1984.
Richly painted pictures and a poetic text describe city and country life with detail about the particular dwellings. For example, sights are shown from apartments in the city and the buildings (barns, stables, tool sheds) are shown beside a country house. This is an important resource book for rural/urban teaching units.

Robbins, Ken. **City/Country**. Viking, 1985.
Clear photographs show town and country houses with a simple text.

Roberts, Sarah. **I Want to Go Home!** Illustrated by Joe Mathieu. Random House, 1985.
Big Bird goes to stay with his grandmother at the beach and is homesick until he makes a new friend.

Schlein, Miriam. **My House**. Illustrated by Joe Lasker. Whitman, 1971.
This is a first-person look at all the touches that make a house a home, such as shelves just the right size, gardens planted by the family, and a tree right outside the window.

Schulz, Charles. **Snoopy's Facts and Fun Book about Houses**. Random House, 1979.
Familiar *Peanuts* characters describe the characteristics of a variety of dwellings all over the world.

Sopko, Eugan. **Townsfolk and Countryfolk**. Faber and Faber, 1982.
Three city friends encounter numerous adventures when they decide to enrich the lives of country folk with their superior scientific knowledge.

Walters, Marguarite. **The City Country ABC**. Illustrated by Ib Ohlsson. Doubleday, 1966.
This turnabout book includes two stories. One is about a ride in the city; the other, about a walk in the country.

Related Activities for Bird's-eye View of Homes

TOWN HOUSE, COUNTRY HOUSE

Make two sets of glove puppets (see p. 32). The country glove has a farmhouse in the palm. On the fingers are a crow, running cat, sheepdog, bee, and person. The city glove has an apartment building. On the fingers are a pigeon, sleeping cat, barking dog, lightning bug, and person.

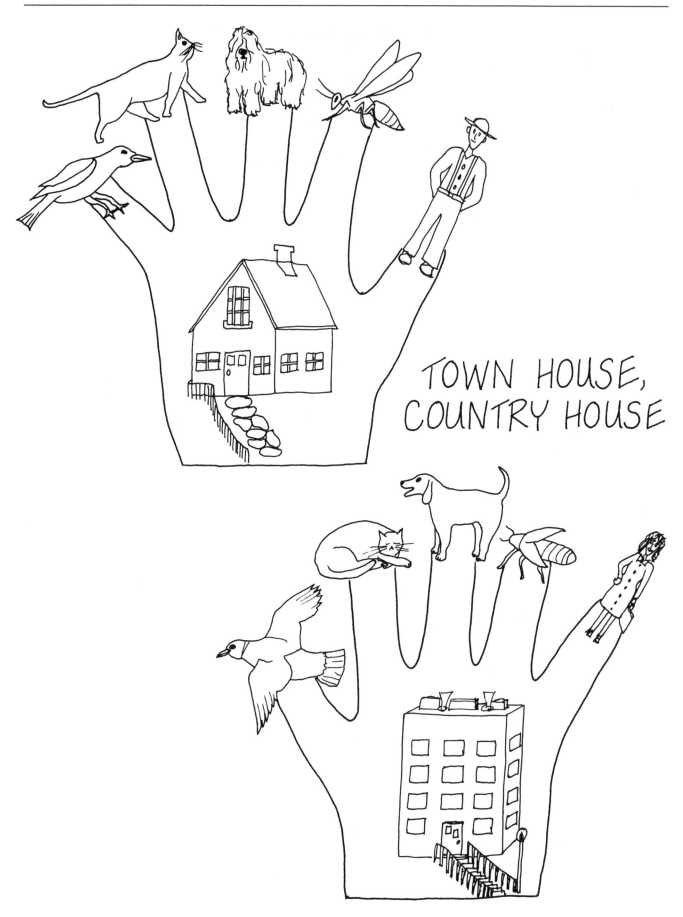

TOWN HOUSE,
COUNTRY HOUSE

Hold up both hands and wiggle the finger with the animal, insect, or person referred to in each line.

Town house, country house,
Let's compare.
Come and meet
Who lives there.

Pigeons on the roof
Are here in town.
Crows in the country
Make a squawking sound.

Town cats sleep on
The window sill.
Country cats keep
The barn mice still.

The city dog cautions
With a warning bark.
The country dog herds
Sheep in by dark.

Lightning bugs flicker
Down city streets.
Honeybees make country
Life more sweet.

Town house, country house—
Different ways.
Visit both
You'll want to stay.

CITY AND COUNTRY HOMES
(Tune: "My Bonnie Lies over the Ocean")

My family lives out in the country.
Our house has a porch all around.
Two floors with a stairway between them—
I like to run upstairs and down.
From my window
I can see fields
Full of corn and beans.
Open spaces
Everywhere that I can see.

My family lives down in the city,
Up high on the thirty-fourth floor.
We ride in a big elevator
And get off right at our front door.
From my window
I can see buses
And lots of cars.
Tall, tall buildings
Reaching way up to the stars.

Some families live out in the country,
And some live with the buses and cars.
If you are with people who love you
Home is wherever you are.
From your window
You may see buildings
Or open land.
City, country
Both places make us feel grand.

TOWN MOUSE AND COUNTRY MOUSE

This story is told with stick puppets of two mice, flowers, nuts and berries, pot of stew, a bus, crowd of people, and a hunk of cheese. Also use a cat puppet. Give each child one stick puppet, keeping the cat hidden for later in the story. Have the country mouse stand with the flowers, nuts and berries, and pot of stew to the left (country side); have the city mouse stand with the bus, crowd of people, and hunk of cheese to the right (city side).

There once were two mice who were cousins. One mouse lived out in the country. He had plenty of corn to eat and the country mouse liked to see the stars shining in the night sky.

The other mouse lived in the city. He had sweet treats of all kinds to eat and the city mouse liked to see the lights of the city glittering at night.

One day the city mouse came out to the country to visit his cousin. (*City mouse moves to country side.*) In the morning they gathered wildflowers. (*Both mice go to flowers.*) In the afternoon they picked nuts and berries. (*Both mice go to nuts and berries.*) At dinner time they made a wonderful stew. (*Both mice go to pot of stew.*) After supper the city mouse said, "What shall we do now?"

"Do?" said the country mouse. "Usually I just relax and watch the sunset. It is very peaceful."

"Peaceful?!" cried the city mouse. "My cousin, you don't know what you are missing! Come with me to the city and I will show you some real excitement!"

(*Both mice move to city side.*) So both mice left the country then and there and traveled to the city. They saw a large bus. (*Both mice go to bus, but then run back to center.*) It was so big it almost ran over the mice, but the city mouse pulled the country mouse out of the way just in time. They scurried along out of the street, but on the sidewalk were lots and lots of people. (*Both mice go to crowd of people, but then run back to center.*) The country mouse almost got stepped on, but the city mouse pulled the country mouse out of the way just in time.

Quickly they ran into the huge house where the city mouse lived. They ran through the walls and there in the kitchen on the table was a big cheese, all ready for them to eat. (*Both mice go to hunk of cheese.*)

"See?!" said the city mouse. "I don't have to gather nuts and berries or make stew. This food is waiting for me. And after we eat I'll show you some real excitement."

The country mouse did like having the cheese all ready and he almost forgot about the bus and the people because the cheese tasted so good.

But suddenly, from out of nowhere came a CAT! (*Leader pulls out cat puppet.*) "Run!" cried the city mouse, and he pulled the country mouse out of the way just in time and back into the wall. (*Both mice run back to center.*)

When they had caught their breath, the city mouse said, "The cat is gone. Now we can have some real excitement!"

"I've had enough excitement for today," said the country mouse. "I'm going back to the country where I can smell the flowers and eat nut-and-berry stew in peace."

And that is just what he did. (*Country mouse goes back to country.*)

TOWN MOUSE &
COUNTRY MOUSE

Books for City Sights

Baker, Jeannie. **Home in the Sky**. Greenwillow, 1984.
    Light, a homing pigeon, lives in a coop on the roof of an abandoned building. He flies away from his owner, is attacked by street pigeons, and is nurtured by a boy he meets on a subway before he instinctively flies back home. The author-illustrator's collage constructions add a distinctive level to the understanding of the story.

Barrett, Judi. **Old MacDonald Had an Apartment House**. Atheneum, 1968.
    When Old MacDonald moves to the city, the familiar rhyme takes on a new twist.

Cobb, Vicki. **Skyscraper Going Up**. Illustrated by John Strejan. Crowell, 1987.
    Paper manipulatives and explanatory text show the construction of a skyscraper, from the digging and pouring of the foundation, to "topping out" (the half-finished stage), working on the core, and finishing the "skin of stone and glass."

Escudie, Rene. **Paul and Sebastian**. Kane/Miller, 1988.
    Paul, a trailer dweller, and Sebastian, from an apartment, renew their friendship on a class trip.

Hawkinson, John. **Little Boy Who Lived Up High**. Whitman, 1987.
    A little boy in a highrise apartment tells how his neighborhood looks from the sky and from the ground.

Heilbroner, Joan. **This Is the House Where Jack Lives**. Illustrated by Aliki. Harper & Row, 1962.
    The house where Jack lives in this modern version is an apartment house. Here a boy and a dog go for a walk, and step by step various surprising events happen, including a falling pail, a man bumped by a mop, and a cook tripped by a cat. Everything leads back to the original perpetrator: Jack in his bath.

Keats, Ezra Jack. **Apt. 3**. Macmillan, 1971.
    The various apartments in the apartment house have different smells, sounds, and people. The noise from Apartment 3 is a harmonica played by a blind man who knows more about his neighbors than anyone else does.

Keith, Eros. **A Small Lot**. Bradbury, 1968.
    A small patch of green grass and a tree provide a nice play area between apartments. When a man contemplates putting a store on the lot, inventive children fit it up to be a park and save their play area.

Raskin, Ellen. **Ghost in a Four-Room Apartment**. Atheneum, 1969.
    Two stories go on at the same time: a simple rhyme about those real people who live in or visit the apartment and a running commentary by the resident ghost. The pictures of the ghost's antics are colorful and fun.

Rice, Eve. **Goodnight, Goodnight**. Greenwillow, 1980.
    Various city dwellers make their way home and slowly the city lights go out.

Schaff, Peter. **An Apartment House Close Up**. Four Winds, 1980.
    Clear photographs show all the parts of an apartment house, from windows, to elevators, to the laundry room.

Schick, Eleanor. **City in the Summer**. Macmillan, 1969.
    Crowded city dwellings are contrasted with the escape a young boy makes to a rooftop sanctuary with an old man and a flock of pigeons. The two take a commuter train to the beach for another escape from the crowds before they head back to the city at night.

Schick, Eleanor. **City in the Winter**. Collier, 1970.

When Jimmy stays home from school because of a blizzard, he watches from his apartment window as birds eat outside and walks to the store with his grandmother. Sights and sounds of a city are carefully described from a child's perspective.

Schick, Eleanor. **5A and 7B**. Macmillan, 1967.

Toby and Sandy live on different floors of a tall apartment building but never meet until one day when their daily schedules change.

Schmidt, Julie Madeline. **The Apartment House**. Illustrated by Anita Riggio. Abingdon, 1988.

Mr. Wong, manager of the apartment house, thinks everyone has forgotten his birthday, but his talented tenants present him with a spectacular array of gifts: piano duets, songs, a painting, and a masterpiece cake.

Stevenson, James. **Grandpa's Great City Tour**. Greenwillow, 1983.

Grandpa takes the children on a tour of the city, using the alphabet as a guide.

Thompson, Kay. **Eloise**. Illustrated by Hilary Knight. Simon & Schuster, 1955.

The precocious and irrepressible Eloise loves the varied attractions of living at the Plaza Hotel, including taking the elevator to the fifteenth floor, ordering room service, and visiting the grand ballroom. This kind of dwelling will make kids want to move right in or at least pay a visit.

Waber, Bernard. **The House on East 88th Street**. Houghton Mifflin, 1962.

Soon after the Primms move into their apartment house, they discover a crocodile in their bathtub. Lyle, the crocodile, wins their hearts quickly by helping out with the chores and performing tricks. Mrs. Primm soon declares that "every home should have a crocodile."

Related Activities for City Sights

CITY LIGHTS
(Tune: "Twinkle, Twinkle, Little Star")

Twinkle, twinkle, city lights,
Shining in the darkest night.
Lights on rooftops,
Lights in stores,
Movie marquees,
Lights galore.
From the windows up so high
Like the stars shine in the sky.

EASY AS PIE
(Flannel-board Story)

Cut an orange felt circle into five pieces and remove one piece each time an animal keeps a piece of the carrot pie.

In the city neighborhood, people like to share with one another. Rabbit lived on the first floor of an apartment building. One morning Rabbit woke up and wanted to do something nice for her neighbor Squirrel, upstairs. So she made a five-piece carrot pie and took it to Squirrel.

"What a nice surprise," said Squirrel. "Thank you so much for the carrot pie."

Now the truth was that Squirrel did not like carrot pie all that much. In fact, she really only wanted one little piece, not a whole pie. But she did not want to waste the rest. So she took out one piece and took the four-piece carrot pie to Owl, upstairs.

"What a nice surprise," said Owl. "Thank you so much for the carrot pie."

Now the truth was that Owl did not like carrot pie all that much. In fact, she really only wanted one little piece, not a whole pie. But she did not want to waste the rest. So she took out one piece and took the three-piece carrot pie to Bear, upstairs.

"What a nice surprise," said Bear. "Thank you so much for the carrot pie."

Now the truth was that Bear did not like carrot pie all that much. In fact, she really only wanted one little piece, not a whole pie. But she did not want to waste the rest. So she took out one piece and took the two-piece carrot pie to Mouse, upstairs.

"What a nice surprise," said Mouse. "Thank you so much for the carrot pie."

Now the truth was the Mouse did not like carrot pie all that much. In fact, she really only wanted one little piece, not a whole pie. But she did not want to waste the rest. So she took out one piece and took the last piece of carrot pie all the way back down to the first floor to Rabbit.

"What a nice surprise," said Rabbit. "Thank you so much for the carrot pie."

And Rabbit ate every bite because it tasted just like her own home-cooking!

CITY LIFE HAS ITS UPS AND DOWNS
(Tune: "My Bonnie Lies over the Ocean")

To put some action in this song, stand on tiptoes on the word "up" and squat on the word "down."

We live high up in an apartment,
With families above and below.
We all ride in one elevator
And here's how we all like to go:
Up, down, up, down.
Push button 12 to go to the top.
Up, down, up, down.
Hoping it never will stop.

One day we came home for our dinner
Our old elevator broke down.
We had to walk to our apartment—
Twelve floors up and twelve more back down.
Up, down, up, down.
We could be walking up all the night.
Up, down, up, down.
Hoping it will be all right.

(*spoken*) And soon!

FINDING THE RIGHT HOUSE
(Cut-and-Tell Story)

Cut a row of houses as shown. Divide each house into rooms as indicated in the story.

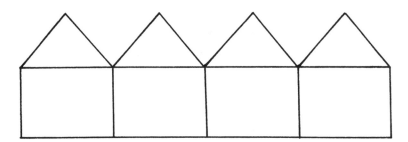

The Anderson family was looking for a new place to live. There were Mr. and Mrs. Anderson, Jeff, Jan, and baby Joy. Five Andersons needed a place to live.

First they looked at an apartment in a tall apartment building. (*Divide the first house into eight sections.*) There were people upstairs and downstairs. There were people to the left and to the right. And the rooms of the apartment were very, very small. Mr. Anderson said,

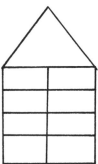

> "Too many people upstairs
> Too many people downstairs
> Too many people side by side
> And not enough room for us."

So they kept looking.

Next they looked at a townhouse. (*Divide the next house into four sections.*) There were no people upstairs, but there were people downstairs and people next door. And the rooms of the townhouse were very small. Mr. Anderson said,

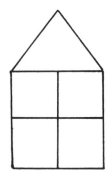

> "There are no people upstairs
> Too many people downstairs
> Too many people side by side
> And not enough room for us."

So they kept looking.

Next they looked at a duplex. (*Divide the next house into two sections.*) There were no people upstairs or downstairs, but there were people next door. And the rooms of the duplex were small. Mr. Anderson said,

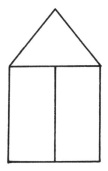

> "There are no people upstairs
> There are no people downstairs
> Too many people side by side
> And not enough room for us."

So they kept looking.

Next they looked at a house. (*Do not divide the next house.*) There were no people upstairs or downstairs. There were no people next door. Instead, there was lots of green grass and a sandbox for baby Joy. And the rooms of the house were just right. Mr. Anderson said,

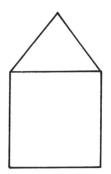

> "There are no people upstairs
> There are no people downstairs
> There are no people side by side
> And just enough room for us."

So they moved right in.

APARTMENT NOISE
(Participation Flannel-board Story)

Use a rectangle of felt for the apartment building. On it draw five squares and label them for the apartments in the story: 5A, 5B, 5C, 4B, and 6B. Point to the squares as you talk about the people who live in each apartment so children who have not seen apartments will understand this type of housing.

The children will enjoy doing all the sounds with you and singing the verses to the tune of "London Bridge Is Falling Down."

Peter lived in a big apartment building in an even bigger city. His apartment was 5B. There were people who lived above him in 6B. There were people who lived below him in 4B. There were people who lived on the left of him in 5A. There were people who lived on the right of him in 5C.

Early one Saturday morning, Peter woke up before anyone else in the apartment building. It was so nice and quiet, Peter wanted to get busy right away. So he decided to play his tuba.

Oom-pa, oom-pa, oom-pa went Peter's tuba.

The man in apartment 6B, above Peter, knocked on the floor and said:

> "You are making too much noise
> Too much noise, too much noise.
> Find some other thing to do
> That is quiet!"

So Peter put his tuba away, but he still wanted to be busy. So he decided to clean the rugs with his vacuum.

Vroooom, vrooooom went Peter's vacuum.

The woman in apartment 4B, below Peter, knocked on the ceiling and said:

> "You are making too much noise
> Too much noise, too much noise.
> Find some other thing to do
> That is quiet!"

So Peter put his vacuum away, but he still wanted to be busy. So he decided to do some exercises.

"One-two-one-two, bend and stretch," said Peter's exercise tape.

The man in apartment 5A, on the left of Peter, knocked on the wall and said:

> "You are making too much noise
> Too much noise, too much noise.
> Find some other thing to do
> That is quiet!"

So Peter put his exercise tape away, but he still wanted to be busy. So he decided to bounce his basketball.

Bump, bump, bump, bump went Peter's basketball.

The woman in apartment 5C, on the right of Peter, knocked on the wall and said:

> "You are making too much noise
> Too much noise, too much noise.
> Find some other thing to do
> That is quiet!"

So Peter put is basketball away, but he still wanted to be busy. So he decided to go out for a walk. All was quiet in Peter's apartment. Before long the people in the other apartments began to wake up. (*Divide into four groups and have each group do a different sound at the same time.*) The man in 6B made coffee. (*Chuch-a-perk, chuch-a-perk.*) The woman in 4B made some pancakes. (*Flip-flap, flip-flap.*) The man in 5A squeezed some orange juice. (*Squeeeeeze, squeeeeeeze.*) The woman in 5C fried some bacon. (*Sizzle, sizzle.*)

When Peter got back from his walk, the apartment was a noisy place! Peter said:

"You are making too much noise
Too much noise, too much noise.
Find some other things to do
That are quiet!"

But then there was a knock on Peter's door. There were all his neighbors with a Saturday morning breakfast for him because he finally found something quiet to do! And they all enjoyed it together.

Books for Country Life

Archambaule, John. **Barn Dance**. Illustrated by Ted Rand. Henry Holt, 1986.
A farm boy enjoys a midnight frolic with all the animals and a scarecrow in the old barn.

Azarian, Mary. **Farmer's Alphabet**. D. R. Godine, 1981.
An alphabet book of woodcuts featuring activities and objects associated with New England farm life. Entries feature the alphabet, from *apple* and *barn* through *zinnia*.

Booth, Eugene. **On the Farm**. Illustrated by Derek Collard. Raintree Children's Books, 1977.
A series of simple questions encourage the reader to look closely at the pictures about farm life.

Brook, Judy. **Tim Mouse Visits the Farm**. Lothrop, 1968.
Tim Mouse and his friend go to the farm for milk, but frighten the cows into running away.

Brown, Margaret. **Country Noisy Book**. Harper & Row, 1940.
Muffin learns about the country through hearing many new sounds. This book is good for children to participate making noises, whether they are city or country raised.

Browne, Caroline. **Mrs. Christie's Farmhouse**. Doubleday, 1977.
Mrs. Christie and Rachel find city life too noisy and lonesome, so they move to the country and find an empty house to live in. They enjoy being disorganized until the king who lives nearby threatens to organize their quiet world. Fortunately he is won over by their chaos, and peaceful disarray reigns once more.

Bunting, Eve. **The Big Red Barn**. Illustrated by Howard Knotts. Harcourt Brace Jovanovich, 1979.
The big red barn that holds all the animals on the farm burns down one night, and the little boy who was attached to that barn has difficulty adjusting to the new barn that takes its place.

Dupasquier, Philippe. **Our House on the Hill**. Viking Kestrel, 1987.
Wordless book shows month-by-month activities of a country family at home.

Gammel, Stephen. **Once upon MacDonald's Farm**. Four Winds Press, 1981.
Old MacDonald tries to make a go of his farm with a lion, a monkey, and an elephant. He does better when a neighbor gives him a cow, a hen, and a horse, but the last picture shows he is still confused enough to hitch the chicken to a plow.

Locker, Thomas. **Family Farm**. Dial, 1988.
A family farm is almost lost until the family raises and sells pumpkins and flowers as well as corn and milk.

Lorenz, Lee. **A Weekend in the Country**. Prentice-Hall, 1985.
Two friends, wishing to escape the city heat by having a weekend in the country, are so intimidated by the risks of various means of transportation that they put the trip off altogether.

Moore, Elaine. **Grandma's House**. Illustrated by Elise Primvera. Lothrop, 1985.
A little girl enjoys her time at the summer home of her grandmother. Picking fruit is a favorite pastime, and they even plant a plum tree together.

Nakatani, Chiyoko. **My Day on the Farm**. Crowell, 1976.
This simple book travels with a child through a day-long trip to the farm.

Noble, Trinka Hakes. **Meanwhile Back at the Ranch.** Illustrated by Tony Ross. Dial, 1987.
Things seemed quiet when a bored rancher left to drive to town, but amazing things are happening to his wife and ranch while he is gone.

Parker, Nancy Winslow. **The Party at the Old Farm**. Atheneum, 1975.
This Halloween story shows the plumber unable to fix anything until he goes to a costume party.

Pearson, Tracey Campbell. **Old MacDonald Had a Farm**. Dial, 1984.
Verse after verse explains the residents of Old MacDonald's farm.

Rylant, Cynthia. **Night in the Country**. Illustrated by Mary Szilagyi. Bradbury, 1980.
This book describes nighttime in the country with all the sights and sounds that make it as busy as the city.

Related Activities for Country Life

FARMHOUSE KEYS
(Draw-and-Tell Story)

Grandma had a big old farmhouse with lots of rooms to take care of. There were nooks and crannies, corners and cubbies. One day Grandma was getting ready for her grandchildren to arrive. Grandma cleaned and waxed and polished every nook and crannie, every corner and cubbie. When the house was all ready, Grandma got ready to go to town to get ice cream for their dessert.

But Grandma could not leave the house because she had lost her keys. So she began to look for them. There were nooks and crannies and corners and cubbies to look in. First Grandma looked in the pantry of the old farmhouse. There were pickles and jams and sacks of flour in the pantry, but there were no keys. (*Draw first line as shown.*)

So Grandma looked in another part of the old farmhouse. There were nooks and crannies and corners and cubbies to look in. Grandma looked in the parlor. She saw a piano and a love-seat and old photo albums with pictures of Great-great-grandma and Great-great-grandpa in the parlor, but there were no keys. (*Continue line as shown.*)

Grandma looked in another part of the old farmhouse. There were nooks and crannies and corners and cubbies to look in. Grandma looked all around in the attic. There were boxes of old hats, trunks of old clothes, and an old washtub in the attic, but there were no keys. (*Continue line as shown.*)

So Grandma looked in another part of the old farmhouse. There were nooks and crannies and corners and cubbies to look in. Grandma went all the way downstairs and looked in the root cellar. There were bags of onions and baskets of potatoes in the root cellar, but there were no keys. (*Continue line as shown.*)

Suddenly Grandma heard a knock at the front door. She looked out the window and saw her grandchildren outside the front door—and then she saw her keys hanging in the keyhole of the front door! (*Complete drawing as shown.*)

"Surprise, Grandma," the children shouted. "We brought you a present!"

When Grandma opened the present, she said, "This is just what I've been needing." It was a key ring with a big heart on it—big enough to find in any nook or cranny or corner or cubby of the big farmhouse. Or even in the front door!

And Grandma and the children went to town for ice cream together.

THE BIG FARMHOUSE
(Tune: "My Bonnie Lies over the Ocean")

My grandmother lived in this farmhouse,
The laundry was way out in back.
She washed all her clothes in a washtub,
And hung them out on a clothes rack.
Those were, those were,
Those were the days in the country.
Those were, those were,
Those were the days on the farm.

My mother once lived in this farmhouse,
The kitchen was always too hot.
She cooked on a black cast-iron skillet
And made coffee in a big pot.
Those were, those were,
Those were the days in the country.
Those were, those were,
Those were the days on the farm.

Now I live right here in the farmhouse,
The washtub and skillet I've saved,
But I love my nice modern kitchen
My washer and new microwave.
These are, these are,
These are the days in the country.
These are, these are,
These are the days on the farm.

HOME ON THE FARM
(Tune: "Twelve Days of Christmas")

On the farm in the country
This is what we see—
A farmhouse just for me.

On the farm in the country
This is what we see—
Two barns for horses,
And a farmhouse just for me.

On the farm in the country
This is what we see—
Three sheds for cows,
Two barns for horses,
And a farmhouse just for me.

On the farm in the country
This is what we see—
Four pens for pigs,
Three sheds for cows,
Two barns for horses,
And a farmhouse just for me.

On the farm in the country
This is what we see—
Five chicken coops,
Four pens for pigs,
Three sheds for cows,
Two barns for horses,
And a farmhouse just for me.

QUIET IN THE COUNTRY
(Tune: "Old MacDonald Had a Farm")

At our farmhouse we can hear
Very little noise.
Except for cars on gravel roads
And they sound like this:
Crunch, crunch here, crunch, crunch there,   *(Pretend to drive car on bumpy road.)*
Here a crunch, there a crunch,
Everywhere a crunch, crunch.
At our farmhouse we can hear
Very little noise.

At our farmhouse we can hear
Very little noise.
Except for laundry on the line
And it sounds like this:
Flap, flap here, flap, flap here,   *(Slap arms against sides.)*
Here a flap, there a flap,
Everywhere a flap, flap,
Crunch, crunch here, crunch, crunch there,
Here a crunch, there a crunch,
Everywhere a crunch, crunch.
At our farmhouse we can hear
Very little noise.

At our farmhouse we can hear
Very little noise.
Except for animals in the barn
And they sound like this:
Moo, moo here, moo, moo there,   *(Each child picks a different animal to imitate.)*
Here a moo, there a moo,
Everywhere a moo, moo.
Close the windows, we can hear
Too much country noise!   *(Put hands over ears.)*

Books for Homes Away from Home

Brown, Marc. **Arthur Goes to Camp**. Little, Brown, 1982.
Arthur is not looking forward to Camp Meadowcroak, and when mysterious things start to happen there, he decides to run away.

Buchanan, Heather. **Emily Mouse's Beach House**. Dial, 1987.
Emily Mouse sets off for adventure but is saved from disaster by George Mouse.

Carlson, Nancy L. **Arnie Goes to Camp**. Viking Kestrel, 1988.
Arnie is sure that he won't survive summer sleep-away camp, but when he arrives he gets some pleasant surprises.

Chorao, Kay. **Lester's Overnight**. Dutton, 1977.
Lester's overnight with Auntie Della is nothing like home.

dePaola, Tomie. **Tomie dePaola's Kitten Kids and the Big Camp-out**. Golden Books, 1988.
Cousin Tom comes for a visit and the cousins camp out in the back yard. What could be scary back there?

Fernandes, Kim. **Visiting Granny**. Annick Press, 1990.
Photographs of baker's-clay people, animals, and household furnishings illustrate this unique picture book about two children who visit Granny's house. Much of the story is centered in the kitchen, and a recipe for Granny's raisin cookies appears at the end of the book.

Henkes, Kevin. **Bailey Goes Camping.** Greenwillow, 1985.
Bailey is too young to go camping with the Bunny Scouts, but his parents take him on a special indoor camping trip.

Koide, Tan. **May We Sleep Here Tonight?** Illustrated by Yasuko Koide. Atheneum, 1983.
When three gophers go hiking they spend the night in a forest cabin and are joined by two rabbits, three raccoons, and Mrs. Bear, who owns the house and gives them all a hot meal.

Krahn, Fernando. **The Family Minus's Summer House**. Parent's Magazine Press, 1980.
A weasel family gets away to nature to have a picnic. They remember to bring along a fully portable, pop-up treehouse, but decide it is safer to camp out on the ground.

Martin, Charles. **For Rent**. Greenwillow, 1986.
A gang of kids fixes up a garage for a summer house. Various experiences with tenants teach them that being landlords is hard work, but they finally find an artist who enjoys the cabin and being their friend.

Rice, Eve. **At Grammy's House**. Illustrated by Nancy Parker. Greenwillow, 1990.
Two children visit their Grammy in her farmhouse and enjoy the pleasures of milking the cow for cream and eating a delicious dinner. Most of the story is set in the old-fashioned farm kitchen, and the endpages of the book are decorated with turn-of-the-century quilts.

Sanders, Sheila. **Beast Goes Camping**. Baker Street, 1985.
Beast and his friends are unprepared to camp but everyone helps, from Beaver, who cuts logs for a shelter, to the lightning bugs, who replace the forgotten flashlight.

Segal, Lore Croszmann. **All the Way Home**. Illustrated by James Marshall. Farrar, Straus and Giroux, 1973.
A little girl's refusal to stop crying attracts a strange procession as her mother leads her out of the park.

Stevenson, James. **The Worst Person in the World at Crab Beach**. Greenwillow, 1988.

When the worst person in the world visits Crab Beach, he tries to make life miserable for everyone in the resort hotel. He is successful in being the worst guest until he meets a woman and her son who are his match.

Waber, Bernard. **Ira Sleeps Over**. Houghton Mifflin, 1972.

Ira does not want to take his teddy bear on his first sleepover, but ghost stories and the realization that his friend sleeps with a toy change his mind.

Wyllie, Stephen. **Monkey's Crazy Hotel**. Illustrated by Maureen Roffey. Harper & Row, 1987.

A thin monkey who runs a hotel in the country assigns rooms with appropriate-size beds to his guests: tall giraffe, small turtle, and fat hippopotamus. But a power failure causes them to find their rooms in the dark and, of course, they bed down in the wrong rooms.

Related Activities for Homes Away from Home

MOTEL FUN
(Tune: "Old MacDonald Had a Farm")

On vacation we have fun
Stopping at motels.
Sometimes there are swimming pools
At the best motels.
With a splash, splash here and a splash, splash there,
Here a splash, there a splash,
Everywhere a splash, splash.
On vacation we have fun
Stopping at motels.

On vacation we have fun
Stopping at motels.
Sometimes there are video games
At the best motels.
With a beep-beep here and a beep-beep there,
Here a beep, there a beep,
Everywhere a beep-beep.
On vacation we have fun
Stopping at motels.

On vacation we have fun
Stopping at motels.
We will get a set of keys
At the best motels.
With a jingle, jingle here and a jingle, jingle there,
Here a jingle, there a jingle,
Everywhere a jingle, jingle.
On vacation we have fun
Stopping at motels.

(*spoken*) Let's all check in now!

ROOM SERVICE

Use a poster or a piece of cardboard with a series of doors to tell this story. Number the doors 1, 2, 3, and 4. Behind door 1 is a towel and soap, behind door 2 is a tray of food, behind door 3 is a TV, and behind door 4 is a bed. Open the doors as directed in the story.

Hippo checked into the nicest hotel in town. He had been traveling all day and he was really tired. Hippo said to Penguin, the manager of the hotel, "I need a hot bath, a good dinner, some relaxing TV, and a comfortable bed. But I do not want to leave my room. Do you have room service?"

Penguin said, "Of course we do. I'll have Monkey see that you get everything you need. And service with a smile."

First Hippo wanted a hot bath. He called out, "Room service." Monkey came right away and said, "Here is what you need, sir. Glad to be of service. We give service with a smile." Monkey gave Hippo dinner on a tray. (*Open door 2.*) Was that the right thing for taking a bath? (*No.*) Hippo did not smile. So Monkey took back the tray of food and brought a towel and soap. (*Open door 1.*) Hippo took a bath with bubbles. Then Hippo smiled.

After Hippo took his bath he was really hungry. He called, "Room service." Monkey came right away and said, "Here is what you need, sir. Glad to be of service. We give service with a smile." Monkey gave Hippo a TV with thirty-two channels. (*Open door 3.*) Was that the right thing for eating dinner? (*No.*) Hippo did not smile. So Monkey took back the TV and brought Hippo a tray of food. (*Open door 2.*) It was delicious. Then Hippo smiled.

Then Hippo wanted to relax in front of a TV. He called, "Room service." Monkey came right away and said, "Here is what you need, sir. Glad to be of service. We give service with a smile." Monkey gave Hippo a roll-away bed. (*Open door 4.*) Was that the right thing for watching TV? (*No.*) Hippo did not smile. So Monkey took back the roll-away bed and brought Hippo a TV with thirty-two channels. (*Open door 3.*) Hippo watched a very funny movie. Then Hippo smiled.

Then Hippo was ready to sleep. He called, "Room service." Monkey came right away and said, "Here is what you need, sir. Glad to be of service. We give service with a smile." Monkey gave Hippo a towel and soap. (*Open door 1.*) Was that the right thing for going to sleep? (*No.*) Hippo did not smile. So Monkey took back the towel and soap and brought Hippo a roll-away bed. (*Open door 4.*) Then Hippo smiled. Hippo was so tired he fell asleep right away.

The next morning Hippo thanked Penguin for his stay at the hotel. Penguin asked, "Did Monkey give you good service?"

"Of course," said Hippo. "This hotel gives great service!" And Hippo himself gave a great big smile.

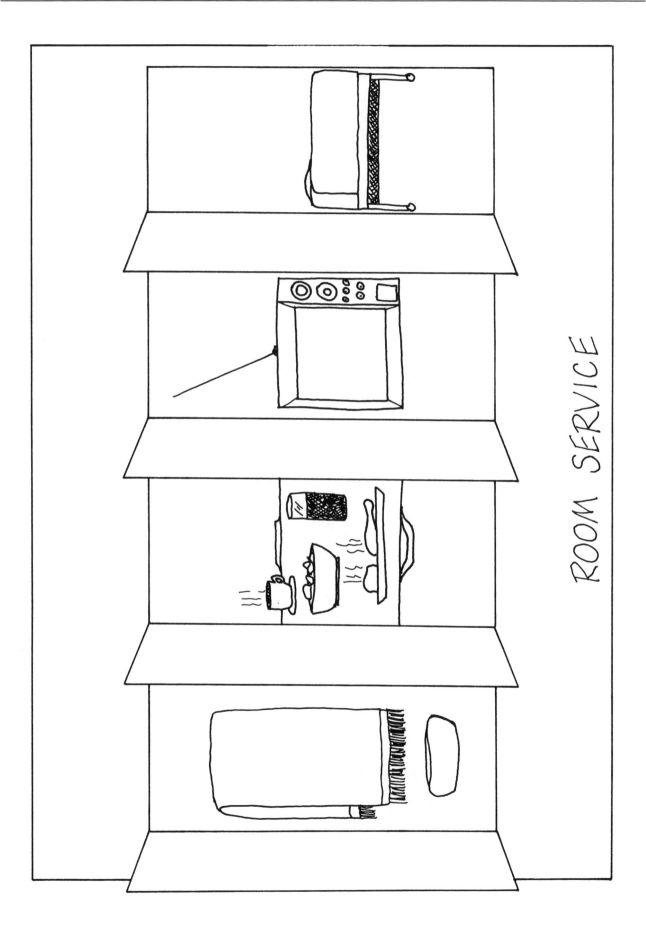

ROOM SERVICE

CAMP MISFORTUNE
(Camp Call)

Children should listen carefully so they can join you on the responses.

Welcome to Camp Misfortune	
We've got food	(*Yum, yum.*)
We've got beds	(*Ahhhh.*)
We've got fun	(*Yea!*)
Here are all the comforts of home	

Welcome to Camp Misfortune	
300 Kids in the dining hall	(*Yum, yum.*)
Cook over an open fire	(*Yum, yum.*)
Take lunches on the trail	(*Yum, yum.*)
Here are all the comforts of home	

Welcome to Camp Misfortune	
Sleeping bags zip up	(*Ahhhh.*)
Tent flaps roll down	(*Ahhhh.*)
Bunk beds line up in a row	(*Ahhhh.*)
Here are all the comforts of home	

Welcome to Camp Misfortune	
Swim every day	(*Yea!*)
Hike and canoe	(*Yea!*)
Catch butterflies	(*Yea!*)
Here are all the comforts of home	

Welcome to Camp Misfortune	
Hot dogs burn over the fire	(*Yuk, yuk.*)
Bunkmates snore all night	(*Zzzzz.*)
Huge mosquitoes bite	(*Ouch! Slap.*)
Won't you be glad to get back	
To all of the comforts of home?	(*Yea!*)

CAMP KITCHEN
(Tune: "Sing a Song of Sixpence")

Sing a song of camp food
Our kitchen is outdoors
Hot dogs on a long stick
Gooey good s'mores
Beans and soup and camp stew
Cooked up in a pot
Hurry with your tin plate
Get your camp food while it's hot

BACK-YARD SLEEPOVER
(Fingerplay)

Begin by holding up five fingers and help children hold up fewer fingers as each child in the story leaves. Whisper "good night" at the end.

Here's a tent with five kids
Sleeping on the floor
One forgot his flashlight
Then there were four

Here's a tent with four kids
Snug as can be
A big mosquito bit one
Then there were three

Here's a tent with three kids
Just a happy crew
One rolled over on a rock
Then there were two

Here's a tent with two kids
Having lots of fun
A ghost story scared one
Then there was one

Here's a tent with one kid
He thought he heard a mouse
Not so brave when all alone
He ran into the house

Goodnight!

GAMES FOR HIGHRISE TO HILLSIDE

CAT AND MOUSE GAME

Seat children in a circle. One child is chosen as the mouse. He walks around the circle touching each child on the head and saying "mouse." When he says "cat" the child tapped chases the mouse. The first one back to the mouse hole (the open space in the circle) is seated and the other becomes the mouse so the game continues.

TOWN OR COUNTRY

Arrange the children as you would for "London Bridge" and sing the following words to that tune. Select one child in the arch to be "town" and the other to be "country."

Do you want to live in town,
Live in town, live in town,
Do you want to live in town,
Or the country?

Children choose town or country and line up behind the appropriate child. When all children have chosen, join hands in a circle and sing the following verse:

When you live with those you love,
Those you love, those you love,
You'll be happy in the town
Or the country!

CRAFTS FOR HIGHRISE TO HILLSIDE

IN TENTS

Use the pattern shown below. Children cut out the tents. Inside they can list all the things they would take on an outdoor sleepover. Younger children may draw pictures or paste in cutouts from magazines.

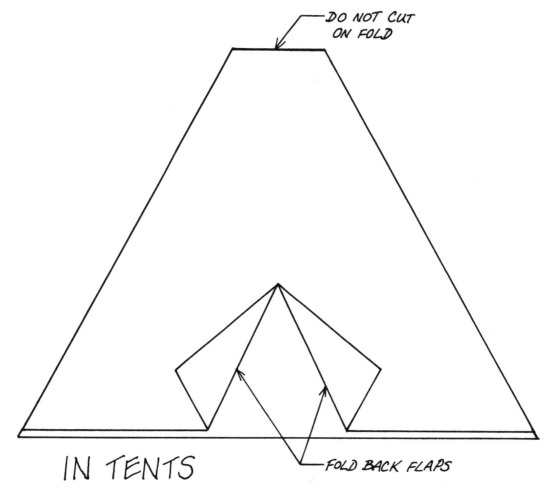

TALK OF THE TOWN

Fold a half sheet of paper accordion style and cut roof lines to make four houses. Children can write the names of family members, put addresses on the houses, draw pictures of the families who live there, or color the houses to resemble their own neighborhoods.

SHOEBOX HIGHRISE

Make apartment houses out of shoeboxes. Cut two slits in the sides of a shoebox, dividing the box in thirds. Insert two pieces of cardboard into the slits for the separate floors. Make an apartment house for each child. Children may decorate the apartments with cutouts or drawings of furniture and people. For extra fun, cut out familiar figures from book jackets or discarded books and let the children paste some famous storybook characters into their apartments.

YOUR VERY OWN HOME

Stack eight rectangles, 5½" × 8½", one on top of the other. Staple the papers together on the left (long) side to form a simple book. Make two diagonal cuts so that the top of the book has the triangular shape of a roof on a simple square house. Children may use each page as a different room of the house or to tell about each person and animal who lives there.

BUDDING ARCHITECTS

Hand out pieces of paper and direct children to draw a map of their own houses. Drawing will not be to scale, but it will help them realize how many rooms they have and how those rooms are located. In each room they can write a sentence telling the kind of activities done there or draw a picture of something found there.

IF YOU COULD CHOOSE YOUR NEIGHBORS

Make cup-puppet neighbors. Give each child a drinking straw, paper cup, and circle of paper. Punch a hole in the bottom of each paper cup with a pencil. Children can draw their own faces on the paper circles and attach these circles to the drinking straws. The straw should be inserted through the hole in the cup so that the face of the child will be inside the cup when the straw is pulled down and can peek out when the straw is pushed up.

PICTURE MY HOUSE

Draw the outline of a simple house on a paper for each child and cut a circle out of the center. Children color their houses to look like the ones they live in and complete the home by inserting their faces in the hole. This is a great chance to take snapshots!

PICTURE MY HOUSE

CITY NIGHT

Use a piece of black construction paper for each child to make an apartment building at night. Either punch windows with a hole punch and lay the black paper over yellow paper or put colored adhesive dots on the black paper for window lights.

FLOOR PLANS FOR HIGHRISE TO HILLSIDE

Focus Book: *The Town Mouse and the Country Mouse*
retold by Lorinda Bryan Cauley

Reading Activities

Compare this version of *The Town Mouse and the Country Mouse* with another edition of this fable by a different author and illustrator. The stories are the same, but how is the setting changed by the illustrations? By the language used?

Encourage children to "read" by noting details (such as the sampler "Make Mine Country" on the wall of the country house and the horse and buggy in the city).

Speaking Activities

Begin by writing the words "town" and "country" on the board or large paper. Brainstorm other words that have similar meaning, for example, "city," "urban," "village," "farm," and "rural." Help the children retell this story using these synonyms. For example, the title might be *The Urban Mouse and the Farm Mouse*.

Do the children picture the mice differently when they use different descriptive words? An urban mouse sounds more modern than a town mouse and a city mouse might be quite sophisticated. Let the children explain their impressions.

Writing Activities

Make a poster with two mouse holes drawn at the bottom. Above one mouse hole write "town"; above the other write "country." Let the children brainstorm any verb, adjective, or noun that comes to mind in either of these categories. They may then pick one word from each list and use it in a sentence about each mouse. A picture may accompany the sentence.

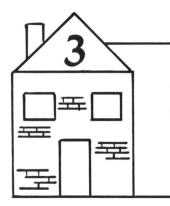

Pyramids and Pagodas

INTRODUCTION

The first homes probably were not much more than shelter against the weather and wild animals. Houses still provide protection from these things but also offer privacy and a place to sleep, eat, and express our lifestyles. This chapter introduces houses through the ages and around the world, providing a springboard for a closer look at housing on your own. Few picture books tell stories about historic houses, so we have written the "Tour of Homes down through the Ages," on page 60, to give a historic overview of houses. Some of these kinds of houses will be more familiar than others, but the mural props will add to children's understanding.

The houses in different parts of the world may be less familiar to children than food or clothing from other countries. Except for igloos and tepees, much of the information will require explanation and pictures when possible. We have written several activities about the more familiar homes, but "Yuri and the Yurt" and "Floating Homes Everywhere," which mentions a sampan, will extend children's knowledge of dwellings.

We have carefully researched and documented the names of Native American tribes and their unique homes so that children will become sensitized to cultural distinctions. This chapter is an introduction, and your discussion and understanding will be needed to help children more fully realize the unique characteristics of people and homes around the world.

The focus book, *Our Home Is the Sea* by Riki Levinson, with illustrations by Dennis Luzak, appropriately combines the two facets of this chapter. This story is about a modern family who live on a sampan, but carry on an ancient way of life.

INITIATING ACTIVITY

MY HOUSE IS YOUR HOUSE
(Mi Casa est Su Casa)

Introduce this Spanish phrase to children with a welcome in the spirit of sharing and world understanding. In a larger sense we all share the world as our home. Stand the children in a circle. After the poem have children say their own names and the names of the streets where they live.

My house is your house
My castle, my tent,
My igloo, my *casa*,
My tall apartment.
Wherever you come from,
Wherever you go,
You're welcome at my house.
Let's all say "hello!"

LITERATURE-SHARING EXPERIENCES

Books for Pyramids and Pagodas

Aardema, Verna. **Who's in Rabbit's House?** Illustrated by Leo and Diane Dillon. Dial, 1977.
The illustrations show west African villagers wearing animal masks as they tell the story "Who's in Rabbit's House," a folk tale in which a "bad thing" takes over Rabbit's house, much to the dismay of the other animals.

Anno, Mitsumasa. **Anno's USA**. Philomel, 1983.
Travel across the United States from west to east (the opposite direction in which the country was settled) and also go back in time. This wordless picture-book journey takes the reader to adobe houses in the desert; frame houses of Hannibal, Missouri, with Tom Sawyer and Huck Finn; row houses in Philadelphia; and even back to the half-timbered front houses of Jamestown.

Brown, Margaret Wise. **Wheel on the Chimney**. Illustrated by Tibor Gergely. Lippincott, 1954.
This book tells about the flight of storks from Africa to northern Europe and how they use homes as stopping places on their path.

Chaffin, Lillie. **We Be Warm till Springtime Comes**. Illustrated by Lloyd Bloom. Macmillan, 1980.
Young Jimmy Jake searches for fuel to keep his mother and sister warm through a severe Appalachian winter.

Dayrell, Elphinstone. **Why the Sun and the Moon Live in the Sky: An African Folktale**. Illustrated by Blair Lent. Houghton Mifflin, 1968.
When Water and all his relations fill the house of the Sun and the Moon, the Sun and the Moon must move to the sky where it is dry.

Emberley, Rebecca. **My House-Mi Casa: A Book in Two Languages**. Little, Brown, 1990.
The rooms and furnishings of a house are captioned in English and in Spanish with brightly colored illustrations.

Goodall, John. **Above and Below Stairs**. Atheneum, 1983.
Contrasting scenes from life above the stairs, with the upper classes, and below the stairs, with the servant class, are shown from the Middle Ages to the present in exterior and interior scenes of typical dwellings.

Goodall, John. **Creepy Castle**. Atheneum, 1975.
A brave young mouse and his lady friend venture into a deserted castle, unaware that an outlaw has been following them.

Goodall, John S. **The Story of an English Village**. Atheneum, 1978.

The changes of history unfold through pictures of an English village from its beginning as a medieval clearing to its present as a modern village with traffic. Two, two-page spreads are devoted to each century with half pages that reveal another scene. Interiors and exteriors of thatch medieval cottages, half-timbered front Renaissance houses, and Victorian rooms are shown.

Grifalconi, Ann. **The Village of Round and Square Houses**. Little, Brown, 1986.

This story, based on the real account of the village of Tos in the hills of the Cameroons in central Africa, tells of a volcanic eruption that left only two houses standing—one round and one square. As the village was being rebuilt, the men stayed in the tall square house, the women in the shorter round house—a tradition that continued, at least for part of each year, even after the other houses were built again. This book has vibrant, color pastel drawings.

Karavasil, Josephine. **Houses and Homes around the World.** Dillon, 1986.

Large photographs and minimal text show fourteen houses around the world, including thatch houses in Japan, houseboats (or sampans) in Hong Kong, houses made of rushes in Peru, and *ghorfas* in Tunisia.

Lent, Blair. **Bayberry Bluff**. Houghton Mifflin, 1987.

A real village with houses grows up on an island where people first spent summers in tents.

LeSeig, Theo. **Come Over to My House**. Illustrated by Richard Erdoes. Random House, 1966.

This rhymed text illustrates houses of all shapes, sizes, and styles the world over, including pink houses in Venice, houseboats in China, palaces in India, and tents in the Sahara.

Levinson, Riki. **Our Home Is the Sea**. Illustrated by Dennis Luzak. Dutton, 1988.

A Chinese boy hurries home from school to his family's houseboat in Hong Kong harbor, anxious to spend the summer fishing with his family.

Lim, John. **At Grandmother's House**. Tundra, 1977.

The artist-illustrator lovingly describes the pleasures of visiting his grandmother in her thatched-roof house in a small village on the island of Singapore in the 1930s. The description of the grandmother's kitchen with an entire wall devoted to a built-in cooking area will intrigue children.

Lobel, Arnold. **Ming Lo Moves the Mountain**. Greenwillow, 1982.

Ming Lo and his wife live in a house at the foot of a mountain in China. Rocks from the mountain make their life difficult, so Ming Lo seeks the advice of a wise man to help him move the mountain. After several unsuccessful attempts, Ming Lo succeeds in the end.

Messenger, Norman. **Annabel's House**. Orchard, 1988, 1989.

Lift the flaps to the doors and drawers in the various rooms of this elegant Edwardian house and you will discover how Annabel and her family live. Family jewels are hidden in a safe behind a picture on the wall. A cat is hidden among towels in the bathroom armoire and a mouse is sitting in a cubby of a rolltop desk. Punch-out people are tucked in the back of the book for children to place in the rooms. This is good for a library display rather than for circulation.

Mitchell, Vanessa. **Homes Then and Now**. Illustrated by Mark Peppe. G. Stevens, 1985.

Including dwellings from prehistoric times to the present, this book surveys homes and the rooms in them.

Montaufier, Poupa. **One Summer at Grandmother's House**. Translated from the French by Tobi Tobias. Carolrhoda, 1983.

This reminiscence about a little French girl who spends summers with her grandmother in Alsace includes memories of a neatly kept house, an attic of treasures, warm kitchens, and eiderdown quilts on the beds.

Nic Leodhas, Sorche. **Always Room for One More**. Illustrated by Nonny Hogrogian. Holt, Rinehart and Winston, 1965.

Based on a Scottish song, this tale concerns Lachie MacLachlan, who hails each traveler who passes his door to "Come awa' in! There's room for one more." After the merry procession bulges out the walls, they raise a bonny new house that will always have room for one more.

Rudstrom, Lennart. **A Home**. With paintings by Carl Larsson. Putnam's, 1974.

This award-winning book is a treasury of fifteen paintings by the beloved Swedish painter of the late nineteenth-century, Carl Larsson. Subjects include his home and family. Detailed text describes the objects and people shown in the rooms, which include Larsson's studio, the old-fashioned kitchen, and his bedroom with a decorative tile oven.

Rylant, Cynthia. **When I Was Young in the Mountains**. Illustrated by Diane Goode. Dutton, 1982.

Life in a simple mountain cabin is a joyful experience for the children growing up there.

Shefelman, Janice. **Victoria House**. Illustrated by Tom Shefelman. Gulliver Books and Harcourt Brace Jovanovich, 1988.

An architect couple and their son buy a Victorian house and have it moved from a deserted lot to the city. There the house is lovingly restored and lived in again.

Shemie, Bonnie. **Houses of Snow, Skin, and Bones**. Tundra, 1989.

The first title in Tundra's promising new series of books on architecture for children describes the four basic shelters—the snow house, the *quarmang* (stone, whale-bone, and skin house), the sod house, and the tent—built by native peoples in the far north. Color illustrations and brief text that could be read aloud for storytime are interspersed with more detailed informational text useful for student study.

Snyder. Dianne. **Boy of the Three Year Nap**. Illustrated by Allen Say. Houghton Mifflin, 1988.

Taro, a lazy boy, plans a deceit so he can marry the daughter of a rich man and get a larger house for her to live in.

Willard, Nancy. **A Visit to William Blake's Inn**. Illustrated by Alice and Martin Provensen. Harcourt Brace Jovanovich, 1981.

This double award-winning book (Newbery Award and Caldecott honor) is a collection of poems about a fantasy inn supposedly owned by the eighteenth-century poet William Blake. The rooms and architecture are vintage English but everything is touched with fantasy from the "rabbit who makes your bed" to the "two dragons (that) bake your bread."

Wood, Audrey. **King Bidgood's in the Bath Tub**. Illustrated by Don Wood. Harcourt Brace Jovanovich, 1985.

The glorious Renaissance setting in King Bidgood's bath shows us elegant court feasts with a procession of entertainers who all try to persuade the jolly king to get out of the bathtub.

Zemach, Margot. **It Could Always Be Worse**. Farrar, Straus and Giroux, 1976.

The humorous retelling of the Yiddish folk tale is set somewhere in eastern Europe in the overcrowded, one-room hut of a family who eventually learns how to share a small living space in peace.

Related Activities for Pyramids and Pagodas

A TOUR OF HOMES DOWN THROUGH THE AGES

Tell the story of how people have built homes throughout the ages by having children take the parts of people who lived in those houses. Use posterboard murals of different houses described in the following songs and poems (see illustrations on p. 61). This can be used as a readers' theater script. The leader can read the narration with children singing the songs in between.

The first humans, who lived four million years ago, slept and ate outdoors. That was fine when the sun was shining and there weren't any saber-toothed tigers around. But when it rained, people needed to be dry. When fierce animals came, people needed to be safe. What did they do?

First Home on the Range
(Tune: "When Johnny Comes Marching Home")

We climbed right up the tallest tree
And hid quite high.
We looked for rock to shelter us
'Neath them we lie
Then one of us
Who's very wise
Discovered right before our eyes
That the caves were safe and
They would keep us dry.

As people began to hunt, they found they had to move often when the animals migrated. They needed homes they could build quickly and live in for a short time. They had to use whatever materials were around. These homes were not very fancy, but they were practically prefab!

Quick and Dirty
(Tune: "Mulberry Bush")

Grass and mud will make a hut,
Make a hut, make a hut,
Quick and dirty, tut, tut, tut!
That's how we make our mud hut.

In the hot climate of Egypt great stone monuments honored the dead, and bricks for homes were made of clay and straw. The first real architects were hired to make the houses for the Egyptians.

In ancient Rome building went on in a big way. Wealthy Romans came home to villas, with hot air heating, bedrooms, and baths with inside toilets.

Ancient Wonders
(Tune: "She'll Be Comin' round the Mountain")

We'll be building homes of stones and straw and clay
We'll be building homes of stones and straw and clay
It will take a long long while
But we'll do it with great style
'Cause we know Rome was not built in just a day

FIRST HOME ON THE RANGE

QUICK AND DIRTY

Mud Hut

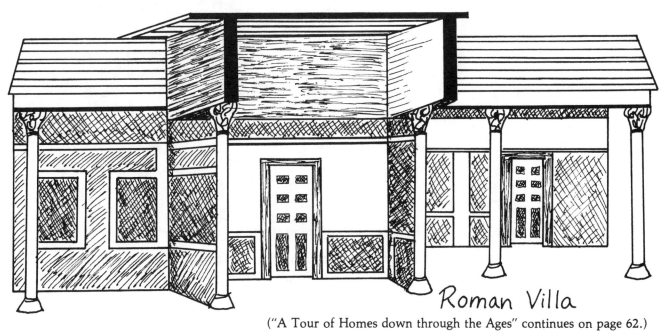

Roman Villa

("A Tour of Homes down through the Ages" continues on page 62.)

Now on the other side of the world, the Plains Indians in North America learned to make truly mobile homes. The tepee was buffalo skin stretched over tall poles. There was a hole to let out the smoke from the fire and to allow natural air-conditioning.

Meanwhile in the southwest United States the Pueblo Indians were farmers and built on the mesas. Native Americans used the materials found in nature and did not damage the land with their construction.

Native American Homes

We're native people with names like Sioux,
Iroquois, and Kickapoo,
Shawnee, Delaware, and Crow,
Hopi, Cheyenne, Navaho.

Building homes of mud and clay,
Poles and sticks to go or stay.
Sod and cedar, buffalo hide.
Close the flap and crawl inside.

Longhouse, tepee, cliff house high,
Totem pole up to the sky.
Pueblo, hogan built with care
For the world that we all share.

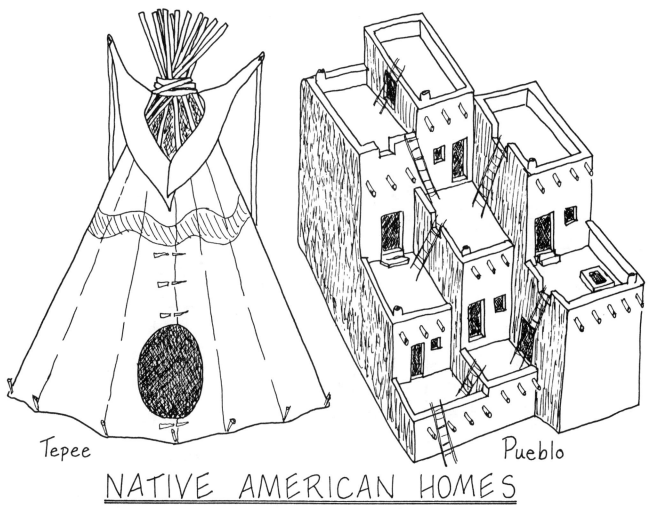

Tepee   Pueblo

NATIVE AMERICAN HOMES

Back in Europe, people in the Dark Ages lived in homes made of wattle and daub—woven sticks covered with mud. In France stones were used for building. As more and more building went on, towns in Europe grew up and up and up. Town houses were soon several stories high with the upstairs rooms overhanging the street. There were no sewer systems, so windows provided a quick exit for all kinds of rubbish.

Once upon a Second Story
(Tune: "My Bonnie Lies over the Ocean")

We live in a two-story building
It hangs far out over the street.
When we have a bucket of garbage
It's easy to keep our house neat.
Out the window,
Throw out the garbage and dump the trash!
Out the window.
Look out below for the splash!

ONCE UPON A
SECOND STORY

("A Tour of Homes down through the Ages" continues on page 64.)

When Europeans came to the New World, they brought housing ideas with them but quickly adapted to the materials most available here. Wood was used for many houses, from log cabins to clapboard houses. Fine Southern mansions were built from brick. Dutch houses in the Hudson Valley had front porches and built-in beds. The frontier was settled. People pushed west until there was no place left to go. When people could no longer move out they moved up, higher and higher in city apartments.

Homes of the Future
(Tune: "Twinkle, Twinkle, Little Star")

City houses reach up high
Tall and pointing to the sky.
Someday we will find a place
We can live in outer space.
Geodesic solar domes,
Lots of shelters we call home.

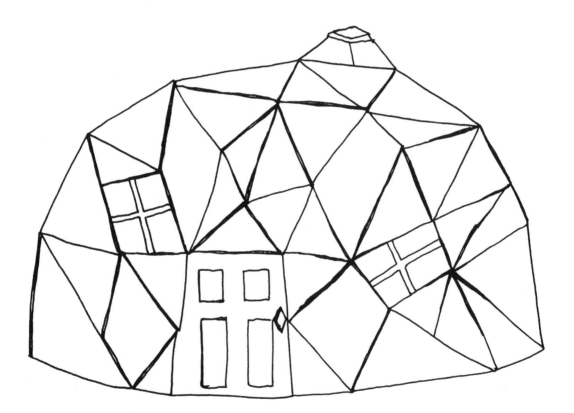

HOMES OF THE FUTURE

CAVE HOMES
(Tune: "On Top of Old Smokey")

The very first house that
Some people did find
Was a cave in the mountains
A bear left behind.

It didn't have comfort.
It didn't have style.
But they had each other,
So they stayed for a while

They had rocks for pillows
And how they did snore!
Their very first watch dog
Was a huge dinosaur.

And when it got dusty
They didn't clean there.
They just packed their things and
They followed a bear.

MUMMY HUNT

We're going on a mummy hunt

We're going to swish through the sand   (*Rub hands together.*)

Swish, swish, swish.

Here we are at the pyramid

Open the creaking door

Eeeeeeek.   (*Move arm as if opening door.*)

Look, there's writing on the walls.   (*Point.*)

It's hieroglyphics—it says walk this way.

Let's tiptoe.   (*Tiptoe in place.*)

Shhhhh, shhhhh.

Here is the inner chamber and

King Tut!

He's having a party.

Let's dance!   (*Dance Egyptian style.*)

Time to go

Better tiptoe out so they don't miss us   (*Tiptoe.*)

Read the hieroglyphics   (*Point.*)

It says "This way out."

Open the door

Eeeek.   (*Move arm as if opening door.*)

And slam it shut

Bang.   (*Clap.*)

Back through the swishing sand   (*Rub hands together.*)

And back to our home.

Brush the sand out of your clothes.   (*Brush self.*)

Do you remember how to dance like King Tut?   (*Dance as before.*)

THIS IS THE CASTLE
(Fingerplay)

This is the castle	
With towers so tall	(*Make pointed roof shape over head with hands.*)
Stones piled so high	
Here are the walls.	(*Place two arms on top of each other, nose level as if you can barely see over the wall.*)
Here is the moat	
Round like a crown.	(*"Draw" imaginary circle with fingers around self, waist high.*)
Here is the drawbridge	
That goes up and down.	(*Left arm parallel to body, elbow of right arm in palm of left hand. Raise and lower right arm like a bridge.*)

CABIN FEVER
(A Story with a Built-in Follow-up Activity)

Before you tell this story, teach children the expression "cabin fever." We usually use the phrase when we mean people feel cooped up inside. In this case the house is quite a small cabin, so there's even more reason to use the phrase "cabin fever" to describe Sarah's grumpiness about small spaces.

Spread out Lincoln logs on a table as you tell this story. Then when Seth and his children begin building the log cabin, begin building a small cabin of your own. At the end of the story point out that this was just a tall tale but if everyone works together you can use the Lincoln logs to build a truly amazing big log cabin—by golly!

Out on the prairie when folks settled down for the night they told tall tales about the way things were or the way they wished things could be. Life was hard settling the prairies so people dreamed of heroes who performed fantastic feats. These tall tales helped people survive those hard times.

Back in the days when people cut down forests to build log cabins in the wilderness and settled the prairies there lived a man, his wife, and seven children. The man's name was Seth and the wife's name was Sarah. The seven children were called Molly, Polly, Solly, Wally, Lolly, Dolly, and By Golly—which was Seth's favorite expression. People always said that amazing things happened every time Seth said "By golly!" Just to show you what I mean, one time there had been a drought for six weeks. Then one day big rain clouds started to roll in. And Seth looked up at the sky and said, "By golly, it's gonna rain." And it did.

Now Seth and Sarah and Molly, Polly, Solly, Wally, Lolly, Dolly, and By Golly lived in a small town that was growing so fast that people said it was going to become a boom town.

"By golly!" said Seth. "There's a whole lot of folks coming." And sure enough there was.

Now Sarah didn't like that. She got grumpy when she didn't have her space. So the family packed up their cooking pots and their rocking chair and their old trunk, put them in a covered wagon, and set out for the wide open spaces.

First they came to a forest. There weren't any people around but there wasn't a lot of space. Now Sarah didn't like that. She got grumpy when she didn't have her space.

"By golly!" said Seth. "There are too many trees." And sure enough there was.

So Seth and Molly, Polly, Solly, Wally, Lolly, Dolly, and By Golly chopped down the trees. Then Seth used those trees to build a snug and sturdy log cabin.

Sarah took one look at the log cabin and said, "Too small. I can't live in a house with no more space than this." She got grumpy when she didn't have her space.

Seth didn't say anything this time. He just looked up into the sky and saw snow beginning to fall. "By golly," said Seth. "Winter's comin'. We'll just have to settle in for the winter anyway."

So Seth and Molly, Polly, Solly, Wally, Lolly, Dolly, and By Golly settled into the snug and sturdy log cabin. Sarah stayed outside. She needed her space. But the snow got deeper and deeper until she got so grumpy that even Sarah came inside for the rest of the winter.

When spring came the snow finally melted. Seth was the first one outside.

"By golly," he said. "An amazing thing has happened. Come see for yourself."

And the amazing thing was this. So much snow had fallen on the log cabin during the winter that the snow had no place to go when it started to melt. The logs in that cabin sucked up all that melted snow and they began to swell. They swelled and they swelled and they swelled. By the time Molly, Polly, Solly, Wally, Lolly, Dolly, and By Golly got outside, the house was seven times its size.

"Come on outside, Ma," called the children. "Come see for yourself how big our house is now."

So Sarah went outside. At first she looked grumpy, but then when she saw that the log cabin was seven times its size, she was grumpy no more. At last she had her space.

"By golly!" said Seth. "This house has enough space for Molly, Polly, Solly, Wally, Lolly, Dolly, By Golly, and even Sarah." And that was the most amazing feat of all.

YURI AND THE YURT

This poem will introduce the yurt, a tent of felt and willow branches used on the Asian steppes. When it is time to move, the tent is collapsed like an umbrella and loaded on camels.

In Asia on the grassy plains
The tent protects against the rains
Like an umbrella opens wide
To let all kinds of friends inside
A yurt is what you call this tent
Here Yuri lived in sweet content.

One day a sheep came running by
"I'm chased by wolves," he loudly cried
"Open up your yurt for me
So I can hide with you, Yuri!"
So Yuri opened up the tent
And two lived there in sweet content.

And then a goat came running by
"I'm chased by wolves," he loudly cried
"Open up your yurt for me
So I can hide with you, Yuri!"
So Yuri opened up the tent
And three lived there in sweet content.

And then a yak came running by
"I'm chased by wolves," he loudly cried
"Open up your yurt for me
So I can hide with you, Yuri!"
So Yuri opened up the tent
And four lived there in sweet content.

And then the wolf came running by
"I'm chasing sheep and goats," he cried
"Do you have a yak for me?
Open this yurt so I can see!"

But Yuri kept the flaps closed tight
The wolf blew hard with all his might
But yurts are made to stand the strain
Of gusts of winds and beating rain

The wolf said, "Please don't make me go.
I only run for fun, you know
And from all meat I stay away
And just eat veggies every day."
So Yuri opened up the tent
And five lived there in sweet content.

HEADS IN THE CLOUD AND FEET ON THE GROUND

In Malaysia are houses standing on stilts
To keep people cool and quite dry.
In Nepal the houses are stone and mud brick
And perched on the mountain so high.
Greek island houses sit up on a hill
White paint reflecting the heat.
When houses are high up the people look out
And see the world spread at their feet.

Near the Sahara are tunnels so deep
To keep people out of the sun.
The houses in outback Australia were mines
Now folks sleep there when work is done.
In Norway the stone houses have to be low;
You can't lift up stones very high.
When houses are low down the people look up
And see the expanse of the sky.

FOUR CITIES OF THE WORLD

Nairobi, Nairobi.
City of wonder.
Skyscrapers rise from the plains
high and higher
reach toward the sky.
Is it any wonder
that the passing giraffe
looks up in wonder
at the tall-necked
creatures,
rising from the plains
high and higher?
Nairobi, Nairobi.

Cairo, Cairo.
Ancient marvel and modern city.
People stacked in highrise dwellings,
a dozen, a hundred in a single building.
Just beyond
a mummy sleeps
alone
in a pyramid
that could house a thousand.
Ancient marvel and modern city.
Cairo, Cairo.

Edinburgh, Edinburgh.
Bagpipes call from ancient walls
surrounded by the noise of traffic.
Split-level city
of castle rock
and contemporary roar.
Can you hear the sound of the piper
If the wind is right?
Edinburgh, Edingurgh.

Rio, Rio,
Rio de Janeiro.
Ocean at your feet
Comes softly washing
Beaches of riches.
While to your back
Sugar Loaf looms
And nestles favelas.
City of contrast.
Rio, Rio,
Rio de Janeiro.

TENT TENANTS
(Mask Story)

Make masks of one sheep, two goats, three camels, and four cobras for children to tell this story. Two other children can join hands to form the entrance to the tent and another child can be Nathaniel to beckon the children in. All the children can join in making the winds blow and blow.

Out in the Sahara Desert it is very hot and very dry and very sandy. And sometimes it is very windy. This story takes place on a windy, sandy day and is about a nomad named Nathaniel.

It was early in the morning when the wind began to blow and blow and blow. It blew the flaps on Nathaniel's tent. It blew his robes until he looked like a big bat about to fly away. The wind blew the sand right up off the ground and into the air until Nathaniel could not see anything but sand, sand, and more sand.

Nathaniel pulled his robe tightly around him and tied the flaps of the tent tight. He would be safe inside from the sand storm.

And the wind blew and blew and blew.

In the middle of the wind came a sound. Not a blowing sound, but a baa-ing sound. It was one lost sheep wanting to come into the tent.

Nathaniel said,

> "The sand is blowing so you can't see!
> Make your home in the tent with me."

"But," Nathaniel added, "no more saying 'baa.'"

The one lost sheep agreed and made his home inside the tent with Nathaniel.

And the wind blew and blew and blew.

In the middle of the wind came a sound. Not a blowing sound, but a bumping sound. It was two lost goats wanting to come into the tent.

Nathaniel said,

> "The sand is blowing so you can't see!
> Make your home in the tent with me."

"But," Nathaniel added, "no more bumping things."

The two lost goats agreed and made their home inside the tent with Nathaniel.

And the wind blew and blew and blew.

In the middle of the wind came a sound. Not a blowing sound, but a galumphing sound. It was three lost camels wanting to come into the tent.

Nathaniel said,

> "The sand is blowing so you can't see!
> Make your home in the tent with me."

"But," Nathaniel added, "no more galumphing about."

The three lost camels agreed and made their home inside the tent with Nathaniel.

And the wind blew and blew and blew.

In the middle of the wind came a sound. Not a blowing sound, but a hissing sound. It was four lost cobras wanting to come into the tent. Nathaniel wasn't sure about letting cobras into the tent, but he did not want them to get lost in the sand storm, so he said,

Goat

Cobra

Masks shown
with elastic
attached

Sheep

Camel

TENT TENANTS

"The sand is blowing so you can't see!
Make your home in the tent with me."

"But," Nathaniel added, "no more hissing."

The four lost cobras agreed and made their home inside the tent with Nathaniel. And they tried, they really did try, but the four cobras could not help hissing. That is just the way cobras are.

And when the three camels heard the four cobras hiss, they began to galumph about.

And when the two goats heard the three camels galumphing about, they began to bump things.

And when the one sheep heard the two goats bumping things, he began to say "baa-baa-baa" as loudly as he could.

And in the middle of all that noise, there was suddenly a new sound. It was not hissing or galumphing or bumping or baa-ing. It was not even the wind blowing.

It was silence. The sand storm had stopped. Carefully Nathaniel looked out of his tent and saw the sunshine. Everything was quiet and safe. So Nathaniel said,

"The sand's not blowing any more
Go find your way to your own front door!"

And he hung a sign on the front of the tent that read

NO baa-ing
NO bumping
NO galumphing
NO hissing
NO ANIMALS ALLOWED
(Except in sand storms)

HOT HOUSES AND COLD STORAGE
(Tune: "My Bonnie Lies over the Ocean")

We live in a hut with a grass roof
The walls are all open and free
The sun is so hot we stay inside
And sit in the shade of a tree
Hot, cold
Hot, cold
Get out of the sun and the wind and snow
Hot, cold
Hot, cold
There are houses wherever you go

Our igloo is made out of ice bricks
We live way up north where it snows
We wrap up in rugs in our ice house
And listen to whistling winds blow
Hot, cold
Hot, cold
Get out of the sun and the wind and snow
Hot, cold
Hot, cold
There are houses wherever you go

NO EXIT

Igloos are built from the inside with the door cut after all the construction is completed. The small tunnel is added so people can get in, but the wind will stay out.

Snow is blowing cold outside.	(*Shiver.*)
Cut the snow blocks—make them wide.	(*Reach arms wide.*)
Place them in a circle round.	(*Make circle with arms.*)
Stack them so they won't fall down.	(*Place one hand on other as if stacking.*)
Stand inside to build this home.	(*Bend elbows, hands at shoulder height parallel to body.*)
Close the top to make a dome.	(*Touch fingertips over head.*)
Now the wind can whistle past	(*Wave arms.*)
Our cozy home we've built so fast.	(*Point to selves.*)
The only problem I can see:	(*Hands on hips, look around.*)
There's no door for you and me!	(*Shake head.*)
We can make one, small and low,	(*Crouch or kneel on floor.*)
Just cut a hole and out we go!	(*Crawl away.*)

FLOATING HOMES EVERYWHERE
(Tune: "Way Down upon the Swanee River")

Way down upon a lazy river
Sailing away,
There you will find some floating houses
That's where the people stay.
Take a trip on the Mississippi
On a houseboat roam.
Or travel down the Peking River,
You'll make a sampan home.

HOME IS WHERE THE HEART IS

Use a long, narrow piece of paper, 11" × 5" folded accordion fashion into four equal panels. Cut out a house shape as shown from the paper, keeping the paper folded. Hold up the house shape as you begin telling the story.

Panel 1

Homer Washington had never traveled far from home. He lived in a small frame house with a flower garden and a house cat. Homer had always lived in his little house in his hometown. People were friendly there, but there wasn't too much change of scenery. One day Homer got the urge to see faraway places and exotic lands, so he bought a ticket to take a round-the-world trip.

His first stop was New York City, where many people live in highrise apartment buildings. (*Open the folded building and on the back side draw windows for apartment building, as shown.*)

Back side
of panel 1

Homer liked the view from the fiftieth floor. He liked looking at all the people in all of the windows, but his heart really wasn't in the city.

He shook his head and said:

"I'm restless and itchy
To travel and roam
But this isn't the place
I want to call home."

So he hopped on the plane and flew to merry old England. (*Unfold next panel and cut according to illustration.*)

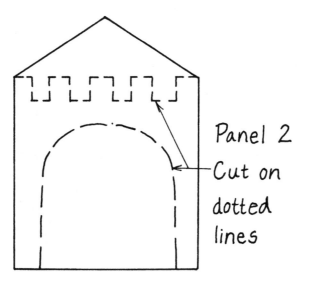

Panel 2
Cut on
dotted
lines

Here he spent a long night in a drafty old castle. It was so drafty that he almost put on one of the suits of armor. His heart really wasn't in the castle.

He shook his head and said:

> "I'm restless and itchy
> To travel and roam
> But this isn't the place
> I want to call home."

So he hopped on the plane and flew to the Yukon. (*Open next panel and cut igloo as shown.*)

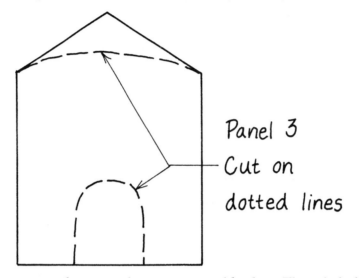

Panel 3
Cut on
dotted lines

There he spent an even longer night in an icy cold igloo. The whale blubber gave him indigestion and the television reception was lousy. His heart really wasn't in the igloo.

He shook his head and said:

> "I'm restless and itchy
> To travel and roam
> But this isn't the place
> I want to call home."

So he hopped on the plane and flew to Egypt. (*Open to last panel and cut pyramid from top half as in illustration. Do not cut through, so pyramid shape will remain intact.*)

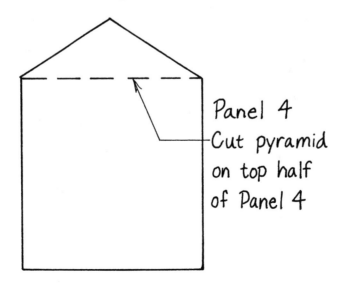

Panel 4
Cut pyramid
on top half
of Panel 4

He spent a day touring the pyramids. But he got sand in his eyes and butterflies in his stomach from the camel ride. His heart really wasn't in the pyramids.

He shook his head and said:

> "I'm restless and itchy
> To travel and roam
> But this isn't the place
> I want to call home."

Homer Washington had come to the end of his worldwide tour. His heart wasn't in the city. It wasn't in the castle. It wasn't in the igloo. And it wasn't in the pyramid. Homer Washington shook his head and said:

> "I was restless and itchy
> To travel and roam
> But now I am ready
> To hurry back home."

So this time Homer hopped on the plane and headed back to his small frame house. After all the exotic places he had been he realized he was really homesick at heart. He missed his flower garden and he missed his house cat. His missed all the friendly people and, for a change, he wanted to see some old familiar scenery. Home was where Homer wanted to be. So that was where he went. And that's where he stayed. (*Fold back pyramid and cut small home with heart as shown.*)

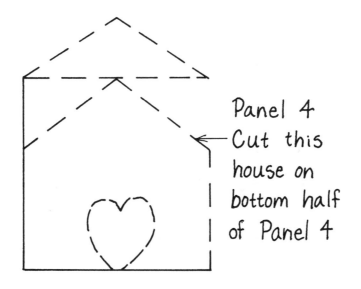

Homer is where his heart is.

GAMES FOR PYRAMIDS AND PAGODAS

TOUR OF HOMES WORLDWIDE

Set up different areas of the room with pictures of homes and books about different parts of the world. Lead the children around the room singing these words to the tune of "Mary Had a Little Lamb."

> Let's go on a tour of homes
> Tour of homes, tour of homes
> Let's go on a tour of homes
> To homes around the world.

Add verses for the various countries you are "visiting."

> Let's all go to Mexico,
> Mexico, Mexico,
> Let's all go to Mexico,
> To homes around the world.

KEEP THE HOME FIRES BURNING

Sit in a circle. The leader rubs hands together as if warming them. The leader then taps the person to the left and both rub hands. Play continues with each one tapped rubbing hands together until the whole circle is keeping the home fires burning and hands are toasty warm.

TENT TIME

Use a bed sheet to play a tenting game. Station children around the edges of a sheet, holding it high enough so other children can pass underneath. Sing the following words to the tune of "London Bridge," lowering the sheet gently at the end of the refrain. Any child under the sheet when it is lowered takes the place of a child holding an edge and play continues.

> Tents on deserts and on plains
> Keep off sun, wind, and rain.
> Take a tent along with you
> When you travel.

CRAFTS FOR PYRAMIDS AND PAGODAS

LOG CABIN PRETZEL HOUSE

Photocopy the house pattern shown in the illustration on page 77, enlarging as you wish, or cut out the shape of the house from lightweight posterboard. Provide pretzels for children to glue to the house, horizontally for the walls and vertically for the door. You may wish to choose different sizes of pretzel sticks (fatter ones, for example) for the door. The roof can be colored or you can provide straw or Easter grass for the roof, since some of the log cabins had sod roofs. Houses can be sprayed with shellac to preserve them or can be left as is.

LOG CABIN PRETZEL HOUSE

ENGLISH COTTAGE

This half-timbered front cottage made of wattle and daub was also the kind of house that the Jamestown settlers built. Older children will enjoy finding pictures of these cottages in some of the resource books.

Cut out the house from tan construction paper using the pattern on page 79. Fold on dotted lines. Then, before you glue the house, attach trim as indicated in the illustration. The timbers and doors are cut from small scraps of brown construction paper. Next, glue section A to the B side of the house. Stand up your house.

Cut out the roof sections from brown construction paper. You may wish to cut out a third small roof section, slightly smaller than the small roof pattern. Create a thatched roof effect by slashing the small roof section on the lines indicated. Fold both roof sections on dotted lines. Glue the large roof section to the house by placing the undersides of the C sections of the roof over the C pitch of the house. Glue the smaller roof section on top of the big roof.

ADOBE OR EGYPTIAN MUD HOUSE

The basic mud or adobe house has been made in many parts of the world where it is hot. This version simplifies the design since large clay slabs instead of individual blocks are used. (See illustration on page 80.) Older children may wish to make the blocks instead.

Simply roll out clay (either commercial or your favorite play dough recipe) to about ½-inch thick and cut four rectangles about four inches by three inches to make the walls of your house. Cut out a door and a few small windows (not many since these houses have few openings so the hot sun won't heat up the house). Join the four slabs and stand up your house. Lay thin dowels or craft sticks across the top of the house so you can attach a stick or grass roof. You might dig up grass and mud or use straw or Easter grass for this. Tiny toothpicks or sticks can be added to the front of the house, as the Pueblo Indian houses use this trim.

PLAINS INDIAN TEPEE

The Plains Indians made tepee covers from buffalo hides that were sewn together. These covers were stretched around poles that had been set in a circular arrangement. The tepee covers were decorated with designs.

The pattern on page 80 is similar to the shape of the tepee cover. Cut out shapes and invite children to decorate them with geometric designs or simple drawings of the buffalo hunt. Overlap sides of the tepee cover and glue or staple together to make your tepee stand up.

CASTLE SIMPLIFIED

Use the simple crenellated, or "toothed," edged wall pattern on page 81 to make your castle. The taller portion is rolled around and glued to make a rounded tower. The shorter section is folded on the dotted lines to make the castle walls. Cut out two pages of these patterns to make a castle enclosure with two towers. You can make many more if you wish a large castle. Add decorations such as flags made of toothpicks and small ribbon banners. Cut out doorways if you wish. (See illustration on page 82.)

PATTERN FOR
ENGLISH COTTAGE

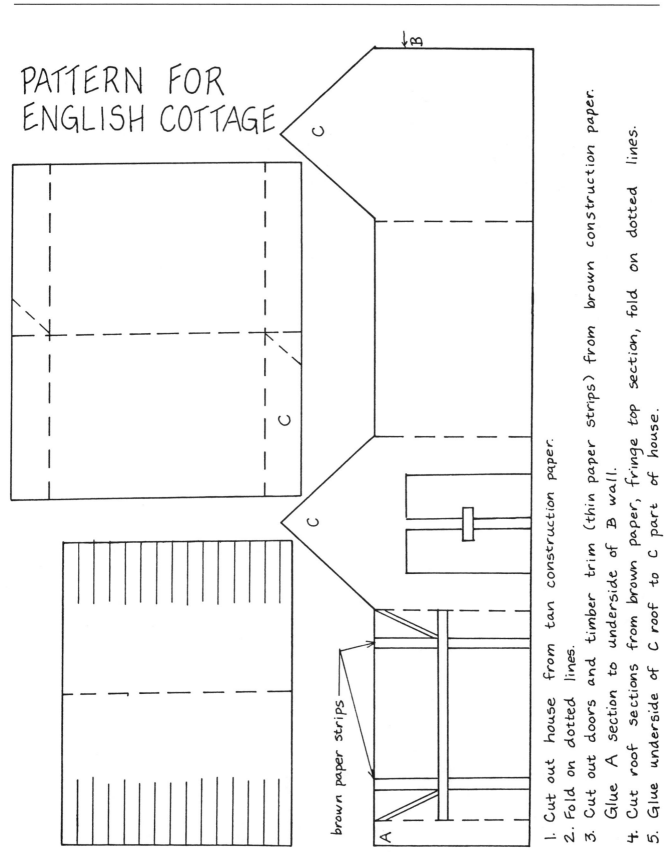

brown paper strips

1. Cut out house from tan construction paper.
2. Fold on dotted lines.
3. Cut out doors and timber trim (thin paper strips) from brown construction paper. Glue A section to underside of B wall.
4. Cut roof sections from brown paper, fringe top section, fold on dotted lines.
5. Glue underside of C roof to C part of house.

ADOBE OR EGYPTIAN MUD HOUSE

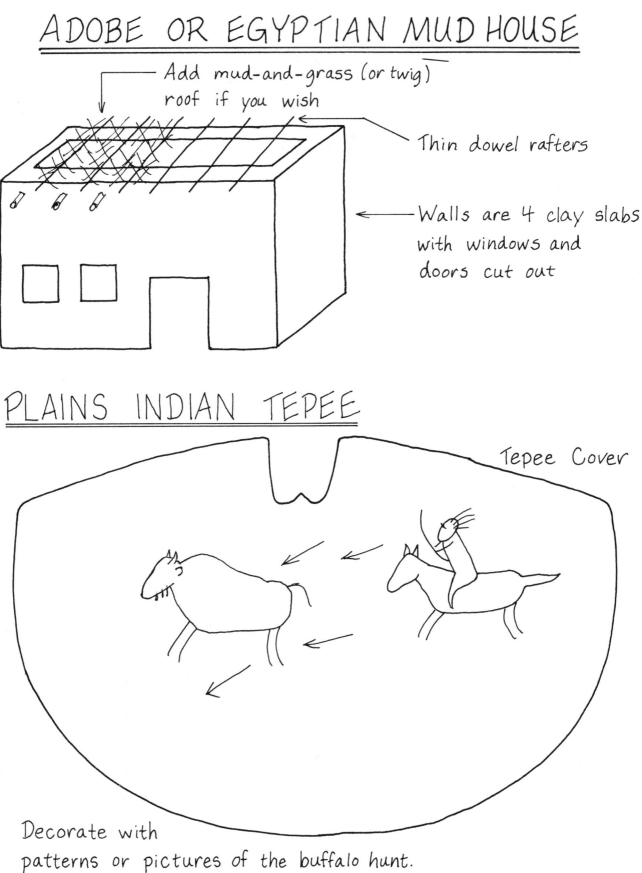

Add mud-and-grass (or twig) roof if you wish

Thin dowel rafters

Walls are 4 clay slabs with windows and doors cut out

PLAINS INDIAN TEPEE

Tepee Cover

Decorate with patterns or pictures of the buffalo hunt.

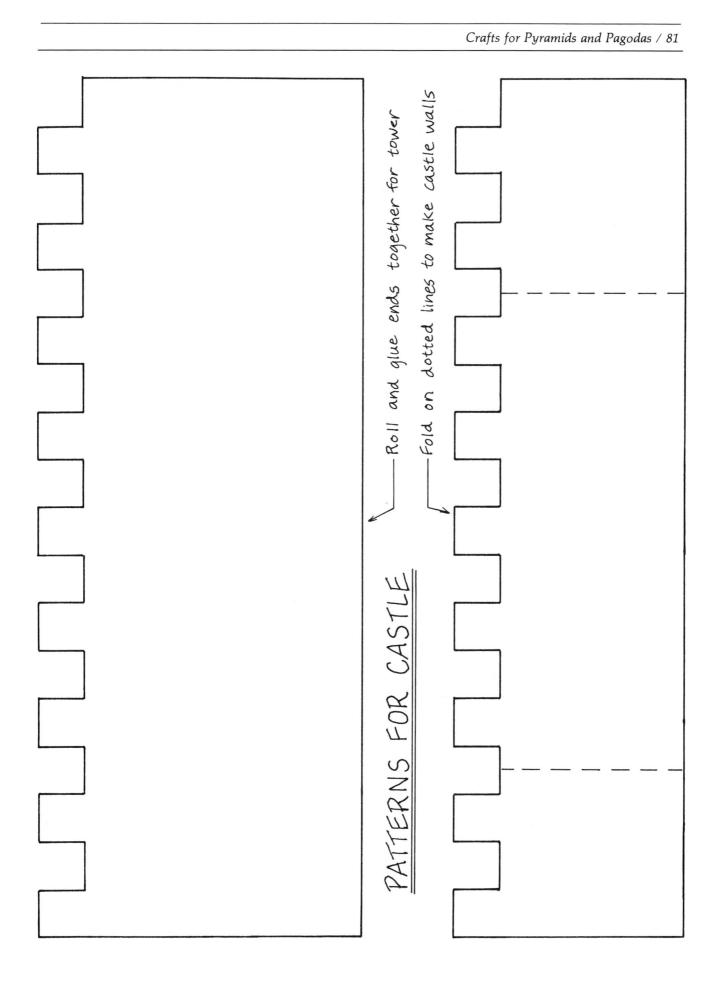

Roll and glue ends together for tower

Fold on dotted lines to make castle walls

PATTERNS FOR CASTLE

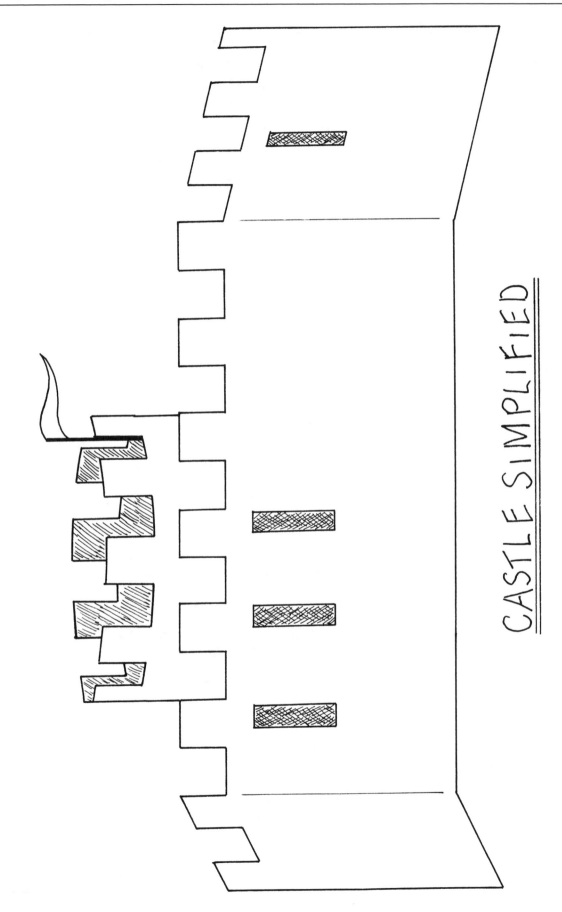

CASTLE SIMPLIFIED

FLOOR PLANS FOR PYRAMIDS AND PAGODAS

Focus Book: *Our Home Is the Sea* by Riki Levinson

Reading Activities

The illustrations in this book are so compelling that it will be worthwhile to linger long and dream quietly about these places. The quiet, warm, and inviting mood is established even on the title and dedication pages.

The first-person telling of this story will make the children identify with the child in the story. The reader should explain to the listeners that the story is set in Hong King so there will be scenes of city life as well as those more removed on the quiet sea. There is also a sharp contrast of modern life and strong tradition.

Four words are introduced before the story begins: *amah* (nurse or maid), *congee* (thin rice soup), sampan (small boat), and tram (double-deck trolly). Ask children to listen for these words as the story is read.

Speaking Activities

Look at the page near the middle of the book that shows the birdmen talking. Read the text on this page again slowly, pointing out where the bird cages have been hung and how the men are seated to talk. Let the children speculate out loud what the men have to say to one another. What do the birds have to talk about?

Writing Activities

The family lives on a houseboat, a unique combination of a home and a way to travel. The multigenerational family in China lives together on this sampan. Ask if any children live in a multigenerational home and encourage them to write about this experience. Children can keep a journal or booklet of their family homes with drawings and a sentence or two describing their families.

All
Spruced Up

INTRODUCTION

Children will either love or hate this chapter! Very young children may like the idea of cleaning as they pick up a broom or mop to model Mom or Dad cleaning the house. As they get older and are expected to take care of their own rooms, children become less enthusiastic about the "chore." Many of the books and activities in this chapter offer humorous consequences of rooms and houses that are not "all spruced up." The other topic in this chapter—house decorating—does have more immediate appeal for children. Trimming the tree for Christmas or being allowed to paint your own room are activities readily enjoyed.

The first subtheme in the chapter, "Clean and Tidy," includes books about cleaning, usually a child's own room. Ideas about what is tidy may not always be the same. Ollie in *The Awful Mess* thinks his "mess" of toy cars and tunnels is actually "neat." Roger keeps a messy room, too, but finds out it can be a problem when he loses his favorite marbles in the book by Gretz, *Roger Loses His Marbles*. Our stories and activities show ridiculous extremes when a boy doesn't clean his room, ways in which the whole family can pitch in, and songs for lightening the load. Books and activities in this section also focus on seasonal house chores such as putting up screen windows in spring and chopping logs for winter. Children can learn sequencing, organizational skills, and logical consequences from these activities.

The second subtheme, "Special Touches and Paint Brushes," gives children the opportunity to decorate the house for Christmas or splash paint on the house in gay abandon. The books range from the simple Appalachian Christmas decorations in *The Year of the Perfect Christmas Tree* to the wildly painted houses in *The Big Orange Splot* and *Oh! Were They Ever Happy*. There is certainly room for a wide variety of choices when it comes to house decoration! Through our stories and activities, children will learn that decorating the house can add to holiday celebration around the year or give us an opportunity for individual creative expression.

The focus book for this chapter, Susanna Gretz's *Roger Loses His Marbles*, sets a perfect humorous tone for the books and activities on this topic. Develop your own language activities using the suggestions in the "Floor Plans" section.

INITIATING ACTIVITY

CLEAN UP

Greet each child upon arrival with a little poem about clean and tidy houses.

> Clean and tidy
> One-two-three
> Can you say your
> Name for me?

LITERATURE-SHARING EXPERIENCES

Books for Clean and Tidy

Berenstain, Stan, and Jan Berenstain. **The Berenstain Bears and the Messy Room**. Random House, 1983.
  The Bear family's treehouse was neat and clean except for Brother Bear's and Sister Bear's rooms. After Mother Bear yells at them to pick things up, Papa Bear comes up with some organizational solutions.

Duke, Kate. **Clean Up Day**. Dutton, 1986.
  The guinea pigs show how to clean house in this little board book.

Gretz, Susanna. **Roger Loses His Marbles**. Dial, 1988.
  The pig family cleans for Aunt Lulu's birthday, especially Roger's room, which is a pigpen. Aunt Lulu helps clean, too, and finally locates Roger's missing marbles in his newly cleaned room.

Hickerman, Martha Whitmore. **Eeps, Creeps, It's My Room**. Illustrated by Mary Alice Baer. Abingdon, 1984.
  Jeffrey Allen hated to clean his room so much that it became a disaster. Everyone in the family tells him to clean it, but only when he can't find things anymore and when his mother finally gives him an ultimatum does he put everything away.

James, Betsy. **What's That Room For?** Dutton, 1988.
  Natalie tries to follow her mother's instructions to clean her room, but has more fun playing with her clothes, toys, and little brother.

James, Simon. **The Day Jake Vacuumed**. Bantam, 1989.
  Jake doesn't like having to vacuum the house until a fiendish idea occurs to him to suck up the cat and everything else in the house. Of course, the vacuum explodes in the end, but Jake doesn't have to vacuum ever again.

Lakin, Patricia. **Don't Touch My Room**. Illustrated by Patience Brewster. Little, Brown, 1985.
  Anticipating a new baby, a little boy becomes possessive of his room. But the redecorating is so successful that the little boy likes it—and the new baby.

Manes, Esther, and Stephen Manes. **The Bananas Move to the Ceiling**. Franklin Watts, 1983.
  When their apartment gets too messy, the Banana family tries to defy gravity by living on the ceiling.

Nerlove, Miriam. **I Meant to Clean My Room Today**. M. K. McElderry Books, 1988.
  What could stop a child from cleaning her room? The girl in this story has lots of reasons!

Parish, Peggy. **Amelia Bedelia**. Illustrated by Fritz Siebel. Harper & Row, 1963.
   Amelia means well when she is hired to clean house for the Rogers family, but "drawing the drapes" and "putting out the lights" have a very literal meaning for her. All is forgiven, of course, when she makes a wonderful lemon meringue pie.

Pearson, Susan. **My Favorite Time of Year**. Illustrated by John Wallner. Harper & Row, 1988.
   Seasonal changes around the house include putting up storm windows for the winter, building fires in the fireplace, mowing the grass in the summer, and having a back-yard barbecue.

Rockwell, Anne. **The Awful Mess**. Four Winds Press, 1980.
   Ollie's mother, father, and the big kids all think Ollie's room is an awful mess, but he meets a boy who thinks the tunnels and traffic jam of toy cars are "neat."

Rockwell, Anne. **Nice and Clean**. Macmillan, 1984.
   Clear drawings show various items used to clean house, from a mop to a scouring pad and powder.

Stanton, Elizabeth, and Henry Stanton. **The Very Messy Room**. Illustrated by Richard Leyden. Whitman, 1978.
   Elizabeth decides to do something with her very messy room: She turns it into a magic forest!

Wilhelms, Hans. **Oh, What a Mess!** Crown, 1988.
   Franklin alone likes a tidy house. His family are pigs, literally. The family clean and redecorate when Franklin draws a prize-winning picture and they need a worthy place to hang it. After that the family is cleaner and Franklin joins them in the mudhole once in a while.

Related Activities for Clean and Tidy

WHAT'S IN THE BED?
(Group Participation Experience)

Teach the children the two-line refrain to say together after each layer is added to the bed. Use an old sheet, a blanket, four pillows, and a bedspread. Start with all children on one side of the room. Choose one child in advance to sit in the middle and prepare him or her to say "Meow" when you ask, "What's that noise?"

> Time to get up, you sleepy heads!
> Time to get up and make the bed.

Who will be the sheet?	(*Look at children.*)
One-two-three-four.	(*Bring four to center.*)
Each take a corner	(*Give each a corner.*)
and spread out	(*Walk as far as they can.*)
smooth and flat.	(*Have them set down the sheet.*)

> Time to get up, you sleepy heads!
> Time to get up and make the bed.

Now we need a blanket—	(*Look at children.*)
king-sized.	(*Spread arms wide.*)
One-two-three-four-five-six-seven-eight.	(*Bring eight to center.*)
start at the center—	(*Give each a corner or side.*)
spread out.	(*Walk as far as they can.*)
Now get the wrinkles out:	(*Stretch blanket tight.*)
up and down,	(*Raise and lower blanket.*)
up and down,	(*Raise and lower blanket.*)
and smooth it out.	(*Set down blanket.*)

Time to get up, you sleepy heads!
Time to get up and make the bed.

Pillows—we need at least	(*Look at children.*)
one-two-three-four	(*Choose four children.*)
round fat pillows.	(*Give each a pillow.*)
Line up at the top of the bed.	(*Have them walk to top of sheet.*)
Fluff them up,	(*Toss pillows in air.*)
Puff them up,	(*Toss pillows in air.*)
set them down.	(*Sit holding pillows.*)

Time to get up, you sleepy heads!
Time to get up and make the bed.

Now a bedspread to cover.	(*Look at children.*)
One-two-three-four	(*Count all the other children.*)
Start at the bottom	(*Line them up opposite pillows.*)
pull it up as you go:	(*Hand edge of spread to children.*)
up	(*Walk to pillows, pulling spread.*)
up	
up	
up over the pillows	(*Cover pillows.*)
and smooth it out.	(*Set down spread.*)

Time to get up, you sleepy heads!
Time to get up and make the bed.

Wait! What's that in the bed?	(*Point to lump in center.*)
Are the sheets smooth?	(*Sheet children say "yes."*)
Are the blankets in place?	(*Blanket children say "yes."*)
Are the pillows fluffed?	(*Pillow children say "yes."*)
Is the bedspread straight?	(*Bedspread children say "yes."*)
What's that in the bed?	(*Point to lump in center.*)
What's that noise?	(*Child in center says "meow."*)
It's the cat playing	
hide and seek!	(*Child in center crawls out.*)

Time to get up, you sleepy head!
Time to get up and make the bed.

After doing this once all the children will understand how to sit in the center and say "meow." Repeat the activity so others have a chance to be the cat in the bed.

UNDER THE BED
(Action Rhyme)

What's that under the bed?	(*Point to floor.*)
What's that under the bed?	(*Point to floor.*)
One old Halloween mask	(*Cover face with hands, peeking out through fingers.*)
Get it out from under the bed.	(*Point to door.*)

What's that under the bed?	(*Point to floor.*)
What's that under the bed?	(*Point to floor.*)
Two smelly stinky socks	(*Hold nose.*)
One old Halloween mask	(*Cover face with hands, peeking out through fingers.*)
Get it out from under the bed.	(*Point to door.*)

What's that under the bed?	(*Point to floor.*)
What's that under the bed?	(*Point to floor.*)
Three spiders on their webs	(*Crawl fingers of one hand up other arm.*)
Two smelly stinky socks	(*Hold nose.*)
One old Halloween mask	(*Cover face with hands, peeking out through fingers.*)
Get it out from under the bed.	(*Point to door.*)

What's that under the bed?	(*Point to floor.*)
What's that under the bed?	(*Point to floor.*)
Four sticky candy canes	(*Open and close hands slowly.*)
Three spiders on their webs	(*Crawl fingers of one hand up other arm.*)
Two smelly stinky socks	(*Hold nose.*)
One old Halloween mask	(*Cover face with hands, peeking out through fingers.*)
Get it out from under the bed.	(*Point to door.*)

What's that under the bed?	(*Point to floor.*)
What's that under the bed?	(*Point to floor.*)
Five fuzzy fluffs of dust	(*Wiggle fingers in air.*)
Four sticky candy canes	(*Open and close hands slowly.*)
Three spiders on their webs	(*Crawl fingers of one hand up other arm.*)
Two smelly stinky socks	(*Hold nose.*)
One old Halloween mask	(*Cover face with hands, peeking out through fingers.*)
Get it out from under the bed.	(*Point to door.*)

I told you your room needed cleaning!

LAZY LUKE AND THE CLEAN GENIES
(Story Theater)

Tell this story and let the children become the different genies in the story. The cleaning actions of the genies can be mimed by individual children or everyone can do them at the same time. By the end of the story there will be plenty of action. It would be a nice touch to bring a harmonica to blow when Lazy Luke plays.

Lazy Luke liked to dream. He liked to dream of flying planes and magic castles and singing songs. Lazy Luke liked to play his harmonica. But he did not like to clean the house. He always waited a long time until the house was really, really dirty, and then he had to work very hard to get it clean.

On Monday, Lazy Luke decided to clean the kitchen sink. He had just bought a new product, Spray Magic Cleaner, and wanted to try it out. He gave it a little squirt. Pfsssst. To Lazy Luke's surprise a genie appeared. The genie was not very big but he could clean the kitchen sink. So the genie cleaned the sink and Lazy Luke played his harmonica.

On Tuesday, Lazy Luke decided to clean the bedroom window. He got out the Spray Magic Cleaner and gave it a medium-sized squirt. Pfsssssssssst. To Lazy Luke's surprise another genie appeared. This genie was not very big and not very little, but he could clean the bedroom window. So the genie cleaned the bedroom window and Lazy Luke played his harmonica.

On Wednesday, Lazy Luke decided to clean the bathroom floor. He got out the Spray Magic Cleaner and gave it a pretty big squirt. Pfssssssssssssssst. To Lazy Luke's surprise another genie appeared. This genie was pretty big and he could clean the bathroom floor. So the genie cleaned the bathroom floor and Lazy Luke played his harmonica.

On Thursday, Lazy Luke decided to clean the basement ceiling. He got out the Spray Magic Cleaner and gave it a big squirt. Pfssssssssssssssssst. To Lazy Luke's surprise another genie appeared. This genie was big and he could clean the basement ceiling. So the genie cleaned the basement ceiling and Lazy Luke played his harmonica.

On Friday, Lazy Luke decided to sweep the entire attic. He knew it was a big job, so he got out the Spray Magic Cleaner and gave it a really big squirt. Pfsssssssssssssssssst. To Lazy Luke's surprise another genie appeared. This genie was enormous. He swept the attic. To Lazy Luke's surprise another genie appeared. Lazy Luke told the second genie to paint the garage. To Lazy Luke's surprise another genie appeared. Lazy Luke told the third genie to mow the lawn. It was then that Lazy Luke realized the nozzle on the can of Spray Magic was stuck. Lazy Luke thought of all the jobs the genies could do. He had one weed the garden and one fix the roof. He had one genie lay new carpet in the living room and another get rid of all the cobwebs in the house. Lazy Luke was so busy thinking of jobs for the genies to do he had no time to play his harmonica. Just as Lazy Luke thought he could not think of one more job for one more genie—pfffffffffft—the can of Spray Magic ran out.

Lazy Luke went to the store to get another can, but he never found another one that had genies inside. But that was all right. The genies had done such a good job that it was a long, long time before Lazy Luke had to clean anything again. He could just play his harmonica.

OUT THE WINDOW
(Tune: "Go In and Out the Window")

My mother likes a clean house,
My mother likes a clean house,
My mother likes a clean house,
It's time to clean for spring!

Where shall we put the papers,   (*Hands shoulder high, palms up.*)
Where shall we put the papers,
Where shall we put the papers,
It's time to clean for spring!

Just throw them out the window,   (*Swing arms wildly to side.*)
Just throw them out the window,
Just throw them out the window,
It's time to clean for spring!

Where shall we put the boxes,   (*Hands shoulder high, palms up.*)
Where shall we put the boxes,
Where shall we put the boxes,
It's time to clean for spring!

Just throw them out the window,   (*Swing arms wildly to side.*)
Just throw them out the window,
Just throw them out the window,
It's time to clean for spring!

Where shall we put the children,   (*Hands shoulder high, palms up.*)
Where shall we put the children,
Where shall we put the children,
It's time to clean for spring!

Don't throw them out the window,   (*Shake head.*)
Don't throw them out the window,
Don't throw them out the window,
They'll clean themselves for spring.

Just put them in the basement,   (*Bend knees to sitting position.*)
Just put them in the basement,
They'll be safe in the basement   (*Fold hands.*)
While mother cleans for spring   (*Ready to listen.*)

SPRING CLEANING
(Tune: "My Bonnie Lies over the Ocean")

It's spring and the windows are dirty.
There are puddles all over the floor.
The dishes we once used to eat on,
Need washing so we can eat more!
Springtime cleaning—
Get out the broom and the mop, the mop!
Springtime cleaning—
I've worked so hard I could drop.
(*spoken*) Plop!

WRECK ROOM
(Object-and-Mask Story)

Bring in the different kinds of junk Kevin collects and pile the items in front of you as you tell the story. Then use masks of a sheep, crocodile, skunk, kangaroo, and cow (see p. 91) for children to take the part of the animals. Scoop up all the trash in a big garbage bag at the end of the story.

Kevin did not like to keep his room clean. Kevin liked to collect things to keep in his room. Sometimes things got so bad that his sister would tell him his room was a wreck, and sometimes his brother would tell him his room was a wreck, and then his mother and his father would tell Kevin his room was the wreck room of the whole house. Kevin got tired of hearing the words "wreck room," but Kevin still did not like to keep his room clean.

skunk

cow

crocodile

kangaroo

sheep

WRECK
ROOM

("Wreck Room" continues on page 92.)

On Monday morning Kevin collected 125 baseball cards to keep in his room. He left the baseball cards all over the floor of his room.

On Tuesday morning Kevin found an old garden hose and a bicycle tire in the garage. He took the garden hose and the bicycle tire up to his room, and he left them on the floor of his room.

Now on Wednesday Kevin had an apple and a banana and a peanut butter sandwich for lunch. He ate all the apple but the core and all the banana but the peel and all the peanut butter sandwich except the crusts, so he took the apple core and the banana peel and the crusts of the peanut butter sandwich up to his room and he left them on the floor of his room.

And on Thursday Kevin dropped his dirty socks, his sneakers, his T-shirt, and an old wet towel on the floor of his room.

By Friday Kevin's room started to smell. But Kevin did not like to keep his room clean. So this is what happened.

There was a knock at the door. Kevin opened it and in came a sheep. "What a heap!" said the sheep.

But before Kevin could say anything there was another knock at the door. Kevin opened it and in came a crocodile. "What a pile!" said the crocodile. "What a heap!" said the sheep.

But before Kevin could say anything there was another knock at the door. Kevin opened it and in came a skunk. "This is junk!" said the skunk. "What a pile!" said the crocodile. "What a heap!" said the sheep.

But before Kevin could say anything there was another knock at the door. Kevin opened it and in came a kangaroo. "P-U!" said the kangaroo. "This is junk!" said the skunk. "What a pile!" said the crocodile. "What a heap!" said the sheep.

But before Kevin could say anything there was another knock at the door. Kevin opened it and in came a cow. Now the cow was so contented to see Kevin's wreck of a room that she said, "I'm moving in now."

Well, when Kevin heard that, he got out a big broom and said, "All right! I'm cleaning my room."

So out came the cow, and out came the kangaroo and out came the skunk and out came the crocodile and out came the sheep.

And after that Kevin kept his room nice and clean. Nobody ever called it a wreck room again. But Kevin did collect lots of hugs and kisses from his whole family.

TIME TO CLEAN
(Tune: "Jingle Bells")

Dust fuzzies, dust fuzzies
Underneath the bed
Stinky sock and wet bath towels
Crusts of old rye bread

Underwear, tennis shoe
Favorite magazines
Stuff you lost and stuff that smells
Do you think it's time to clean?

CLEANING CREW
(Fingerplay)

Hold up one finger for each member of the cleaning crew.

Daddy washes dishes,
Mom gets sinks to scrub.
Brother vacuums carpet,
Sister wipes the tub.
But when it comes to cleaning
Just watch our doggie, Thor!
He licks up all the tasty crumbs
That fall upon the floor!
Yip!

FIXING THE HOUSE SONG
(Tune: "Go In and Out the Window")

Let's fix the house for winter,
Let's fix the house for winter,
Let's fix the house for winter,
Now tell me what to do?

(Children suggest chores and sing these in the following manner:)

Chop the logs for fire,
Chop the logs for fire,
Chop the logs for fire,
Now tell me what to do?

(If you are "stuck," here are some other ideas:)

Rake the leaves and burn them

Put blankets on your bed

Get out your big snow shovel

(When you have made all preparations, you can sing this verse:)

Now we're all set for winter,
Now we're all set for winter,
Now we're all set for winter,
In our happy homes!

Let's fix the house for springtime,
Let's fix the house for springtime,
Let's fix the house for springtime,
Now tell me what to do?

(Children suggest springtime fix-ups as they did before. Here are some suggestions:)

Put screens on your windows,
Put screens on your windows,
Put screens on your windows,
Now tell me what to do?

(There are many fix-ups children could suggest, but here are a few of our ideas:)

> Put away the blankets
>
> Time to plant the garden
>
> Get out the lawn mower

(Now end with this verse:)

> Now we're all set for springtime,
> Now we're all set for springtime,
> Now we're all set for springtime,
> In our happy homes!

MORE BLANKETS!
(Tune: "London Bridge")

Select two children to form a bridge in the traditional "London Bridge" way. Sing the first two verses as the children march through the bridge, catching a child on the word "winter" in the last line.

> Wintertime is coming near,
> Coming near, coming near.
> Wintertime is coming near,
> Get the blankets.
>
> Put the blankets on the bed,
> On the bed, on the bed.
> Put the blankets on the bed
> For the winter.

The child who is caught can choose a favorite color or use a color he or she is wearing. Sing this verse as he or she goes to stand by the mattress cutout.

> Put a (red) one on the bed,
> On the bed, on the bed.
> Put a (red) one on the bed
> For the winter.

Continue in this manner until all the children are part of the bed. Last to join the line are the two who formed the bridge. Hand the last child a pillow and sing this verse.

> Now the bed is warm enough,
> Warm enough, warm enough.
> Now the bed is warm enough
> For the winter.

It would be fun to take a picture of the children forming the many-blanketed bed. Display the picture sideways so it looks like the children are lying on the mattress with the pillow on top.

BLANKET FULL OF LOVE
(Flannel-board Story)

Tell this flannel-board story using two squares of cloth in each color: red, yellow, green, blue, and one square of purple. They can be plain or whatever is in your scrap bag. Place the pieces on the board as indicated in the story.

Mrs. North had five children—five growing children. With so many children, she could not afford to waste food or clothing. She saved all the leftover food in little containers in the refrigerator. She put all the scraps of used clothing in the rag bag.

On Monday, Jennifer noticed she had outgrown her red dress. Mrs. North cut the red dress into pieces and put them in the rag bag. (*Place red scraps on the board.*)

On Tuesday, when Jason tore the knee of his yellow pants, Mrs. North cut the yellow pants into pieces and put them in the rag bag. (*Place yellow scraps on the board.*)

On Wednesday, when Jeffrey's pen leaked in the pocket of his blue shirt, Mrs. North cut the blue shirt into pieces and put them in the rag bag. (*Place blue scraps on the board.*)

On Thursday, when Jill lost one green sock, Mrs. North cut one green sock into pieces and put them in the rag bag. (*Place green scraps on the board.*)

And on Friday, Jeremy spilled mustard on his purple jacket. There wasn't much jacket not covered with mustard, but Mrs. North found one piece and put it in the rag bag. (*Place purple scrap on the board.*)

On Saturday, it turned very cold. Mrs. North got out all the blankets for the beds. There was one for Jennifer, one for Jason, one for Jeffrey, and one for Jill. But when they found Jeremy's blanket it had a big hole in the middle and a big spot on one end. Jeremy could not use the blanket like that.

So Mrs. North got out the rag bag. Jeremy said, "I can't sleep in a pile of rags." But Mrs. North just smiled and started to sew.

She sewed a red piece to a yellow piece to a green piece to a blue piece. She sewed a blue piece to a red piece to a yellow piece. She sewed a green piece to a purple piece to a red piece. (*Assemble small squares into a larger square as you talk.*) Then she sewed the blanket to the back of all the pieces and Jeremy had a wonderful, colorful new blanket. It was a blanket full of warmth.

Jeremy used that blanket for years and years until he and all the other children were grown and had homes of their own. Even then Mrs. North kept the colorful blanket because (*point to pieces as you name the colors*) the red piece reminded her of Jennifer, the yellow piece reminded her of Jason, the blue piece reminded her of Jeffrey, the green piece reminded her of Jill, and the purple piece reminded her of Jeremy. It was a blanket full of memories.

And that is what a quilt is—a blanket full of warmth, a blanket full of memories, and a blanket full of love.

BLANKETS FOR MY BED
(Tune: "Farmer in the Dell")

Use this little add-on song as an action rhyme by having children mime the adding of blankets and the wind blowing and the snow snowing.

A blanket on my bed   (*Arm parallel across chest.*)
A blanket on my bed
Hey ho, I'm cozy-o   (*Hug self.*)
A blanket on my bed

The wind blows tonight	(*Blow.*)
The wind blows tonight	(*Blow.*)
Hey ho, I'm freezing-o	(*Shake all over.*)
The wind blows tonight!	(*Blow.*)

Two blankets on my bed	(*Arm over parallel arm.*)
Two blankets on my bed	
Hey ho, I'm cozy-o	(*Hug self.*)
Two blankets on my bed.	

The wind blows and howls	(*Blow and howl.*)
The wind blows and howls	
Hey ho, I'm freezing 'cause ♂	(*Shake all over.*)
The wind blows and howls	

Three blankets on my bed	(*Arm over arm three times.*)
Three blankets on my bed	
Hey ho, I'm cozy-o	(*Hug self.*)
Three blankets on my bed.	

Now it starts to snow	(*Wiggle fingers like snow.*)
Now it starts to snow	
Hey ho, I'm freezing 'cause ♂	(*Shake all over.*)
Now it starts to snow.	

Four blankets on my bed	(*Arm over arm four times.*)
Four blankets on my bed	
Hey ho, I'm cozy-o	(*Hug self.*)
Four blankets on my bed.	

The wind blows the snow	(*Blow and wiggle fingers.*)
The wind blows the snow	
Hey ho, I'm freezing 'cause ♂	(*Shake all over.*)
The wind blows the snow	

Five blankets on my bed	(*Arm over arm five times.*)
Five blankets on my bed	
Hey ho, I'm cozy-o	(*Hug self.*)
Five blankets on my bed!	

The snows doesn't snow
The wind doesn't blow
Hey—okey dokey-o
Take the blankets off my bed!
The blankets have to go.

Books for Special Touches and Paint Brushes

Adler, David. **The House on the Roof: A Sukkot Story**. Bonim Books, 1976.
   Despite the protests of his landlady, an old man builds a Sukkot for himself and his grandchildren on the roof of an apartment building.

Blos, Joan. **Old Henry**. Illustrated by Stephen Gammel. Morrow, 1987.
    Old Henry causes quite a scandal in the neighborhood when he doesn't fix up his house. He finally moves out, but his neighbors miss him, and vice versa.

Bond, Felicia. **Christmas in the Chicken Coop**. Crowell, 1983.
    It takes the magic of Christmas starlight to make the hens in the coop see why they should decorate a tree for Christmas. But once they do, they love the result. A very small book in format, but with colorful pictures and a touching story.

Climo, Shirley. **The Cobweb Christmas**. Illustrated by Joe Lasker. Crowell, 1982.
    When the old German Tante decorates, she wants everything beautiful for all the animals. The spiders come and enjoy the tree leaving their webs all over it, then Father Christmas touches the webs, changing them to gold, and they look like the tinsel we use today.

Cole, Joanna, and Philip Cole. **Hank and Frank Fix Up the House**. Illustrated by William Van Horn. Scholastic, 1988.
    Hank and Frank, the Fix-up Brothers, fix up houses like new, but Hank's speed sometimes causes them to make silly mistakes.

Duvoisin, Roger. **The House of Four Seasons**. Lothrop, 1956.
    When the family can't decide what color to paint the house, they think it would be fun to paint each side a different color for each of the four seasons. After experimentation in mixing colors, they decide on a white house with a variety of colorful trim on window shutters and doors.

Francis, Frank. **The Magic Wallpaper**. Abelard Schuman, 1970.
    A little boy walks into adventure down the path pictured on his new wallpaper.

Houston, Gloria. **The Year of the Perfect Christmas Tree**. Illustrated by Barbara Cooney. Dial, 1988.
    An Appalachian tale of how the tradition of decorating a pine tree and putting a lace angel on top came to one family. A lovely quiet story that is perfect for holiday reading to grade-school children.

McGraw, Sheila. **This Old New House: Graham Learns about Renovating**. Annick Press, 1989.
    When the people next door renovate an old house, Graham learns all the details, from plumbing to painting.

Pinkwater, Daniel. **The Big Orange Splot**. Hastings House, 1977.
    All the houses are the same on Mr. Plumbeam's street until a seagull drops a bucket of orange paint on Mr. Plumbeam's house. When the neighbors complain about the orange splot, Mr. Plumbeam paints his whole house like "a rainbow," a jungle, and an explosion. At first the neighbors object, but eventually they change their houses so everyone ends up with a different and unique dream house.

Spier, Peter. **Oh! Were They Ever Happy**. Doubleday, 1970.
    One Saturday morning while their parents are away, the children decide to paint the house—with colorful results!

Spier, Peter. **Peter Spier's Christmas**. Doubleday, 1983.
    Wordless but detailed look at decorating for the holidays, from the tree, to the mall, to the church.

Related Activities for Special Touches and Paint Brushes

THE VERY HEIGHT OF FASHION
(Flannel-board Story)

Cut squares of felt: five blue, four yellow, three pink, two green, and one purple. Place on the board as indicated in the story.

Mrs. Featherstone wanted to be at the height of fashion. She always had the best clothes and the newest shoes and the fanciest car. Everyone said she was a trend setter. But Mrs. Featherstone wanted her house to be at the height of fashion, too.

So in January she went to the home of Mrs. Teal. Mrs. Teal had a lovely blue house. "Well," thought Mrs. Featherstone, "blue must be the color at the height of fashion for houses." So Mrs. Featherstone went home and painted her living room and dining room and bedroom and bathroom and kitchen blue. (*Place five blue squares on board.*)

In February she went to the home of Mrs. Maize. Mrs. Maize had a lovely yellow house. "Well," thought Mrs. Featherstone, "yellow must be the color at the height of fashion for houses." So Mrs. Featherstone went home and painted her living room and dining room and bedroom and bathroom yellow. (*Replace four blue squares with yellow ones.*) By the time she got to the kitchen, though, she was too tired to paint anymore. So she left the kitchen blue.

In March she went to the home of Mrs. Fuchsia. Mrs. Fuchsia had a lovely pink house. "Well," thought Mrs. Featherstone, "pink must be the color at the height of fashion for houses." So Mrs. Featherstone went home and painted her living room and dining room and bedroom pink. (*Replace three yellow squares with pink ones.*) By the time she got to the bathroom, though, she was too tired to paint anymore. So she left the bathroom yellow, and the kitchen blue.

In April she went to the home of Mrs. Mint. Mrs. Mint had a lovely green house. "Well," thought Mrs. Featherstone, "green must be the color at the height of fashion for houses." So Mrs. Featherstone went home and painted her living room and dining room green. (*Replace two pink squares with green ones.*) By the time she got to the bedroom, though, she was too tired to paint anymore. So she left the bedroom pink. She left the bathroom yellow. And she left the kitchen blue.

In May she went to the home of Mrs. Lilac. Mrs. Lilac had a lovely purple house. "Well," thought Mrs. Featherstone, "purple must be the color at the height of fashion for houses." So Mrs. Featherstone went home and painted her living room purple. (*Replace one green square with a purple one.*) By the time she got to the dining room, though, she was too tired to paint anymore. So she left the dining room green. She left the bedroom pink. She left the bathroom yellow. And she left the kitchen blue.

In June Mrs. Featherstone gave a party and all her friends came. They were amazed at the lovely decorating Mrs. Featherstone had done. "Well, you know," said Mrs. Featherstone, "a rainbow house is at the very height of fashion." And since Mrs. Featherstone was too tired to paint anymore, the rainbow house was at the height of fashion for a very long time.

DECORATING FOR OWL'S PARTY
(Story with Masks)

Make five masks: owl, bear, mouse, duck, and possum (see p. 99). Give each of five children a mask and have them move as indicated in the story.

DECORATING FOR OWL'S PARTY

duck

possum

mouse

Attach shape to front of paper bag

owl

bear

("Decorating for Owl's Party" continues on page 100.)

Owl was having a birthday party for all his friends. He invited Bear, Mouse, Duck, and Possum. The invitation said:

Come to my tree
at half past three
We'll have tea
And a party for ME!
    Signed, OWL

The animals hurried to Owl's house as soon as they got the invitations. They all asked, "What would you like us to do to help get ready for the party?"

Owl said, "Bear, you blow up the balloons. Mouse, you put out the tablecloth, Duck, you hang the streamers, and Possum, you get the centerpiece. I'll get the cake."

And everyone hurried to get ready for Owl's party. Bear got bags and bags of balloons—red and blue and yellow. Bear said, "I got lots of balloons to decorate for Owl's party. What's a party without balloons for decorations?"

Mouse got a long, long, long green tablecloth with yellow flowers on it. Mouse said, "I got a long tablecloth to decorate for Owl's party. What's a party without a tablecloth for decoration?"

Duck got yards and yards of crepe-paper streamers—pink and purple. Duck said, "I got yards and yards of streamers to decorate for Owl's party. What's a party without streamers for decorations?"

Possum had trouble thinking of a centerpiece. He thought of a branch full of birds, but the birds might fly away. He thought of the tomatoes growing in the garden because they were such a nice color, but maybe the pots of tomatoes would spill and the dirt would get all over. Finally he thought of a vase of flowers.

"Perfect!" said Possum. He picked bunches and bunches of flowers—red and blue and green and yellow and pink and purple. Possum said, "I got bunches and bunches of flowers to decorate for Owl's party. What's a party without flowers for decorations?"

Owl baked the cake. (*Move owl off to one side.*)

At half past three, all the animals gathered at the tree. Bear began to blow up balloons. Blow, blow, blow.

Mouse began to spread out the tablecloth. Spread, spread, spread.

Duck began to hang the streamers. Hang, hang, hang.

Possum waited until the last minute to pick the flowers so they would be nice and fresh. Pick, pick, pick. Then he brought his bunches and bunches of flowers to the party and set them on the table.

Owl stayed in the kitchen and baked the cake.

But there were party crashers at the party. They did not mean to be there, and they certainly were not invited, but there were bees on the flowers Possum picked. Lots and lots of bees! Buzz, buzz, buzz.

The bees buzzed out of the flowers and began to swarm around Possum's head. "Yow!" called Possum and ran away from the flowers. What a mess! (*Have possum sit down.*)

He ran right into the stool Duck was using to hang streamers. Duck fell off the stool and the streamers came with him—wrapped all around him. What a mess! (*Have duck sit down.*)

Duck could not see where he was going, and he crashed into Mouse. When she saw the bees around Possum she was so frightened she rolled herself up in the tablecloth to hide. What a mess! (*Have mouse sit down.*)

As Mouse rolled herself up in the tablecloth she rolled too far and crashed right into Bear, who was still blowing up balloons. Bear sat down with a thud and all the balloons he had blown up burst. POP! What a mess! And all those balloons popping scared the bees away. (*Have bear sit down.*)

Bear and Mouse and Duck and Possum looked at the mess. What's a party without decorations? All the animals began to cry.

Owl heard all the commotion and heard his friends crying. He came out carrying the cake. (*Bring back owl.*) When owl saw the mess and heard how it happened, he said, "A party is more than decorations—pink and green and red and blue and yellow and purple. A party is four good friends. (*Have all children stand up.*) Four good friends to share my birthday cake!"

DECORATE WITH HEARTS AND LACE
(Tune: "Twinkle, Twinkle, Little Star")

> Paper chains
> Cards of lace
> Violets, roses,
> Smiling face
>
> With Cupid's arrow
> Love we send
> Take my hand
> And be my friend
>
> Red hearts
> Say won't you be mine
> Let's decorate
> For Valentine's!

PAINT THE TOWN RED
(A Story for Valentine's Day)

Grays Gulch was a shabby town. No one came to visit and no one wanted to stay, until the new mayor, Hank, decided to change the image. He called a meeting of the town council. First they changed the name of the town. They thought of Hollywood, but they heard tell there was a town by that name already. They thought of Silver Creek, but there was no creek nearby and no silver anywhere. They wanted a name that would make people come and feel really good, feel like celebrating. Happy something—Happy Heart—Happy Heart Hollow! That was the new name for the town.

Now they needed a reason for people to come there. Happy Heart sounded like a perfect spot to spend Valentine's Day. One of the town council members suggested they get lots and lots of love birds: love birds cooing in the park, love birds cooing in the City Hall, love birds cooing at the library. So Mayor Hank ordered lots and lots of love birds: love birds cooing in the park, love birds cooing in the City Hall, love birds cooing at the library. There were so many love birds no one could sleep with all that cooing. And no one came to Happy Heart Hollow to see the love birds.

Another council member suggested they get lots and lots of sweet chocolate: chocolate in the milk, chocolate on the spare ribs, chocolate in the chop suey. So Mayor Hank ordered lots and lots of sweet chocolate: chocolate in the milk, chocolate on the spare ribs, chocolate in the chop suey. There was so much chocolate no one could eat anything with all that sweetness. And no one came to Happy Heart Hollow to taste the chocolate.

Another council member suggested they get lots and lots of honeysuckle perfume: spray perfume on the statue of General Stinkbine riding his horse, spray perfume on the door of the school, spray perfume on all the pigeons in the town square. So Mayor Hank ordered lots and lots of honeysuckle perfume. They sprayed perfume on the statue of General Stinkbine riding his horse, sprayed perfume on the door of the school, and sprayed perfume on all the pigeons in the town square. There was so much perfume no one could stand to smell it. And no one came to Happy Heart Hollow to smell the honeysuckle perfume.

Finally Mayor Hank got an idea. "What we need," he said, "is fun and excitement. We need to paint the town red!" So they painted red houses and a red cafe. There were red streets with red cars and red dogs. And they rolled out the red carpets. Finally lots of people came to celebrate Valentine's Day at Happy Heart Hollow.

It was a red-letter day!

WHERE'S THE LAST EGG?

Teach remembering skills with this Easter Bunny story. Use six eggs (real or cut out of paper) in purple, red, pink, yellow, green, and blue. You will also need a crumpled piece of blue tissue paper.

At night while Stacy was sleeping the Easter Bunny brought six eggs to her house. (*Line the eggs up in front of you as you name the colors.*) He brought a purple one and a red one and a pink one and a yellow one and a green one and a blue one—six pretty Easter eggs.

The Easter Bunny looked high and low for good hiding places for the eggs.

He hid one in the family room under the sofa. (*Place purple egg in a visible spot in the room.*)

He hid one in the bedroom behind the lamp. (*Place red egg in a visible spot in the room.*)

He hid one beside the railing on the stairs. (*Place pink egg in a visible spot in the room.*)

He hid one in the laundry hamper in the hall. (*Place yellow egg in a visible spot in the room.*)

He hid one on the back porch between the flower pots. (*Place green egg in a visible spot in the room.*)

The last one he hid in the kitchen behind the stove. (*Place blue egg in a nonvisible place where blue tissue paper has been hidden.*)

When the sun came up Stacy ran downstairs and got her Easter basket. She began to look for the eggs. Can you help her?

Where was the purple egg? (*Under the sofa.*) (*Get purple egg and place in front.*) Now Stacy had one egg.

Where was the red egg? (*Behind the lamp.*) (*Get red egg and place in front.*) Now Stacy had one-two eggs.

Where was the pink egg? (*Beside the railing.*) (*Get pink egg and place in front.*) Now Stacy had one-two-three eggs.

Where was the yellow egg? (*By the laundry hamper.*) (*Get yellow egg and place in front.*) Now Stacy had one-two-three-four eggs.

Where was the green egg? (*Between the flower pots.*) (*Get green egg and place in front.*) Now Stacy had one-two-three-four-five eggs.

Stacy looked and looked and looked for that last blue egg, but she could not find it. Do you remember where it is? (*Behind the stove.*) Well, I'm glad you know, but Stacy could not find it. She even got her mother to help, but they could not find it. Stacy's mother said, "Don't worry, the egg will turn up. Somehow we'll know where it is." And she went out to the kitchen to cook Easter dinner.

Pretty soon Stacy smelled the Easter ham beginning to bake. Then she smelled another smell—like an egg cooking. Like an egg cooking too much. Like an egg about to ...

BANG—KAPOW!

(*Show blue crumpled tissue paper.*) The blue egg exploded behind the stove. And that is how Stacy found her last egg that Easter.

CELEBRATE THE FOURTH

Hang the flags
Parades march by
Brass bands play on
The Fourth of July

Stars and Stripes
Red, white, and blue
Come celebrate
With a barbecue

Late at night
On the Fourth of July
Fireworks shower
Decorating the sky

SPOOKY DECORATIONS
(Action Rhyme)

Decorate for Halloween—
Hang a ghost up high.   (*Wiggle fingers in air.*)
Put a scarecrow on the porch   (*Arms out, shoulder height.*)
To watch the spooks go by.   (*Circle eyes with fingers.*)
Ooooooh!

Light your jack-o-lantern,   (*Circle face with hands.*)
In the moonlight he will gleam.   (*Touch fingertips overhead.*)
Now put on your costume—quick!   (*Clap on "quick."*)
It's time for Halloween.
Ooooooh!

CHRISTMAS CHEER
(An Echo Chant to Help Get Ready)

Leader: Christmas comes but once a year
          So let's get ready—give a cheer!
          Yea, Christmas! (*Point to group to repeat.*)

Group: Yea, Christmas!

Leader: Got the holly?

Group: Got the holly!

Leader: Mistletoe? Candy canes?

Group: Mistletoe! Candy canes!

Leader: Christmas stockings?

Group: Christmas stockings!

Leader: Cranberry-and-popcorn chains?

Group: Cranberry-and-popcorn chains!

Leader: Got the wreath?

Group: Got the wreath!

Leader: A great big fat Christmas tree?

Group: A great big fat Christmas tree!

Leader: Deck the halls! Light the candles!

Group: Deck the halls! Light the candles!

Leader: For our Christmas holidays!

Group: For our Christmas holidays!

Leader: Yea, Christmas!

Group: Yea, Christmas!

DECKED OUT FOR THE HOLIDAYS
(Tune: "Deck the Halls")

At Christmas children love as much glitz and sparkle as the season can provide. Here's how the house could look if you really went all out decorating!

Deck the house for holidays
Fa-la-la-la-la-la-la-la-la!
Garland string in the hallways
Fa-la-la-la-la-la-la-la-la!
Get a tree that's tall and green
Fa-la-la-la-la-la-la-la-la!
Hang the stockings to be seen
Fa-la-la-la-la-la-la-la-la!

There's a wreath upon the door
Fa-la-la-la-la-la-la-la-la!
Outside we need something more
Fa-la-la-la-la-la-la-la-la!
Six-foot candy canes? A few
Fa-la-la-la-la-la-la-la-la!
Soldiers dressed in red and blue
Fa-la-la-la-la-la-la-la-la!

Place a Santa up on top
Fa-la-la-la-la-la-la-la-la!
Lights that flash and never stop
Fa-la-la-la-la-la-la-la-la!
Now we need to cover all
Fa-la-la-la-la-la-la-la-la!
With a giant white snowfall
Fa-la-la-la-la-la-la-la-la!

EAT YOU OUT OF HOUSE AND HOME
(A Puppet Story)

Tell this story with a vacuum-cleaner sock puppet and the objects mentioned in the story (see patterns on page 106)—a bow, two Christmas stockings, a turkey leg, a candy cane, a cranberry-and-popcorn chain, a toy train, a Christmas tree (small artificial one), and a stuffed dog and cat. You could substitute other items in the story if you cannot locate any of the above. As the vacuum cleaner sucks up the different things, stuff them into the mouth of the puppet, then pull them out when the vacuum cleaner coughs in the end. See illustration for making the puppet. For extra fun, have children make sucking sounds as the vacuum cleaner sucks up each item!

It was the day after Christmas in the Moore house. It had been a wonderful Christmas. Everyone had opened stacks of presents. And everyone had eaten plates and plates of food. And everyone had played with the new toys underneath the Christmas tree. But now that Christmas was over, the house was a mess.

Deep in the dark corner of the hall closet sat Super Deluxe Clean Supreme, the vacuum cleaner. Super Deluxe peeked through the keyhole and saw all the ribbons and wrapping, the crumbs and the Christmas leftovers. What a feast for a super-deluxe-clean-supreme vacuum cleaner! Super Deluxe got so excited that his motor began to hum and his hose started to vibrate all by itself.

Super Deluxe crashed open the door of the closet and snaked his way around the living room. He saw a big red bow left under the tree.

"Christmas is over except for the crumbs. I'm going to eat you out of house and home," he snarled. And he sucked up the bow.

Next, Super Deluxe saw two child-sized Christmas stockings—empty and dropped on the hearth by the fireplace.

"Christmas is over except for the crumbs. I'm going to eat you out of house and home," he snarled. And he sucked up the Christmas stockings.

Then, Super Deluxe saw a candy cane and a cranberry-and-popcorn chain that had fallen off the Christmas tree. And, would you believe it, he even found a turkey leg under the dining room table.

"Christmas is over except for the crumbs. I'm going to eat you out of house and home," he snarled. And he sucked up the candy cane, the cranberry-and-popcorn chain, and the turkey leg.

Super Deluxe next saw a little toy train with an engine, one boxcar, one coal car, one tank car, and one caboose. It had been left on the tracks underneath the Christmas tree by the little boy of the house. But Super Deluxe didn't care.

"Christmas is over except for the crumbs. I'm going to eat you out of house and home," he snarled. And he sucked up the little toy train with an engine, one boxcar, one coal car, one tank car, and the caboose, too.

Well, Super Deluxe was getting stuffed, but he was on a roll. So when he looked up at the Christmas tree—all decorated with candies and gingerbread boys and tinsel—he said (and you can help me say the words)—

"Christmas is over except for the crumbs. I'm going to eat you out of house and home," he snarled. And, somehow, he sucked up the Christmas tree with all of its candies, its gingerbread boys, and its tinsel trimming.

Super Deluxe should have been content with all that he had eaten, but then he saw the dog and the cat asleep by the fire.

"Christmas is over except for the crumbs. I'm going to eat you out of house and home," he snarled. And he sucked up the dog and the cat.

But that was a terrible mistake, because the minute the dog and the cat got inside the vacuum cleaner, they started to fight. And that made Super Deluxe start to cough.

EAT YOU OUT OF HOUSE & HOME

Vacuum-cleaner Sock Puppet

← Tuck funnel or plastic vacuum cleaner attachment inside closed end of sock and tape or glue in place

And when he coughed, out came the big red bow; out came two child-sized Christmas stockings; out came one candy cane, one cranberry-and-popcorn chain, and one turkey leg; out came one toy train with an engine, one boxcar, one coal car, one tank car, and one caboose; and out came the Christmas tree with the candies, the gingerbread boys, and the tinsel trimmings. And, finally, out came the dog and the cat, too.

As for Super Deluxe Vacuum Cleaner—he was put back in the closet with a blown gasket. Months later he was repaired, but he had learned his lesson. He never did try to eat the Moore family out of house and home again.

GAMES FOR ALL SPRUCED UP

GOOD, CLEAN FUN

Assemble the following for two to five relay teams: buckets, sponges, rubber gloves, clean soap container. Each team member must run to the bucket, put on the gloves, pretend to squirt soap and wipe with the sponge, put everything back into the bucket, and run back and tag the next team member.

WHAT'S UNDER THE BED

All sorts of things get stored under the bed! Play this variation of "I Packed My Grandmother's Trunk" thinking of all under-the-bed things there could be. Older children will enjoy trying to remember the entire list of objects or making the list in alphabetical order.

Under the bed, what's under the bed?

What will I find looking under the bed?

I found an apple core, box of crayons, cat fur, dustball, elegant slipper ...

BIRTHDAY PARTY STREAMER GAME

Give each child a length of colored crepe-paper streamer. Play a variety of music—some slow and ballet-like, some with a strong drum beat. Have the children wave the streamers to the music. For variety, move to some music in pairs or in a circle.

EVERYTHING-YOU-EVER-WANTED-IN-A-CLEANING MACHINE

Brainstorm different cleaning functions and the appropriate actions with children. Each child will become a different part of this incredible cleaning machine. For example, one child could be a rotary brush, another could be a mechanical broom, another could be a jet spray of water. At the sound of a whistle or as you begin playing music such as "Syncopated Clock," the parts of this cleaning machine gear up. You could decide to have everyone move at once or you could make this a chain reaction type of machine: One part begins, then touches the next part, which begins, and so on until everyone in the room is actively helping to clean the house!

CRAFTS FOR ALL SPRUCED UP

A ROOM OF YOUR OWN CRAFT

Give each child a shoebox along with bits of wallpaper and carpet samples and smaller boxes from which to cut furniture. They can design their own shoebox room. Help them cut windows or cut items from magazines to paste on.

KNOCK, KNOCK CRAFT

Trace one of the patterns on page 109 to make a door-knob decoration out of posterboard or felt. Decorate with scraps that fit the season, adding eyes to the ghost and decorations for the tree.

NOT-JUST-LIKE-EVERYBODY'S HOUSE CRAFT

Fold a piece of paper in half twice, folding horizontally both times. Cut a roof shape. Open to have four identical houses as shown in the illustration on page 110. Decorate each house with its own special look using crayons, markers, or pieces of cutout paper.

CLEAN UP YOUR ACT CRAFT

Make individual wastebaskets using large ice cream containers. Give one to each child to be decorated with wallpaper, strips of colored tape, and large stickers. Or cover the entire basket with cutouts from magazines. You can use spray shellac to provide a durable surface. Inside the wastebasket tuck a reminder to the child to keep his or her room clean.

PAINT THE TOWN RED CRAFT

Make potato stamps by cutting a potato in half and carving a raised heart on the cut surface of one potato and a raised house shape on the other half. Use red stamp pads or sponges soaked in red paint. The children can use the stamps to decorate greeting cards or wrapping paper for Valentine's Day. Suggest phrases like "home is where the heart is" for the greeting cards.

LEND ME A HAND CRAFT

Have children trace around their hands on bright colors of construction paper. List five clean-up chores they can do to help around the house. Younger children can dictate these to the teacher and older children can write this list themselves. Give children stars, hearts, and little stickers to make their helping hands look especially attractive.

KNOCK KNOCK CRAFT

Tree can be glued in front of house for Christmas

Ghost can be glued on roof for Halloween

cut out this portion

NOT-JUST-LIKE-EVERBODY'S
HOUSE CRAFT

FLOOR PLANS FOR ALL SPRUCED UP

Focus Book: *Roger Loses His Marbles* by Susanna Gretz

Reading Activities

Because the illustrations in this book are full of details that add to the humor of the story, you won't want to miss the fun that begins even before the story itself. Point out the endpapers and illustrations on the title page. This is a story that has several storylines: text set in type, the picture that elaborates on the text, and comments by the characters themselves in speech balloons that add humorous insight into the emotions of the characters beyond the text. You may want to point out these features as you read the story or go back and emphasize them later. The tone and mood of this book will be enhanced by changing your voice for the various characters, especially Aunt Lulu.

Speaking Activities

Turn to the two-page spread where some of the pigs are wishing Aunt Lulu happy birthday. If there were speech balloons over the heads of some of the other pigs, what would they be saying? These comments may or may not relate to giving birthday greetings, but they do need to be appropriate for the action in the picture. For example, the little pig on the floor might be saying, "I wonder how high I can build this tower."

Writing Activities

This book has a number of wonderful puns and plays on words in it. Turn to the page where Aunt Lulu takes a look at Roger's room and calls it a pigpen. To point out the humor of this line, talk about what a real pigpen looks like. How is the term used differently to describe Roger's room? Have the children draw two pictures: one of a real pigpen with pigs and another of Roger's pigpen room. Label the pictures "Pigpen" and "Roger's Pigpen."

To focus on another play on words, write on the board the text from the page where Roger's father is doing the dishes, leaving a blank for the word "trot." List the possible words that could fill the blank: run, go, walk. Why is the word "trot" so appropriate? (Note that the hoofs of a pig are called his trotters.)

More Room!
More Room!

INTRODUCTION

Now here is a chapter packed with action! Building houses and moving to new ones captures the fancy of children who are filled with restless activity themselves. Young children will enjoy the interactive stories, songs, and rhymes that allow them to participate in the theme. Older children will be fascinated especially with the books on designing and building houses, particularly those who dream of becoming future architects. Books in the resource bibliography at the end of this book provide additional direction for children with this interest.

The first subtheme, "Build It Up, Tear It Down," includes books about house building as well as house wrecking. Most of the books annotated in this section tend to be simple in order to provide a quick overview of the topic for a read-aloud. Longer, informational books about building houses appear in the resource bibliography. David Macaulay's fascinating *Unbuilding* (Houghton Mifflin, 1980) has not been included since it treats a skyscraper rather than a house that people live in. The stories and activities we have created include stories about room additions and about planning dream houses. Use these as springboards for children in your classroom or library to brainstorm about houses they might like to build.

The second subtheme, "Moving Experiences," focuses on a common experience for many children today. "The Big Move" teaches counting the days until the move as the child eagerly gets packed. "Animal Squatters" and "The Whole Kitten and Kaboodle" engage in language play as animals get into the act. If you are particularly interested in developing a program or unit on the theme of moving, use "Everything and the Kitchen Sink" and "On the Move Craft" from one of our previous resource books, *Full Speed Ahead* (Libraries Unlimited, 1988). The focus in *Raising the Roof* is on leaving one house and getting settled into a new one.

I Can Build a House!, our focus book for this chapter, provides whole language learning for younger children. Try some of the ideas regarding sequencing and encouraging children to create dialogue on their own with another book, *Anno's Counting House*, if you are working with older children. Anno's wordless books are sophisticated enough to use with even middle school children, but they are also of interest to primary age.

INITIATING ACTIVITY

OPEN HOUSE
(Tune: "Muffin Man")

Greet children with this song. Give children house-shaped nametags as they say their names in response to the last line of the song.

Welcome to our open house,
Open house, open house.
Welcome to our open house.
Come in and say your name.

LITERATURE-SHARING EXPERIENCES

Books for Build It Up and Tear It Down

Alley, R. W. **The Clever Carpenter**. Random House, 1988.
Despite the objections of his neighbors, an eccentric carpenter builds the perfect retirement home for a sea captain.

Barton, Byron. **Building a House**. Greenwillow, 1981.
The steps in building a house are briefly described.

Cauley, Lorinda Bryan. **The New House**. Harcourt Brace Jovanovich, 1981.
The woodchuck family consider moving to a new house until they realize how much they love their old one.

Cobb, Vicki. **Skyscraper Going Up**. Crowell, 1987.
This pop-up book tells about building construction. The skyscraper literally goes up!

Dauer, Rosamond. **Bullfrog Builds a House**. Illustrated by Byron Barton. Greenwillow, 1977.
Not wanting to forget any important items in his new house, Bullfrog seeks the advice of Gertrude. Together they make a wonderful house—except for one important thing.

Flory, Jane. **The Bear on the Doorstep**. Houghton Mifflin, 1980.
Young Bear is adored by the Rabbits who find him on the doorstep and adopt him, but his size soon becomes a problem in their crowded little house.

Gibbons, Gail. **The Magnificent Morris Mouse Clubhouse**. Watts, 1981.
Morris the Mouse's tail gets in the way until he learns how to use it when he builds his own clubhouse.

Gibbons, Gail. **Up Goes the Skyscraper!** Four Winds Press, 1986.
Through simple text and illustrations the building of a skyscraper is described.

Horwitz, Elinor. **How to Wreck a Building**. Photographs by Joshua Horwitz. Pantheon, 1982.
Clear photographs show the tearing down of a building.

Kotzwinkle, William. **The Supreme, Superb, Exalted and Delightful, One and Only Magic Building**. Illustrated by Joe Servello. Farrar, Straus and Giroux, 1973.
   The emperor looks down on the carpenter after the magnificent palace of the ruler's design is constructed.

Manley, Deborah. **A New House**. Illustrated by Julie Simpson. Raintree Children's Books, 1979.
   Simple text and illustrations show a new house being built and a family moving and settling into the neighborhood.

Maynard, Joyce. **New House**. Illustrated by Steve Bethel. Harcourt Brace Jovanovich, 1987.
   Andy watches all summer as a new house is built on his road and at the same time builds a treehouse for himself.

Mendoza, George. **Need a House? Call Ms. Mouse!** Illustrated by Doris Susan Smith. Grosset and Dunlap, 1981.
   Ms. Mouse, house builder-architect-designer par excellence, creates such unusual dwellings as a watery underworld resembling Atlantis for Trout, an above-ground mole hole, a miniature apartment inside a pear for Worm, and a beach house for Lizard.

Merriman, Eve. **Bam-Zam-Boom! A Building Book**. Walker and Co., 1972.
   Unrhymed poetry and lots of sound effects tell about construction and destruction in the city.

Robbins, Ken. **Building a House**. Four Winds Press, 1984.
   From the initial architectural design to final installation of fixtures, this book traces the building of a house.

Tison, Annette. **Barbapapa's New House**. World Publishers, 1972.
   The Barbapapa family have many adventures building a new house.

Watanabe, Shigeo. **I Can Build a House!** Illustrated by Yasuo Ohtomo. Philomel Books, 1983.
   Bear looks until he finds just the right thing to build his very own house.

Related Activities for Build It Up and Tear It Down

JUST EXACTLY ALIKE
(Draw-and-Tell Story)

Sis and Sal were identical twins. They looked alike. They talked alike. And they shared the same room and the same birthday. They liked to be exactly alike.

When Sis and Sal had their tenth birthday, they got many nice gifts. Daddy built them new matching beds. (*Draw two rectangles apart from one another.*) They were just alike, just exactly alike.

Mama made them matching quilts. (*Draw one vertical and one horizontal line inside each rectangle.*) They were just alike, just exactly alike.

Grandma painted the walls on Sis's side of the room bright green. (*Draw a vertical wall on one side. See illustration.*)

Then she painted the walls on Sal's side of the room bright green. (*Draw the other vertical house wall. See illustration.*) They were just alike, just exactly alike.

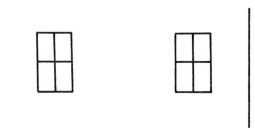

Uncle Ralph bought Sal a matching green carpet for her side of the room. (*Draw one half of the floor of the house. See illustration.*)

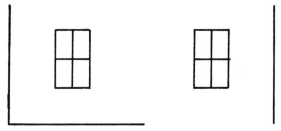

He bought Sis a matching green carpet for her side of the room. (*Draw the other half of the floor of the house. See illustration.*) They were just alike, just exactly alike.

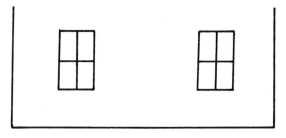

Auntie Kate bought Sal a big, soft, triangle pillow to read books in bed. (*Draw triangle for one side of roof, according to illustration.*)

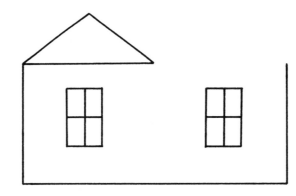

And she bought Sis a big, soft, triangle pillow to read books in bed. (*Draw other triangle to complete roof, according to illustration.*) They were just alike, just exactly alike.

Then Grandpa came. He said, "When you are ten years old, it is good to be alike, but not exactly alike." He did not buy any presents. Instead he made the presents.

Grandpa said to Sis, "I made you a bird feeder so we can feed the birds together." (*Draw one rectangle for one side of front door. See illustration.*)

Grandpa said to Sal, "I planted an apple tree for you in the front yard. We can water it together." (*Draw another rectangle for the other side of front door. See illustration.*)

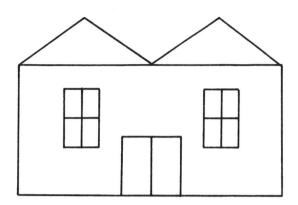

Sis and Sal were not sure they wanted to do anything that was not exactly alike. But Sis went to feed birds with Grandpa. Sal went to water the tree with Grandpa. Much to their surprise they found they enjoyed themselves.

And this is the house Sis and Sal live in. (*Point to drawing of house.*)

Sis and Sal are still twins. They still look alike and talk alike. They still share the same room and the same birthday. But now Sis and Sal say (at exactly the same time), "It is good to be alike, but not exactly alike."

FIX IT UP
(Tune: "Mulberry Bush")

This is the way we fix the house,
Fix the house, fix the house.
This is the way we fix the house
With hammer and paint and saw.

This is the way we saw and saw,   (*Move arm back and forth in sawing motion.*)
Saw and saw, saw and saw.
This is the way we saw and saw,
Saw and saw the house.

This is the way we hammer loud,   (*Pound one fist into other hand.*)
Hammer loud, hammer loud.
This is the way we hammer loud,
Hammering the house.

This is the way we paint and paint,   (*Move arm up and down in painting motion.*)
Paint and paint, paint and paint.
This is the way we paint and paint,
Paint and paint the house.

Now we've used the saw and paint,
Saw and paint, hammer, too.
Now it looks like we're all through—
We've fixed up the house!

RAISE THE ROOF
(Tune: "Three Blind Mice")

Raise the roof!
Raise the roof!
Nice and high,
Nice and high.
We all get together and work all day,
Then under the new roof we laugh and play.
We'll dance and we'll sing till the break of day,
And raise the roof!

NEW HOUSE
(Tune: "London Bridge")

Let's all build a brand new house,
Brand new house, brand new house,
Let's all build a brand new house.
Let's get started!

First we'll dig a great big hole,
Great big hole, great big hole,
First we'll dig a great big hole.
Let's keep going!

Then we'll put in walls and floors,
Walls and floors, walls and floors,
Then we'll put in walls and floors.
Let's keep going!

Now it's time to raise the roof,
Raise the roof, raise the roof,
Now it's time to raise the roof.
Let's keep going!

Then put out the welcome mat,
Welcome mat, welcome mat,
Then put out the welcome mat,
And have a party!

BUILDING OUR DREAM HOUSE
(Action Rhyme)

Building our dream house   (*Raise arms high over head.*)
Let's add lots of nooks
For hide and seek places   (*Peek through hands in front of face.*)
To read favorite books.   (*Palms up, waist high like a book.*)

Stairs to climb up   (*Mime climbing stairs.*)
Windows and doors   (*Place palms together then spread them apart.*)
Attics and cellars
We'll want to explore.   (*Cup hand over eyes as if exploring, crouch down slightly.*)

So help me get started
Let's all lend a hand   (*Take another person's hand.*)
We're raising the roof   (*Raise hands high.*)
On our dream house so grand!

GARAGE SALE JUNKIE
(Flannel-board Story)

Make flannel-board pieces of all the garage sale items from the patterns shown on pages 120-21: frames for house and garage, dishes, chair, sofa, washing machine, twelve Christmas trees, chandelier, two dog dishes, dog. Place them on the board as indicated in the story.

Mr. Packrat had a bumper sticker on his car that said, "I brake for garage sales." And he really did! Whenever Mr. Packrat saw a garage sale on any street in any part of town, he stopped to look around. And he almost always found something to buy. Whatever it was, Mr. Packrat said, "It will come in handy someday." So he brought it home to his house. (*Place frame of house on board.*)

One time it was a set of dishes with only the cups missing. (*Place dishes on board.*) One time it was a chair that still had three good legs. (*Place chair on board.*) One time it was a dog dish in perfect condition. (*Place dog dish on board.*) Except Mr. Packrat did not have a dog.

What Mr. Packrat did have was a family who were getting tired of garage sales. Mrs. Packrat wanted cups with her dishes. Their son, Paul, wanted to study on a chair with all four legs. And little Paula wanted a dog to go with the dog dish.

But Mr. Packrat just smiled and said, "It will come in handy someday."

So it went with garage sales and Mr. Packrat. A sofa with no cushions. (*Place sofa on board.*) A washing machine that leaked. (*Place washing machine on board.*) Twelve plastic Christmas trees each missing only a few branches. (*Place trees on board.*) A crystal chandelier that was too big for the dining room. (*Place chandelier on board.*) And another dog dish in perfect condition. (*Place other dog dish on board.*) Mr. Packrat just smiled and said, "It will come in handy someday."

Finally the Packrat house was so full of things Mr. Packrat had collected that no one could move around. That is when Mrs. Packrat got an idea. She took Paul and Paula and went to a garage sale herself.

That night at dinner she said, "Mr. Packrat, it is too crowded in this house for any more things from garage sales. But I know that you will not stop buying things that will come in handy someday. So today we went to a garage sale, too. Come outside."

There behind the house Mr. Packrat saw what the family had bought. They had gone to a garage sale and bought him a GARAGE! (*Place frame of garage on board.*) "Now," said Mrs. Packrat, "you can keep your garage sale things where they belong. In a garage!"

(*Take items out of the house frame as they are mentioned and put them in the frame of the garage.*) So out of the house came the set of dishes with the cups missing. Out came the chair with three legs. Out came the sofa with no cushions, and the washing machine that leaked, and the twelve plastic Christmas trees each missing only a few branches. Out came the crystal chandelier that was too big for the dining room. (*Only the dog dishes are left in the house.*)

And what happened to the dog dishes in perfect condition? Mr. Packrat finally found a brand new puppy for Paula at a garage sale. (*Place dog in house by dog dishes.*) "See," said Mr. Packrat with a smile, "I knew that would come in handy someday."

(Text continues on page 122.)

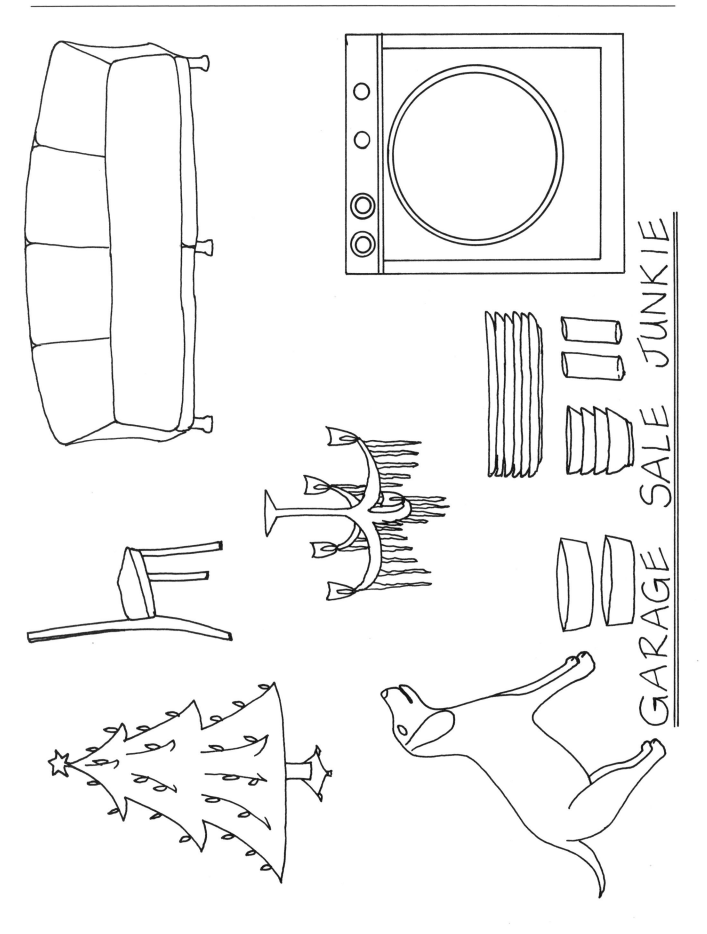

GARAGE SALE JUNKIE

MORE ROOM! MORE ROOM! A "HARE-RAISING" ADVENTURE
(Object Story)

To add extra interest to this story, bring in the following objects that the Rabbit relatives carry into the house: weights; a cello or violin; and a hairbrush, blow dryer, and can of hairspray. If you can't locate some of these items, make large cutouts from posterboard. Distribute these items to children so they can actively participate in the story.

The Rabbit family lived in a house in the forest. There was a room for eating, a room for sleeping, and a room for talking by the fire. That was just enough for the Rabbit family.

One day Cousin Jack Rabbit came for a long visit. "This is a nice house," he said, "but where can I work out with my weights? You need an exercise room."

So the Rabbit family added on to their house. Now they had a room for eating, a room for sleeping, a room for talking by the fire, and a room for exercising. That was just enough for the Rabbit family, plus Jack.

One day Uncle Harry came for a long visit. "This is a nice house," he said, "but I play 'long-hare' music. Where can I practice my cello? You need a music room."

So the Rabbit family added on to their house. Now they had a room for eating, a room for sleeping, a room for talking by the fire, a room for exercising, and a room for playing "long-hare" music. That was just enough for the Rabbit family, plus Jack and Uncle Harry.

Then one day the Bunny sisters—Fluffy, Muffy, and Buffy—came for a long visit. "This is a nice house," they said, "but we spend a lot of time washing and drying and styling our hair. Where can we do our hair? You need a dressing room with lots of mirrors."

So the Rabbit family added on to their house. Now they had a room for eating, a room for sleeping, a room for talking by the fire, a room for exercising, a room for playing "long-hare" music, and a dressing room for grooming and styling hair. That was just enough for the Rabbit family, plus Jack and Uncle Harry and the Bunny sisters—Fluffy, Muffy, and Buffy.

And before any more Rabbit relations could come for a long visit, Mr. Rabbit took his own little family into the room for talking by the fire. "We don't need an exercise room or a music room or a dressing room. What we need is fewer rabbits in this house!"

So quick as a bunny, Mr. Rabbit got Cousin Jack Rabbit a room at the local gym. He got Uncle Harry a room at the local music conservatory. And he found places for the Bunny sisters—Fluffy, Muffy, and Buffy—at three beauty parlors.

All the Rabbit relations were happy in their new homes. The Rabbit family went back to using just the room for eating, the room for sleeping, and the room for talking by the fire. That was just enough for the Rabbit family. And the only times they used the other parts of the house were when their Rabbit relations came for a SHORT visit.

BUILD A HOUSE—QUICK!
(Action Rhyme)

Teach the actions to this busy rhyme and then get faster each time you say it.

Dig the hole.	(*Squat, scooping arms to floor.*)
Lay the floor.	(*Stand, move hands as if patting ground.*)
Raise the roof.	(*Reach arms overhead.*)
Open the door.	(*Bend elbow as if opening door.*)

MOUSE HOUSE
(Flannel-board Story)

For this story cut a square, rectangle, triangle, half circle, and circle from felt. Adjust the story to the color felt you use for each shape. Place them on the flannel-board as Mollie builds her house.

Mollie Mouse resided in the mansion of the Swathmore family. But she wanted her own cozy little house. She looked around the playroom of the Swathmore children for a cozy little house.

First she tried the jack-in-the-box, but there was already somebody living there. Next she tried the doll house, but it was too big to keep clean. Next she tried a music box, but the noise level was too much. Finally Mollie Mouse said, "I'll have to build a cozy little house all by myself."

So she went to the toy box and found a red square block. (*Place red square block on flannel-board.*) "Perfect," she said, "but it still doesn't feel like home."

So she went back to the toy box and found a green half-circle block. (*Place green half circle below blue rectangle to form welcome mat.*) "Perfect," she said, "but it still doesn't feel like home."

This time Mollie went back to the kitchen and brought back a yellow round cheese. (*Place yellow circle beside house.*) "Perfect," she said. "Now it finally feels like home. A cozy little mouse house." And she moved right in.

This time Mollie went back to the kitchen and brought back a yellow round cheese. (*Place yellow circle beside house.*) "Perfect," she said. "Now it finally feels like home. A cozy little mouse house." And she moved right in.

Books for Moving Experiences

Anno, Mitsumasa. **Anno's Counting House**. Philomel Books, 1982.
    This wordless book can be used to make up stories and to teach counting, as you turn the pages and reveal ten children leaving one house and going to another.

Asch, Frank. **Goodbye House**. Prentice-Hall, 1986.
    Baby Bear goes back to look for something in his old house and Papa and Mama help him remember where everything used to be. To help him feel closure, Papa Bear takes him from room to room to say goodbye to everything.

Burton, Virginia Lee. **The Little House**. Houghton Mifflin, 1942.
    A country house is unhappy when the city, with all its buildings and traffic, grows up around it.

Demarest, Chris. **Benedict Finds a Home**. Lothrop, 1982.
    Benedict leaves his crowded nest to search for the perfect home.

Gerstein, Mordicai. **The Room**. Harper & Row, 1984.
    Presents glimpses of a room and the many people who inhabit it over the years.

Gretz, Susanna. **Teddy Bear's Moving Day**. Four Winds Press, 1981.
    Moving to a new house is painful for Robert because he loses things all over town on the way, but the other teddy bears persuade him to join them in the end rather than camp out in the back yard.

Hickman, Martha. **I'm Moving**. Illustrated by Leigh Grant. Abingdon, 1974.
    William explains what he has brought with him and what he had to leave behind when the family moved to a new town.

Isadora, Rachel. **The Potter's Kitchen**. Greenwillow, 1977.
    The Potter family has to make a few adjustments when they move from the country to the city, but it is a happy time for them.

Joerns, Consuelo. **The Lost and Found House**. Four Winds Press, 1979.
    A mouse suffers one mishap after another with his house until a boy with a model train provides a whole new life.

Keyworth, Cynthia. **New Day**. Illustrated by Carolyn Bracken. Morrow, 1986.
    Moving to a new place means learning a new street, house, neighbors, and lots of other surprises.

Klein, Norma. **Dinosaur's Housewarming Party**. Illustrated by James Marshall. Crown, 1974.
    Dinosaur's friends treat him to an array of housewarming presents when he moves into his new penthouse.

Kwitz, Mary. **Rabbits' Search for a Little House**. Illustrated by Lorinda Cauley. Crown, 1977.
    Mother Rabbit and her son look for a tiny and cozy winter home.

Malone, Nola. **A Home**. Bradbury, 1988.
    Molly does not feel comfortable in her new house until she makes a new friend.

Milord, Sue. **Maggie and the Goodbye Gift**. Lothrop, 1979.
    The family is lonely in their new town until Maggie uses the gift her friends gave her in their old place.

O'Donnell, Elizabeth. **Maggie Doesn't Want to Move**. Illustrated by Amy Schwartz. Four Winds Press, 1987.
    Simon is feeling sad about moving, but he says it is his sister Maggie who doesn't want to go.

Provensen, Alice. **Shaker Lane**. Viking Kestrel, 1987.
    When the town decides to build a reservoir on their land, the residents of Shaker Lane decide to move away rather than fight to keep their homes.

Sharmat, Marjorie Weinman. **Mitchell Is Moving**. Illustrated by Jose Aruego and Arian Dewey. Macmillan, 1978.
    Mitchell the dinosaur is determined to move away because everything looks the same in his old house. Margo, his next-door neighbor, tries to discourage him, but Mitchell moves anyway. Once resettled, Mitchell misses his next-door neighbor so much that he ends up building her a new house next to his.

Shefelman, Janice. **Victoria House**. Illustrated by Tom Shefelman. Harcourt Brace Jovanovich, 1988.
    An architect couple and their son buy a Victorian house and have the old house moved from a deserted lot to the city, where the house is lovingly restored and lived in again.

Singer, Marilyn. **Archer Armadillo's Secret Room**. Illustrated by Beth Lee Weiner. Macmillan, 1985.
    Archer Armadillo refuses to leave his secret room when the rest of the family moves to a new burrow.

Wahl, Jan. **More Room for the Pipkins**. Illustrated by John Wallner. Prentice-Hall, 1983.
    Mr. and Mrs. Pipkins and their two children live with Grandpa Gus in a cozy little house, but they decide everyone needs a separate room to pursue various hobbies. Once everyone is tucked away in isolated places, life loses its merriment, until Mr. Pipkin comes up with a new project.

Wilhelm, Hans. **A New Home, a New Friend**. Random House, 1985.
    Michael's anxieties over moving to a new house are lessened when he meets a large dog.

Ziefert, Harriet. **A New House for Mole and Mouse**. Illustrated by David Prebenna. Puffin, 1987.
    In this easy reader Mole and Mouse move into a new house and try everything out, including the piano, the bathtub, and the light. Everything is working fine until balloons are delivered to the door.

Related Activities for Moving Experiences

NEW NEIGHBORS
(Tune: "Mulberry Bush")

Use this song to review the names of children. Each joins the circle as his or her name is sung in the last line.

We're all moving into town,
Into town, into town.
We're all moving into town.
Say "hello" to (child's name).

ANIMAL SQUATTERS
(Action Rhyme)

Once there were homeowners who went away
For winter vacation one snowy day,
And while they basked in the Florida sun
Said a bunch of animals, "Let's have fun!"

In came a skunk	*(Hold nose.)*
With a pile of junk.	*(Arms outstretched.)*
Moved to the house that snowy day	
When the owners were far away.	

In came a pig	*(Puff out cheeks.)*
With a bag this big.	*(Curl arms around imaginary bag.)*
In came a skunk	*(Hold nose.)*
With a pile of junk.	*(Arms outstretched.)*
Moved to the house that snowy day	
When the owners were far away.	

In came a fox	*(Tap nose.)*
With a heavy box.	*(Lower arms as if carrying box.)*
In came a pig	*(Puff out cheeks.)*
With a bag this big.	*(Curl arms around imaginary bag.)*
In came a skunk	*(Hold nose.)*
With a pile of junk.	*(Arms outstretched.)*
Moved to the house that snowy day	
When the owners were far away.	

In came a toad	*(Stick out tongue several times.)*
With another load.	*(Throw pack over back.)*
In came a fox	*(Tap nose.)*
With a heavy box.	*(Lower arms as if carrying box.)*
In came a pig	*(Puff out cheeks.)*
With a bag this big.	*(Curl arms around imaginary bag.)*

In came a skunk	(Hold nose.)
With a pile of junk.	(Arms outstretched.)
Moved to the house that snowy day	
When the owners were far away.	

Last said the ape	(Flex muscles.)
"It's time to escape."	(Beckon others to come.)
So out went the toad	(Stick out tongue several times.)
With another load.	(Throw pack over back.)
Out went the fox	(Tap nose.)
With a heavy box.	(Lower arms as if carrying box.)
Out went the pig	(Puff out cheeks.)
With a bag this big.	(Curl arms around imaginary bag.)
Out went the skunk	(Hold nose.)
With a pile of junk.	(Arms outstretched.)
Moved from the house that snowy day	
When the owners were far away.	

THE WHOLE KITTEN AND KABOODLE
(Tune: "Jingle Bells")

Moving day, moving day,
Time to pack the van.
Bring the boxes, bring the bags,
Bring the pots and pans.
Moving day, moving day.
Pack your coat and hat,
Don't forget to check each room,
And bring along the cat.
Meow!

PACKING CHANT

Set the rhythm for this chant by tapping on knees. After you have done the verses listed, have children suggest more items to take to the new house. Then finish with the last stanza.

We're moving to a new house
With lots of room inside.
Help to pack the moving van,
Then come and take a ride.

Don't forget the sleeping bags.
(repeat: sleeping bags)
Help to pack the moving van,
Then come and take a ride.

Don't forget the pizza pans.
(repeat: pizza pans)
Help to pack the moving van,
Then come and take a ride.

Don't forget the bird cage.
(repeat: bird cage)
Help to pack the moving van,
Then come and take a ride.

(Children can suggest more verses.)

Now we're at the new house.
Here's our brand new street.
We'll unpack the moving van,
Then sit right down to eat.

GYPSY THE MOTH AND THE BRIGHT LIGHTS
(Participatory Story)

On paper plates mount pictures of the following objects (see patterns on p. 128): house with a porch light, car with a headlight, street lamp, and restaurant with a pink neon light that says "Eat Here." Also use stick puppets of a firefly and Gypsy the moth cut out of cardboard. Attach Velcro to the back of Gypsy and the front of all the other pieces. Move Gypsy as indicated in the story.

(*Hold up Gypsy.*) Gypsy the moth was on the move. She constantly flew from one place to another and was never really happy. Gypsy said, "I'm searching for the bright lights of the city. When I find the right light, then I'll be happy.

> Gotta fly, gotta flit
> Gotta flee, flee, flee
> Where's the light that's
> Meant for me?"

(*Attach Gypsy to house with porch light.*) Gypsy the moth first landed on a porch light of a small house in the city. It was a soft yellow light, but it was not bright enough for Gypsy. (*Remove Gypsy from house with porch light.*) She said,

> "Gotta fly, gotta flit
> Gotta flee, flee, flee
> Where's the light that's
> Meant for me?"

(*Attach Gypsy to car with headlight.*) Then Gypsy landed on the headlight of a car. It was bright enough, but the car moved so fast Gypsy could not hang on. This was not the right light for Gypsy. (*Remove Gypsy from car with headlight.*) She said,

> "Gotta fly, gotta flit
> Gotta flee, flee, flee
> Where's the light that's
> Meant for me?"

(*Attach Gypsy to street lamp.*) Then Gypsy landed on a street lamp. It was nice and bright, but it made a buzzing sound. The noise was too much. This was not the right light for Gypsy. (*Remove Gypsy from street lamp.*) She said,

> "Gotta fly, gotta flit
> Gotta flee, flee, flee
> Where's the light that's
> Meant for me?"

(*Attach Gypsy to restaurant with neon sign.*) Next Gypsy landed on a neon sign on a restaurant. It was pink and said "Eat Here." Gypsy liked the pink light and thought she was happy, but when the restaurant closed, the owner turned off the sign and Gypsy was left in the dark. That was not the right light for Gypsy. She said,

> "Gotta fly, gotta flit
> Gotta flee, flee, flee
> Where's the light that's
> Meant for me?"

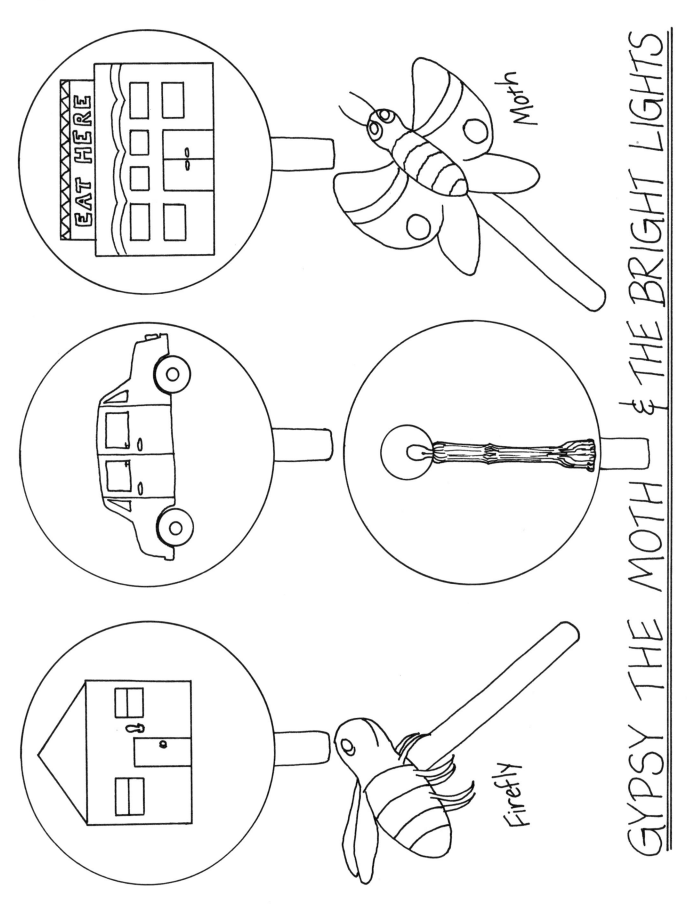

Moth

Firefly

GYPSY THE MOTH & THE BRIGHT LIGHTS

EAT HERE

While she sat on the dark sign and felt sad, she saw a new light, a wonderful bright light that blinked on and off, on and off. The light flew through the air and landed next to her. It was Frank the firefly. (*Hold up the firefly stick puppet.*) "What a wonderful light," said Gypsy. (*Remove Gypsy from restaurant with neon sign and attach to firefly.*)

> "Gotta fly, gotta flit
> Gotta flee, flee, flee
> This is the light that's
> Meant for me!"

(*Move Gypsy and firefly off together.*) So they flew off together to a lighthouse by the ocean where they had a bright and happy future.

HOME RUN
(Prop Story)

Cut out four posterboard houses of red, blue, green, and yellow for Red Rooster, Blue Heron, Green Frog, and Yellow Chameleon (see illustrations on p. 130). Then cover the tops of four boxes with construction paper of the same colors. You may wish to use cake boxes since these can be purchased from bakeries and take little room to store as they are collapsible. If you wish, you may place red, blue, green, and yellow fabric in each to stand for the red rug, blue bedspread, green bathmat, and yellow curtains.

Elephant Moving was a good company. Elephant moved all the boxes himself and always got them to the right house. But business was so heavy that Elephant decided to go on a vacation. He hired Chicken to take over the run while he was gone. Chicken wanted to do things right, but did not stop to think before he delivered the boxes.

On Monday Chicken delivered a red box to Blue Heron's new house. Blue Heron opened up the box expecting to find his blue bedspread, but inside the box was a red rug.

"Chicken, this is not right," said Blue Heron. "Stop and think for a minute before you make your next run. This is not my box."

"Dear me," said Chicken. "I want to get things right. Just let me try again."

On Tuesday Chicken delivered a blue box to Green Frog's new house. Green Frog opened up the box expecting to find his green bathmat, but inside the box was a blue bedspread.

"Chicken, this is not right," said Green Frog. "Stop and think for a minute before you make your next run. This is not my box."

"Dear me," said Chicken. "I want to get things right. Just let me try again."

On Wednesday Chicken delivered a green box to Yellow Chameleon's new house. Yellow Chameleon opened up the box expecting to find her yellow curtains, but inside the box was a green bathmat.

"Chicken, this is not right," said Yellow Chameleon. "Stop and think for a minute before you make your next run. This is not my box."

"Dear me," said Chicken. "I want to get things right. Just let me try again."

On Thursday Chicken delivered a yellow box to Red Rooster's new house. Red Rooster opened up the box expecting to find his red rug, but inside the box was a pair of yellow curtains.

"Chicken, this is not right," said Red Rooster. "Stop and think for a minute before you make your next run. This is not my box."

"Dear me," said Chicken. "I want to get things right. Just let me try again."

The next day was Friday. Chicken had to unscramble the whole mess before Elephant got home. So Chicken put her head on straight and picked up the boxes.

First Chicken went back to Yellow Chameleon's house and picked up the green box. He took this to Green Frog's house. Green Frog was happy to get his own green bathmat.

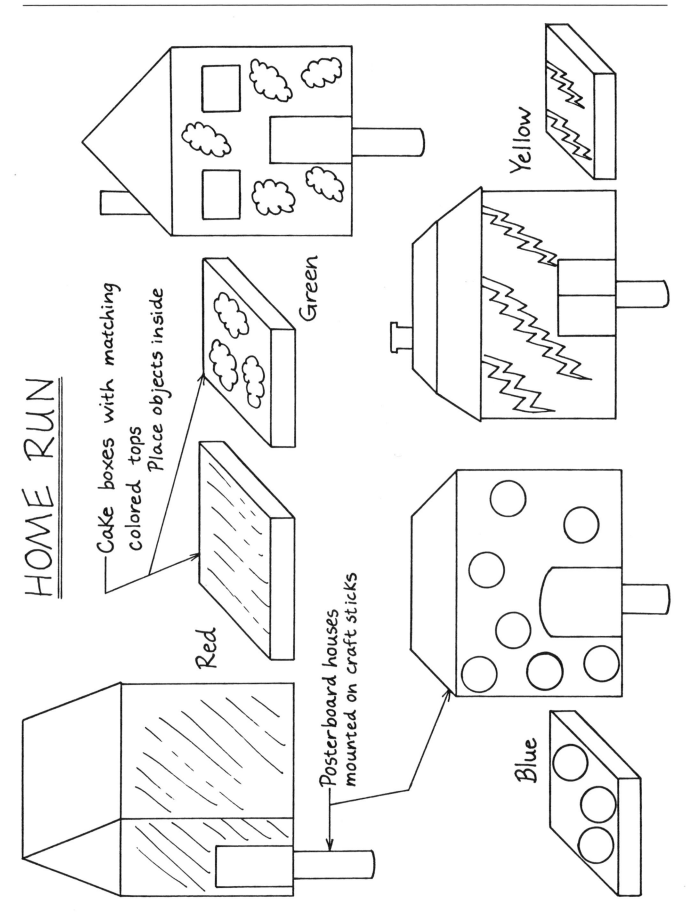

HOME RUN

Cake boxes with matching colored tops
Place objects inside

Posterboard houses mounted on craft sticks

Green

Red

Yellow

Blue

Then Chicken picked up the blue box and delivered it to Blue Heron's house. Blue Heron was happy to have his old blue bedspread.

Then Chicken picked up the red box and delivered it to Red Rooster's house. Red Rooster was so glad to get back his red rug that he crowed and crowed.

Then Chicken picked up the yellow box and delivered it to Yellow Chameleon's house. Yellow Chameleon was so happy to have her yellow curtains that she hung them up and invited Chicken to stay for lunch.

But Chicken said, "I've got to run home. I want everything to be right when Elephant gets there."

When Chicken got back to Elephant Moving Company, Elephant was just unloading his suitcases from the trunk of his limousine.

"Did you get all the boxes delivered to the right houses?" asked Elephant.

"Oh, yes," said Chicken. "I got everything right. I made a home run!" And he did, too.

THE BIG MOVE
(Object Story)

Use a packing box and the following objects to tell this story: baseball glove, goldfish bowl, hippo poster, sleeping bag, toothbrush. If you do not have these items, change the story to match the items you can find. Put the items in the box as Danny packs and then have the children see how many items they can remember when it is finally time for Danny to move.

Danny was excited about moving. He looked at the calendar every day and counted until the day the moving van would come take them to their new home.

When there were five days left, Danny put his baseball glove in a big box. "I'm all packed," said Danny. "Can we move now?"

"Not yet, Danny," said his mother. "There are still five more days."

When there were four days left, Danny put his goldfish bowl in a big box. "I'm all packed," said Danny. "Can we move now?"

"Not yet, Danny," said his mother. "There are still four more days."

When there were three days left, Danny put his hippo poster in a big box. "I'm all packed," said Danny. "Can we move now?"

"Not yet, Danny," said his mother. "There are still three more days."

When there were two days left, Danny put his sleeping bag in a big box. "I'm all packed," said Danny. "Can we move now?"

"Not yet, Danny," said his mother. "There are still two more days."

When there was one day left, Danny put his toothbrush in a big box. "I'm all packed," said Danny. "Can we move now?"

"Almost ready, Danny," said his mother. "There is only one more day."

So when the morning of the big move came, Danny was ready. Can you name all the things in his box? (*Baseball glove, goldfish bowl, hippo poster, sleeping bag, toothbrush.*) Good! Danny and all his things moved to the new house, and it took Danny much less than five days to unpack!

FIVE LITTLE BOXES
(Fingerplay)

Five little boxes
Sitting by the door.
The movers came and took one,
And then there were four.

Four little boxes
Some are really heavy.
The movers came and took one,
And then there were three.

Three little boxes
Some are old and some are new.
The movers came and took one,
And then there were two.

Two little boxes
Now we're almost done.
The movers came and took one,
And then there was one.

One more box left,
Full of pots and pans.
The movers came and took it—
Let's get into the van!

GAMES FOR MORE ROOM! MORE ROOM!

MOVING IN AND OUT

Form a circle and sing these words to the tune of "Farmer in the Dell." Choose a child to be in the center. This child is the new child in the neighborhood. Sing the following verse; then the child chooses someone else to get in the center, too.

Welcome to our street
Welcome to our street
Choose another boy or girl
We would like to meet.

PACKING GAME

Everyone sits in a circle. One child is selected as the child who is planning to move. Repeat the following verse, then ask the child to name something to put in the moving box. This child then chooses another to come to the center and continue the packing game.

Look at all the boxes
What a great big stack!
Tell me what you put in
When you start to pack.

CRAFTS FOR MORE ROOM! MORE ROOM!

CARPENTER ANT TOOLBOX

Use a center-cut file folder and decorate the outside with pictures of little ants. An ant can be made easily by making thumbprints and drawing the legs on with magic markers. Inside the folder toolbox, paste pictures of tools from catalogs or invite children to draw their own versions of tools a carpenter ant might need to build a house.

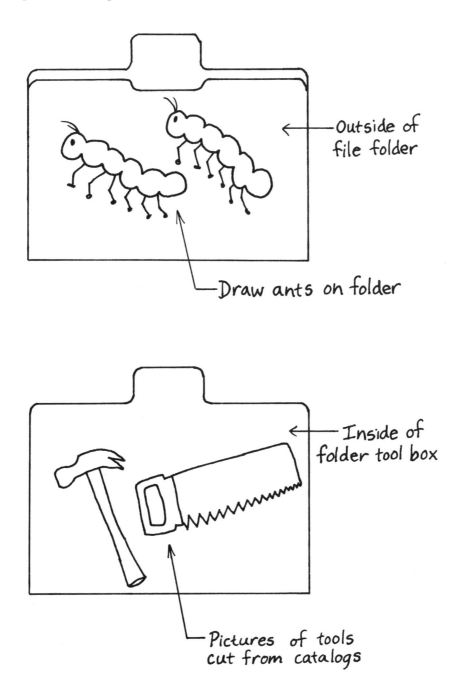

GETTING YOUR HOUSE IN SHAPE

Provide children with a number of different shapes of colored paper—red squares, blue rectangles, yellow triangles, green circles, etc. Children construct their own houses by pasting shapes on paper (see suggestions in illustrations below). When houses are finished, you can distribute gold seals as "good housekeeping" seals of design.

MY OWN FLOOR PLAN

Provide children with simple floor plan outlines and ask them to label the different rooms. Children can draw in furniture or cut out pictures from catalogs.

FLOOR PLANS FOR MORE ROOM! MORE ROOM!

Focus Book: *I Can Build a House!* by Shigeo Watanabe

Reading Activities

This brief text will be read by many of the children themselves. Read through the text with the children several times, focusing their attention on the words. The large type will make it easy for even beginning readers to see clearly and follow along.

Point out the cause and effect relationship of each sequence of pictures (building with blocks, cushions, box). Then photocopy pages 10-17. Mount each picture on paper and allow children to sequence the pictures to show the four steps in construction and destruction of a house made of cushions.

Speaking Activities

Cover the text on pages 18-19. Let children suggest what the little bear might be saying upon finding the box. Comments may or may not have to do with the storyline. The bear could be saying, "I bet this box has a big present in it." Record all these possible captions and read them aloud as a group.

There are three houses in the book. The first two fall down. Help the children practice communicating the frustration and disappointment the bear experiences by having them say the words ("uh-oh" and "oh, no") with you, expressing great feeling. Show the last page and let the children say "I did it all by myself!" with great pride.

Writing Activities

There are five pictures in the box-building sequence of the story. Use the pictures only and let the children make up their own words, either as a group or as individuals, to retell the sequence on paper.

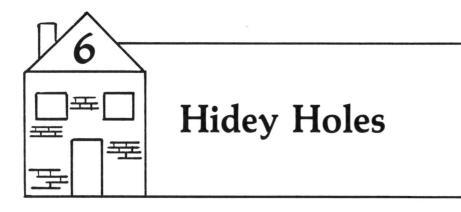

Hidey Holes

INTRODUCTION

Even the youngest child who plays peek-a-boo understands the fun of finding a hideaway. As children grow and become more imaginative, the hiding place becomes more elaborate. It can be a temporary sheet-thrown-over-a-card-table hidey hole or it can be a treehouse sturdy enough to last for years of enjoyment. Even after children outgrow their small hiding places, as teenagers they nest in bedrooms with closed doors as if they are receding into "the cave years," as one of our colleagues humorously described adolescence. Everyone will understand the fun in this chapter!

The books written on this theme are usually treehouse stories or imaginative books about different hideaways. The cadenced text of Liesle Moak Skorpen's *We Were Tired of Living in a House* tells of children moving to a tree, a pond, a cave, and even the sea with such appeal that even the most entrenched homebody would pack a bag for these hiding places. We have created stories, songs, and rhymes about even more hidey holes that children enjoy. Basements, attics, and closets are parts of houses that make perfect hiding places for children. We can still fondly remember hours of play spent in these places during our childhoods. Not every child will be lucky enough to have a treehouse or a child-sized playhouse, but a refrigerator carton gives everyone an opportunity to create a house.

The focus book of this chapter, *A Little House of Your Own* by Beatrice deRegniers, encourages children to create their own places using everyday objects and an active imagination. Let the ideas in this book and the activities in this chapter foster even more creative language and learning experiences in your school or library.

INITIATING ACTIVITY

HIDEY HOLE HELLO

Peek-a-boo!
Come inside.
Here's a secret
Place to hide.

Tell your name
Quietly.
Then sit down
Right next to me.

LITERATURE-SHARING EXPERIENCES

Books for Hidey Holes

Aruego, Jose. **We Hide You Seek**. Greenwillow, 1979.
Hidden animals add to the fun of this colorful book about animal homes.

Baylor, Byrd. **Your Own Best Secret Place**. Scribner, 1979.
What is your favorite hiding place: a hollow tree, gully, or sand dune?

Berson, Harold. **The Rats Who Lived in a Delicatessen**. Crown, 1976.
A rat is happy living in the delicatessen until he begins to let other rats come to live there.

Brodsky, Beverly. **Secret Places**. Lippincott, 1979.
Despite the sound of a clanging radiator and neighbors' quarrels in nearby apartment, a girl makes her own secret dream places in a big-city apartment house.

deRegniers, Beatrice. **A Little House of Your Own**. Illustrated by Irene Haas. Harcourt Brace, 1954.
Secret hiding places are explored, from treehouses and tents to more temporary and unusual places such as under the blankets, in a box, or behind a chair in a corner.

Fisher, Timothy. **Hammocks, Hassocks, and Hide Aways: Furniture Kids Can Build for Themselves**. Addison-Wesley, 1980.
This nonfiction book includes instructions for making furniture such as shelves and lampshades from easily available materials.

Fleisher, Robbin. **Quilts in the Attic**. Illustrated by Ati Forberg. Macmillan, 1978.
Attics are places for playing imaginative games and for curling up in a cozy quilt, as two sisters discover one rainy day.

Gerstein, Mordicai. **William, Where Are You?** Crown, 1985.
At bedtime William hides and his parents look all over the house for him.

Hogrogian, Nonny. **Handmade Secret Hiding Places**. Overlook Press, 1975.
Directions are given for making ten unusual hiding places, including a pole-bean tepee, a leafy lean-to, and a "behind the stairs" hideout.

Joerns, Consuelo. **The Lost and Found House**. Four Winds Press, 1979.
When his treehouse blows away, Cricket the mouse searches for the perfect house. The one he finds and repairs is carted away and lost several times until a kind boy rescues both Cricket and the house.

Kirk, Barbara. **Grandpa, Me, and Our House in the Tree**. Macmillan, 1978.
Grandpa can't climb up into the treehouse he built for Nico since his illness, but he makes a tin-can telephone so they can still stay in touch.

Krahn, Fernando. **The Family Minus's Summer House**. Parents' Magazine Press, 1980.
On a trip to the country, the Minus family puts up a portable treehouse but then decides it's safer to live on the ground.

Lane, John. **How to Make Play Places and Secret Hidey Holes**. Doubleday, 1979.
Presents directions for constructing a castle, lemonade stand, covered wagon, and other play places from cardboard.

McCoy, Elin. **Secret Spaces, Imaginary Places: Creating Your Own Worlds for Play**. Illustrations by Lynn Sweat. Macmillan, 1986.
   Instructions for pirate ships, castles, and secret hideouts made with free or inexpensive materials.

Mayer, Mercer. **There's a Nightmare in My Closet**. Dial, 1968.
   Strange creatures come out of the closet at night until the boy bravely confronts his fears.

Schertle, Alice. **In My Treehouse**. Illustrated by Meredith Dunham. Lothrop, 1983.
   A little girl describes the pleasures of living in a treehouse, including sharing her lunch with tree ants, lowering a bucket for mail, hearing night sounds, and swaying—house and all—on a windy day.

Skorpen, Liesle Moak. **We Were Tired of Living in a House**. Illustrated by Doris Burn. Coward-McCann, 1969.
   In this gently cadenced text, some children "tired of living in a house" pack a bag "with sweaters and ... mittens and woolen caps" and move to a tree, where a breeze ripples the roof until they tumble out. They pack their bag and move to a pond ... until they sink. Then they move to a cave but meet a bear, so they move to the sea until the tide comes in. Finally they go back to living in a house.

Soya, Kiyoshi. **A House of Leaves**. Illustrated by Akiko Hayashi. Philomel Books, 1986.
   When Sarah is playing in her yard, it begins to rain, so she crawls in a leafy enclosure (her "house to hide in") and is joined by a beetle, a lady bug, a praying mantis, and a host of other garden creatures.

Tudor, Bethany. **Samuel's Tree House**. Colling, 1979.
   A duckling who wants to build a treehouse all by himself accepts some help from his friends.

Tusa, Tricia. **Maebelle's Suitcase**. Macmillan, 1987.
   Maebelle, who is 108 years old, builds a treehouse so she can live happily among the birds. When one of the birds tries to fly south with Maebelle's suitcase, Maebelle persuades him to leave behind some of the treasures so she can decorate a hat she is creating for a contest.

Vigna, Judith. **The Hiding House**. Whitman, 1979.
   Barbara and Marybeth, two best friends, have their own hiding house that they decorate and sleep in and keep exclusively for themselves. But when a new girl moves into the neighborhood, Marybeth is reluctant to invite her to share the hiding house.

Related Activities for Hidey Holes

POCKET HOMES
(Tune: "Paw-Paw Patch")

Use finger puppets and a rock with eyes painted on it to sing this song about the original "mobile homes."

> There's a home inside my pocket.
> Who is hiding in my pocket?
> Who is hiding in my pocket?
> Listen carefully so you will know.

(*spoken*) Meow. Meow. What is it? A kitten!

There's a kitten in my pocket.
Made her home inside my pocket.
Something else is in my pocket.
Listen carefully so you will know.

(*spoken*) Ribbit. Ribbit. What is it? A froggie!

There's a froggie in my pocket.
Made his home inside my pocket.
Something else is in my pocket.
Listen carefully so you will know.

(*spoken*) Bow-wow. Bow-wow. What is it? A puppy.

There's a puppy in my pocket.
Made his home inside my pocket.
Something else is in my pocket.
Listen carefully so you will know.

(*silence*) What is it? Can you tell? (*Show rock.*)

It's a pet rock in my pocket!
Made its home inside my pocket.
Now you know what's in my pockets!
All these creatures call my pockets "home."

SAVE EVERYTHING!
(Tube Story)

Cut out the following objects to attach to rings of cardboard: girl, nose cone, control panel, rocket ship, flame coming out of rocket, space creature. Slip the rings over a paper-towel roll as shown in the illustration on page 140. Flip each object up as it is mentioned in the story.

Patty lived in an average house on an average street in an average town. The only thing un-average about Patty was that she liked to save things—lots of things. She hid them away in her room, under the bed and in the closet and behind the dresser. Other than that, her life was very, very average.

Then one day Patty opened the closet door, and there sat a space creature. She was only about half Patty's size and such a pretty shade of green that Patty forgot to be frightened and just said, "Hello."

"Jello," said the creature. She had not planned to visit the planet Earth and was still having trouble with the language.

"Where did you come from?" asked Patty.

"Zars," said the creature. She could have meant either "Mars" or "the stars," but before Patty could ask, the creature said, "Flow grom. Flow grom."

"Flow grom?" asked Patty. Could that mean "go home"? "Do you want to go back?" Patty asked.

The creature nodded.

"Okay," said Patty, although she thought it might have been fun to show the creature off to some of her friends. "What do you need?"

The creature thought a minute. "Hose bone," she said.

"Hose bone," said Patty. Could that mean nose cone? Patty got some cardboard from behind the dresser and made a cone. Then she found some tinfoil in her bottom drawer and covered the nose cone. "There you are," she told the space creature. "A nose cone complete with heat shield."

The creature smiled.

"What else do you need?" asked Patty.

"Bargoles," said the creature.

"Bargoles," said Patty. Could that mean controls? Patty got an old clock from under the bed and took out the face and hands. Then she added some nuts and bolts she had been saving in her piggy bank. "There you are," she told the space creature. "A full set of cockpit controls."

The creature smiled.

"What else do you need?" asked Patty.

"Flockit drip," said the creature, who was getting very excited.

"Flockit drip," said Patty. Could that mean rocket ship? Patty got some metal strips from the closet and in a little while she had put together a rocket ship with glue that was hidden in a shoebox. "There you are," she told the space creature. "A rocket ship ready to fly."

The creature smiled.

"Anything else?" asked Patty.

"Mule," said the creature.

"A mule," said Patty. Could that mean a school? Or a tool? Or a rule? What do you think the creature meant? (*Let children guess.*) Yes, the rocket needed fuel. As luck would have it, Patty had some chemicals hidden behind the bathtub. Soon Patty said, "There. Now you have a good supply of fuel for the flight."

The creature smiled.

Patty assembled all the things together and let the creature climb in. They counted backward together (with the creature getting most of the numbers right)—ten-nine-eight-seven-six-five-four-three-two-one—BLAST OFF! The creature headed through the sky and off to Mars, or the stars, or wherever. (*Flip girl down. Move rocket through air.*)

(*Show girl only.*) And Patty made it a point to keep saving things in hiding places in her room: even in an average house on an average street, amazing things could happen.

GAZEBO HOME
(Tune: "In the Good Old Summertime")

I am sipping lemonade,
My hammock's cool and light,
Listening to the crickets chirp,
Everything is right.
I'll drift and dream the day away,
This house has no walls or doors,
Gazebo is my summer home,
Who could ask for more?

BUGS IN THE BASEMENT
(Tune: "Skip to My Lou")

Bugs in the basement, what'll we do?   (*Wiggle fingers all around.*)
Bugs in the basement, what'll we do?
Bugs in the basement, what'll we do?
They're hiding in the basement.

Tried to stamp 'em—shoo, bugs, shoo,   *(Stamp floor.)*
Tried to stamp 'em—shoo, bugs, shoo,
Tried to stamp 'em—shoo, bugs, shoo,
They're hiding in the basement.

Tried to spray 'em—phew, bugs, phew,   *(Hold nose.)*
Tried to spray 'em—phew, bugs, phew,
Tried to spray 'em—phew, bugs, phew,
They're hiding in the basement.

They won't go, what can we do?   *(Palms up in helpless gesture.)*
They won't go, what can we do?
They won't go, what can we do?
They're hiding in the basement.

Make them pets, in a jar or two,   *(Cup hands or show jar with paper bug in it.)*
Make them pets, in a jar or two,
Make them pets, in a jar or two,
So they're not in the basement.

RAIN HOUSE
(Action Rhyme)

I've got a little house to keep me dry   *(Point two hands over head.)*

When raindrops fall down from the sky.   *(Wiggle fingers down as rain falls.)*

My umbrella is just the thing   *(Point two hands over head.)*

To hide me from the rains of spring.   *(Pull two arms together and move down to hide face.)*

PUP TENT
(Participatory Story)

For this story use a large sheet for the pup tent, and assemble the following articles: a flashlight, a canteen, a bag of popcorn, and a stuffed dog or dog puppet. Select four kids to take part in the story. At the end of the story, the leader hands the dog to the one child left in the tent. Begin the story as one child crawls under the sheet.

Rick got a big pup tent for his birthday and he could hardly wait to set it up in his own back yard. He unrolled the tent, set up the stakes, stretched out the canvas, and climbed inside. It was a wonderful pup tent—nice and big with lots of room inside. So much room that Rick wished a friend would come visit him in his pup tent home.

Before long Rick heard a noise outside. And a voice said, "Hi, Rick! It's Joe. Is this tent new? I'll get in and share with you."

And Rick said, "Come on in. There's room to spare as long as you've got stuff to share. *(Second child climbs under the sheet.)*

Joe pulled his flashlight out of his back pocket and climbed inside the tent. The two boys had a wonderful time shining the flashlight all around the tent.

Before long Rick heard a noise outside. And a voice said, "Hi, Rick! It's Tim. Is this tent new? I'll get in and share with you."

And Rick said, "Come on in. There's room to spare as long as you've got stuff to share. (*Third child climbs under the sheet.*)

Tim had a canteen hooked on his belt. He climbed inside the tent with Rick and Joe. The three boys had a wonderful time shining the flashlight and sharing the lemonade out of the canteen.

Before long Rick heard a noise outside. And a voice said, "Hi, Rick! It's Sam. Is this tent new? I'll get in and share with you."

And Rick said, "Come on in. There's room to spare as long as you've got stuff to share." (*Fourth child climbs under the sheet.*)

Sam had a bag of popcorn. He climbed inside the tent with Rick and Joe and Tim. The four boys had a wonderful time shining the flashlight and sharing the lemonade and popcorn.

Before long Rick heard voices outside calling, "Joe! Tim! Sam! Time to come home now!"

So Joe and Tim and Sam left the tent and ran right home. (*Second, third, and fourth children climb out from the sheet.*)

Rick was left all alone in the pup tent. It was a wonderful pup tent—nice and big with lots of room inside. So much room that Rick wished a friend would come visit him in his pup-tent home.

Before long Rick heard a noise outside. "Ruf! Ruf! Ruf!"

Rick opened up the flap on the front of the pup tent. In jumped Rufus, Rick's big puppy dog. (*Hand dog puppet to first child and pull back the sheet so the other children can see the dog and the child.*)

"Oh, Rufus," said Rick. "You are the best friend to share a pup tent!"

SECRET PLACES I LIKE TO HIDE
(Tune: "Skip to My Lou")

Every child creates secret hiding places, especially when they don't want Mom or Dad to find them. Use this little song to allow children to brainstorm about their hiding places, adding other verses to the ones given here.

Secret places I like to hide,
Secret places I like to hide,
Secret places I like to hide,
When my mommy calls me.

In the closet behind my clothes,
In the closet behind my clothes,
In the closet behind my clothes,
Shh! She'll never find me!

In the doghouse with the dog,
In the doghouse with the dog,
In the doghouse with the dog,
Woof! She'll never find me!

In my treehouse with the birds,
In my treehouse with the birds,
In my treehouse with the birds,
Chirp! She'll never find me!

In the attic with the bats,
In the attic with the bats,
In the attic with the bats,
Help! Mommy, please come find me!

NO PLACE LIKE HOME
(A Draw-and-Tell Story)

Draw the figures as indicated to find Larry's secret hiding place.

Larry was having a terrible morning. First his mom lost one of his favorite tube socks in the laundry so he only had one sock to wear. Then Larry's dad made him make his bed before Larry could come down to breakfast. And breakfast turned out to be oatmeal. Larry hated oatmeal.

"This is an awful place!" said Larry. "I think I'll run away from home. There must be a better place for me!"

So Larry put his comic books, a sweatshirt, one half of a granola bar, and a monster mask in his backpack, and he ran away from home. He didn't even leave a note. He wasn't planning to come back. He was going to find a better place to stay.

First Larry went down the sidewalk to the end of the block. (*Draw a vertical line as shown.*)

He stopped at the O'Connor house. The O'Connor family lived in a big two-story house with a front porch. Under the front porch was a hiding place where no one would find Larry.

"A hidey hole!" said Larry. "A porch hidey hole is a perfect place to run away." So Larry crawled under the porch. Then he got out his comic books to read. But it was so dark under the porch that Larry couldn't see anything.

"This is no place for me to stay and hide," said Larry. So he crawled out from underneath the porch and cut across the back of the O'Connor yard until he came to the city park. (*Draw diagonal line as shown.*)

The city park was surrounded by a circle of maple trees that had just dropped their bright yellow leaves because it was fall.

"A leaf-house hidey hole!" said Larry. "A leaf-house hidey hole is a perfect place to run away."

So Larry crawled under a pile of maple leaves to hide. After a while he got cold and sneezy. Achoo! Larry put on his sweatshirt, but he was still cold and sneezy.

"Achoo! This is no place for me to stay and hide," said Larry. So he cut across the park and went to the baseball diamond on the other side. (*Draw diagonal line as shown.*)

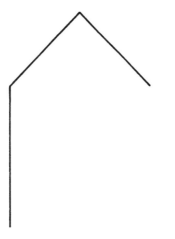

Next to the baseball diamond were a lot of bleachers.

"A bleacher-place hidey hole!" said Larry. "A bleacher-place hidey hole is a perfect place to run away."

So Larry crawled under the bleachers. By this time he was getting hungry, so he took out his half of a granola bar and ate it up. It wasn't very much to fill up a runaway boy. He was so hungry that he almost ate the wrapper, too. And he was also getting a little bored under the bleachers. There really wasn't very much going on down there.

"This is boring," said Larry. "This is no place for me to stay and hide." So he walked out of the park and down the street until he came to a big abandoned house at the bottom of a hill. (*Draw vertical line as shown.*)

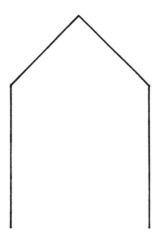

"A haunted house hidey hole!" said Larry. "What a perfect place to run away! There must be a lot of neat things going on inside here!"

So Larry walked up the front steps, opened the door of the abandoned house, and tiptoed inside. It was very dark and creepy in there. Larry heard strange sounds. "OOOOOOOOOO!

EEEEEEE! Ooooooo! We're coming to catch yoooooooooou!" Larry put on his monster mask, but the sounds got louder. "OOOOOO! EEEEEE! Ooooooo! We're coming to catch yoooooooou!"

"Oh, no, you're not," said Larry. "This is no place for me to stay and hide. There must be a better place for me to stay."

So Larry ran and he ran until he ran straight back to his own house. (*Draw horizontal line as shown.*)

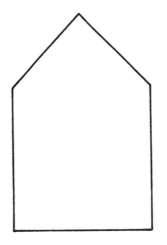

There was a hiding place under his own porch, a pile of leaves in the front yard, a big back yard where he could play catch, and inside the house his mother and father were waiting for him.

Larry opened the front door and smelled something good to eat. (*Draw door as shown.*)

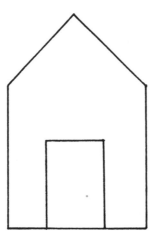

"Chicken noodle soup!" said Larry. "I love chicken noodle soup."

So Larry decided then and there that of all the hidey holes and places that he might run away to this was the best place for him to stay (*point to drawing of completed house*) because there's no place like home.

QUIET AS A MOUSE
(Flannel-board Story)

In preparation for this flannel-board story, make felt cutouts of the following articles: a teddy bear, a cat, a frog, a dog, and a mouse. Place the articles on the flannel-board according to the directions.

QUIET AS A MOUSE

Ted the Bear

Frog

Mouse

Pat the Cat

Og the Dog

("Quiet as a Mouse" continues on page 148.)

Ned lived in a little crackerbox of a house. So many people and so many things were stuffed in Ned's house that sometimes he couldn't find any quiet place to get away from it all.

One day when his baby brother spilled cereal all over Ned's favorite stuffed toy, Ned crawled under his bed. He took with him Ted the bear. (*Place teddy bear on flannel-board.*)

"Poor Ted," said Ned. "Let's stay under my bed so no one can bother us."

And that's just what they did—all morning. But then somebody slammed the front door, and Pat, the family cat, got her tail caught in the door. Pat scampered under the bed. (*Place cat on flannel-board.*)

"Oh, Pat, poor cat! Poor Ted," said Ned. "Let's all stay under my bed so no one can bother us."

And that's just what they did—all afternoon. But then, just about dinner time, Ted's pet frog leaped under the bed because Og, the family dog, was chasing him. (*Place frog and dog on flannel-board.*)

"Oh, Og, silly dog! Poor Frog! Oh, Pat, poor cat! Poor Ted," said Ned. "Let's all stay under my bed so no one can bother us. But you will all have to settle down."

And that's just what they did—for a while. But pretty soon, just about bedtime, a little brown mouse scurried under the bed because Mother was chasing it with a broom. (*Place mouse on flannel-board.*)

"Oh, Mouse, this isn't your house," said Ned. "Come on Og, silly dog (*take off dog from flannel-board*). Come on Frog (*take off frog from flannel-board*). Come on Pat, poor cat (*take off cat from flannel-board*). Come on Ted (*take off teddy bear from flannel-board*)," said Ned. "Let's all cuddle up in my bed. So we can get a good night's sleep without anybody bothering us anymore."

And that's just what they did—all night long. Nobody bothered them because the whole house was finally as quiet as—(*Point to mouse left on flannel-board*) a mouse. Shh!

THIS PLACE IS FOR THE BIRDS
(Participatory Story with Bird Masks)

Make masks using the patterns on page 149 for the birds in this story. Distribute the masks to children so they can take active part in the story. Be sure to practice the bird sounds with children so they can say those lines right along with you as the story progresses.

Rosie and Hannah were best friends. They wanted to build a treehouse for their own special hideaway. They got boards and hammers and saws and nails. They found the perfect tree in Hannah's back yard. They climbed up in the tree and started to build the treehouse.

Just as they put the floor in place, two little bluebirds landed on a branch high in the tree.

> "Chirp! Chirp!
> What do we see?
> Whose house is this
> Up in our tree?"

Rosie and Hannah didn't answer. They kept right on working to finish their treehouse.

Just as they put the walls in place, four red-headed woodpeckers landed on a branch high in the tree.

> "Rat-a-tat-tat!
> What do we see?
> Whose house is this
> Up in our tree?"

Rosie and Hannah didn't answer. They kept right on working to finish their treehouse.

THIS PLACE IS FOR THE BIRDS

CUCKOO

BLUEBIRD

WOODPECKER

GULL

("This Place Is for the Birds" continues on page 150.)

Just as they put the roof in place, six gray gulls landed on a branch high in the tree.

"Squawk! Squawk!
What do we see?
Whose house is this
Up in our tree?"

Rosie and Hannah still didn't answer. They kept right on working to finish their treehouse. Just as they put the ladder in place, eight crazy cuckoo birds landed on a branch high in the tree.

"Cuckoo! Cuckoo!
What do we see?
Whose house is this
Up in our tree?"

Rosie and Hannah didn't answer. But this time the eight crazy cuckoo birds said again, "Cuckoo! Cuckoo!" And the six gray gulls said, "Squawk! Squawk!" And the four red-headed woodpeckers said, "Rat-a-tat-tat!" And the two bluebirds said, "Chirp! Chirp!" Then all together they said,

"What do we see?
Whose house is this
Up in our tree?"

They all swooped down and sat on the roof of the treehouse.
"Yikes!" said Rosie and Hannah. "Let's get out of here. This house is for the birds."
And that's just who lived there—happily ever after!

INSIDE PENELOPE'S CLOSET
(A Cut-and-Tell Story)

Fold a piece of 8½" × 11" paper in half and cut according to the drawings.

Penelope was looking all around the house for something to take to school for show-and-tell. She looked everywhere but could not find anything she was very excited about.

"Why don't you look in the closet?" said Mother. "Closets have amazing things hiding inside." (*Hold up folded paper.*)

So Penelope went to the closet and reached inside. The first thing she pulled out of the closet was a baseball bat. (*Make first cut as shown.*)

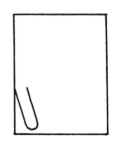

"Oh, groan! A baseball bat is really boring. Isn't there anything more exciting than this hiding in the closet?"

So Penelope went to the closet and reached inside. The next thing she pulled out of the closet was a tube sock. (*Make second cut as shown.*)

"Oh, groan! A tube sock is really boring. Isn't there anything more exciting than this hiding in the closet?"

So Penelope went to the closet and reached inside. The next thing she pulled out of the closet was a hockey stick. (*Make third cut as shown.*)

"Oh, groan! A hockey stick is really boring. Isn't there anything more exciting than this hiding in the closet?"

So Penelope went to the closet and reached inside. The next thing she pulled out of the closet was a foot-long hot dog. (*Make fourth cut as shown.*)

"Oh, groan! A foot-long hot dog is really boring. Isn't there anything more exciting than this hiding in the closet?"

So Penelope went to the closet and reached inside. The next thing she pulled out of the closet was a ping-pong ball. (*Make last cut as shown.*)

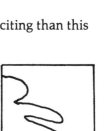

"Oh, groan! A ping-pong ball is really boring. Isn't there anything more exciting than this hiding in the closet?"

So Penelope went to the closet and reached inside. This time she found just what she had been looking for. It was not boring. It was exciting. It was just right for show-and-tell. Everyone in Penelope's class loved her new pet spider! (*Open the paper and wiggle the spider vigorously.*)

SECRET HIDING PLACES
(Action Rhyme)

Invite children to mime the actions suggested by the words in this little rhyme.

It's raining, raining
Out today
We have to stay
Inside to play.

Come with me
And take a look
In every corner,
Crack, and nook.

In the attic
Behind the stairs
Under the table
Around the chairs

Down in the cellar
Behind a drape
In the tub
Under a cape.

We'll have fun
In secret spaces
Finding special
Hiding places!

HOME IN A TRUNK
(Fingerplay)

Hold up the appropriate number of fingers for each stanza and invite children to do the actions with you.

One old trunk
Let's look inside
Blow off the dust
And open wide.

Two black shoes
With buttons galore
Are these the ones
That Grandma wore?

Three feathered hats
From long ago
Four parasols
Each with a bow.

Way down in the corner
Of the trunk so deep
Live five baby mice
All fast asleep.

Down in trunk
The old and the new
Mice make their home
In Grandma's shoe.

GAMES FOR HIDEY HOLES

HIDEY HOLE HIDE-AND-SEEK

Stretch your imagination with this mental hide-and-seek game. One child is chosen to be the "hider." He or she thinks of a place to hide. It can be a real hiding place or an imaginary place to hide such as under a plant leaf. Other children guess the hiding place by asking questions that must be answered "yes" or "no." The one to guess the correct location becomes It.

WHO WILL HIDE WITH YOU?

Stand in a circle. One child stands in the center as the following song is sung to the tune of "Go In and Out the Window."

Oh, where will you be hiding?
Oh, where will you be hiding?
Oh, where will you be hiding?
And who will hide with you?

The child in the center names a place and selects a friend to come to the center, too. This child is the next one to name a place and choose another friend. Play continues until everyone is in the center and has lots of good ideas for places to hide.

MY VERY OWN HIDING PLACE

Provide children with large boxes, blankets over tables, clotheslines with sheets draped over, even oversized clothing like a cape. Children create their own hiding places. This free-play activity is a good follow-up after reading deRegniers's *A Little House of Your Own*.

CRAFTS FOR HIDEY HOLES

CLOSET CRAFT

Provide each child with a sheet of construction paper. Fold the paper in half lengthwise to make a closet. Attach a brass paper fastener to the front of the closet for a door knob. Ask children to draw pictures inside of special things they might hide in their closets.

TRUNK COLLAGE CRAFT

Have children cover shoeboxes or other sturdy rectangular boxes with old greeting cards, photographs, maps, or assorted pictures. Attach the lid of the box to the bottom with masking tape in the back, as if it were a hinge. Cover the tape with a gold gummed seal. Use another seal in the front for a lock. This trunk "hidey hole" can be covered with clear self-adhesive paper for a finished project.

HIDEAWAY MASK

Children can hide in paper-bag masks. First cut off the end of the paper bag so that it clears the child's shoulders. Make eye holes large enough and help younger children cut these out. Provide bright-colored construction paper, yarn, and other materials so children can make disguises for their own personal hideaways.

PUPPY'S PUP TENT

Use a rectangular piece of paper twice as long as it is wide. Fold the paper in half to form a square. Staple shut at the bottom. At the bottom center cut a slit half way up the square in the top layer only. Fold back corners of slit to create flaps and draw a dog in the opening to make a real "pup" tent.

FLOOR PLANS FOR HIDEY HOLES

Focus Book: *A Little House of Your Own* by Beatrice deRegniers

Reading Activities

The small format of this book, its quiet tone, and its theme of secret little places encourages reading to smaller groups with a soothing voice. Because more than one picture appears on some pages, it will be important to point to the picture that corresponds to the words.

Speaking Activities

Generate a list of all the things from the book that are used to make houses. Encourage children to choose the ones they would like to make a hiding place from and tell the group why.

Writing Activities

Children can use this book as a jumping-off point to write about the things they would like to do or friends they would invite to a hiding place all their own.

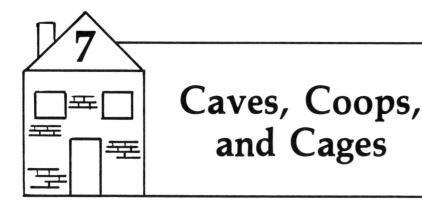

Caves, Coops, and Cages

INTRODUCTION

Animal homes can be a far-reaching topic if we were to include the entire earth, ocean, and air for dwellings in natural habitats as well as the range of human-made dwellings from fishbowls to zoos. Some of this breadth is suggested in the variety of books listed and the activities provided. In school settings the topic of animal homes may be an early introduction to ecology and social order. Art appreciation is another natural link as children linger over the detailed and accurate drawings in McCloskey's classic *Make Way for Ducklings* or are intrigued by the underwater world in Carle's *A House for Hermit Crab*. Lionni books invite children to try their hand at fingerpainting, collage, and simple printmaking.

The first subtheme, "Hollow Logs and Holes," covers homes that animals build for themselves. Some of the books listed are realistic renderings; others describe actual homes but treat the subject with humorous exaggeration, such as Jack Kent's kangaroo tale *Joey* or Leo Lionni's story about two fleas living on a dog in *I Want to Stay Here! I Want to Go There!* An almost endless list of books might be used if the purpose of the unit or program is as broad as natural habitats. The purpose here is mainly to introduce some different kinds of animal homes.

The second subtheme, "Barns and Birdhouses," includes homes people build for animals. These may range from large dwellings such as zoos and barns to small places like doghouses and fishbowls. One of the interesting facets of this topic is that animals may not necessarily feel comfortable in the homes that are created for them. Arthur, the dog in "Welcome Home, Arthur," our flannel-board story, seems typical of the many pets we have known that end up "ruling the roost" in the eventual choice of their own place in the sun. With this story as an opener, encourage children to tell stories of places where their pets have lived. Oral and written language activities grow naturally from this theme.

Make Way for Ducklings, the focus book of the chapter, provides the natural culmination for the topic. The story begins with Mr. and Mrs. Duck looking for a place to build their nest and start their family and ends with the family settling down peacefully for the night on their own little island. Children will be interested to know that McCloskey's fictional ducklings have been given a permanent home in Boston as statues that can be seen in the public garden, a perfect tribute to this landmark in children's literature.

INITIATING ACTIVITY

WHERE DO THEY LIVE?

Birds live in nests.	*(Form small circle with hands.)*
Fish live in bowls.	*(Form larger circle with arms.)*
Bats live in caves.	*(Form larger circle over head with arms.)*
Mice live in holes.	*(Form little circle with fingers.)*
Chicks live in coops.	*(Bend elbows, hold palms flat, shoulder high.)*
Pigs live in pens.	*(Move hands further apart.)*
Cows live in barns.	*(Move hands further apart.)*
Bears live in dens.	*(Form large circle over head with arms.)*
Animal houses,	
Some big and some small,	*(Spread arms wide then bring hands close together.)*
For all kinds of animals:	
Short, fat, or tall.	*(Squat, stand and pat tummy, then stretch tall.)*

LITERATURE-SHARING EXPERIENCES

Books for Hollow Logs and Holes

Bartoli, Jennifer. **In a Meadow, Two Hares Hide**. Whitman, 1978.
 Two young hares living in a meadow survive the changing seasons and their natural enemies.

Batherman, Muriel. **Animals Live Here**. Greenwillow, 1979.
 This book describes animals' homes below and above ground.

Carle, Eric. **A House for Hermit Crab**. Picture Book Studio, 1987.
 When Hermit Crab outgrows his shell house, he moves into a new one that he decorates with different sea creatures.

Coats, Laura. **The Oak Tree**. Macmillan, 1987.
 Birds, bats, and people find a home in the oak tree in one day.

Duvoisin, Roger. **The Crocodile in the Tree**. Knopf, 1973.
 A crocodile befriended by barnyard animals tries to prove to the farmer's wife that he will not hurt her.

Facklam, Margery. **I Go to Sleep**. Little, Brown, 1987.
 While a child prepares to go to bed, the various bedding places of animals are described.

Fisher, Aileen. **Best Little House**. Crowell, 1966.
 Various animal houses are described in rhyme before the best house, and the new dog inside, are revealed.

Georgiou, Constantine. **The Nest**. Illustrated by Bethany Tudor. Harvey House, 1972.
 Mother Robin builds her nest with great care for the baby birds who will soon live in it.

Ginsburg, Mirra. **Which Is the Best Place?** Illustrated by Roger Duvoisin. Macmillan, 1976.
    Adapted from a Russian version, this story is about a rooster and a goose who argue about which is the best place to live. But each friend they ask has a different opinion, too!

Kent, Jack. **Joey**. Prentice-Hall, 1984.
    Joey, a young kangaroo, becomes bored playing alone in his mother's pouch and invites some friends over to play with him.

Kent, Jack. **Joey Runs Away**. Prentice-Hall, 1985.
    Joey runs away from his mother's pouch and various other animals try to move in.

Killion, Bette. **The Apartment House Tree**. Harper & Row, 1989.
    A tall tree in the woods is the home of all sorts of animals and birds.

Lionni, Leo. **The Biggest House in the World**. Pantheon, 1968.
    Snail gets carried away in his wishes for a bigger and grander shell.

Lionni, Leo. **Fish Is Fish**. Pantheon, 1970.
    When his friend the tadpole becomes a frog and leaves the pond to explore the world, the little fish decides that maybe he doesn't have to remain in the pond either.

Lionni, Leo. **I Want to Stay Here! I Want to Go There!** Pantheon, 1977.
    Two fleas who live on a dog have different desires. One wants to go on an adventure. The other wants to stay home.

McCloskey, Robert. **Make Way for Ducklings**. Viking, 1941.
    When Mr. and Mrs. Mallard are ready to have a new family, they make an island their home. The ducklings have an adventure with traffic and a kind police officer as they move to the Public Garden. Brown and white illustrations show actual sites in the Boston area.

McDonald, Megan. **Is This a House for Hermit Crab?** Illustrated by S. D. Schindler. Watts, 1990.
    Crab tries many new things as he looks for a new house until he finds an empty snail's shell.

Maris, Ron. **Better Move on Frog!** Watts, 1982.
    A frog searches for a home for himself but all the holes he finds seem to be taken.

Minarik, Else. **Percy and the Five Houses**. Greenwillow, 1989.
    None of the five different houses Percy receives from the House of the Month Club proves to be as perfect as his own beaver home.

Nussbaum, Hedda. **Animals Build Amazing Homes**. Random House, 1979.
    The homes and construction methods of 15 different animals are examined.

Vevers, Gwynne. **Animal Homes**. Illustrated by Wendy Bramall. Bodley Head, 1980.
    This naturalist book looks at the home of the swallow, the water spider, the beaver, and others.

Wildsmith, Brian. **Animal Homes**. Oxford University Press, 1980.
    Animals from armadillo and walrus to beaver and eagle are pictured in their homes.

Related Activities for Hollow Logs and Holes

GARDEN JUNGLE
(Cumulative Action Rhyme)

Who lives out in the garden,
Under the flowers and trees?
Who lives out in the back yard,
Feeling the sun and the breeze?

There's a creeping ant   *(Wiggle fingers up arm.)*
Crawling up a plant
It's a jungle garden home.

There's a wiggly worm   *(Wiggle all over.)*
Watch him squirm
There's a creeping ant
Crawling up a plant
It's a jungle garden home.

There's a digging mole   *(Palms together in front, wiggle wrists.)*
Scooting into his hole
There's a wiggly worm
Watch him squirm
There's a creeping ant
Crawling up a plant
It's a jungle garden home.

There's a buzzing bee   *(Wiggle fingers by ear.)*
Hey! Don't sting me!   *(Clap on word "hey.")*
There's a digging mole
Scooting into his hole
There's a wiggly worm
Watch him squirm
There's a creeping ant
Crawling up a plant
It's a jungle garden home.

That's who lives in the garden,
Under the sky so blue.
It's a jungle out there in the garden
Watch out or they'll get you!

TREE FULL OF HOUSES
(Tune: "Paw-Paw Patch")

Who, oh, who lives in the branches?
Who, oh, who lives in the branches?
Who, oh, who lives in the branches?
Birds build nests up in the trees so tall.

Who, oh, who lives in the tree trunk?
Who, oh, who lives in the tree trunk?
Who, oh, who lives in the tree trunk?
Squirrels store nuts and live in hollow trees.

Who, oh, who lives in the tree roots?
Who, oh, who lives in the tree roots?
Who, oh, who lives in the tree roots?
Chipmunks scurry back to make their homes.

Can you think of other houses,
Can you think of other houses,
Can you think of other houses,
Built by animals in parts of a tree?

HOME SPUN
(Tune: "Twinkle, Twinkle, Little Star")

Spider, spider, weave and spin,
Make your web with threads so thin,
Work nonstop throughout the night,
Moon and stars your only light.
Morning comes your web is done—
It will sparkle in the sun.

BEDTIME FOR BABY BEAR

Cut a hole in a colorful sheet and slip the sheet over the head of the child who will be Baby Bear. Other children are selected to be the ball, the top, and the jack-in-the-box. They go under the sheet and come out as indicated in the story. You will also need a teddy bear at the end of the story.

It was quarter till November and Mama Bear had to get the cave all ready for winter. It was time for the Bear family's long winter nap.

She swept the corners. She fluffed the pillows. And she set the alarm clock for half past March.

She called Baby Bear to climb into his snug little bed. But Baby Bear was a busy bear and he was not ready to go to sleep.

"Can I take something to bed with me this winter?" asked Baby Bear.

"Well, you can take one thing, just one thing, but hurry up," said Mama Bear.

So Baby Bear chose a big red ball—a big red ball that bounced. Baby Bear and the big red ball snuggled down together under his balnket. (*Child with ball sits under sheet with Baby Bear.*)

"Mama, can I take one more thing to bed with me this winter?" asked Baby Bear.

"Well, you can take two things, just two things, but hurry up," said Mama Bear.

So Baby Bear chose a shining blue top—a blue spinning top that went around and around. Baby Bear and the big red ball and the shining blue top snuggled down under his blanket. (*Child with top sits under sheet with Baby Bear.*)

"Mama, can I take one more thing to bed with me this winter?" asked Baby Bear.

"Well, you can take three things, just three things, but hurry up," said Mama Bear.

So Baby Bear chose a jack-in-the-box—a funny, pop-up jack-in-the-box. Baby Bear and the big red ball and the shining blue top and the funny, pop-up jack-in-the-box snuggled down under his blanket. (*Child with jack-in-the-box sits under sheet with Baby Bear.*)

Mama Bear turned out the light and said, "Good night."

But as soon as the light was out, the big red ball started bouncing. (*Child with ball hops up and down.*) The shining blue top started spinning. (*Child with top turns around and around.*) And the jack-in-the-box popped up. (*Child with jack-in-the-box jumps up in air.*) This made Baby Bear laugh so loud that Mama Bear came running back and said, "Dear, dear, this will never do. Baby bears need their rest."

Mama Bear lifted up the blanket, and out bounced the big red ball (*child with ball runs out to seat*), out spun the shining blue top (*child with top runs out to seat*), and out popped the jack-in-the-box (*child with jack-in-the-box runs out to seat*).

Then Mama Bear said, "Here is something you can take to bed with you for the winter. Something to give you a nice quiet bear hug." (*Hand child in sheet a teddy bear.*) Mama Bear gave Baby Bear his very own teddy bear and Baby Bear went right to sleep.

BATS IN THE BELFRY

Bats in the belfry, can we count them?
Bats in the belfry, can we count them?
Bats in the belfry, can we count them?
Watch them as they fly!

One bat, two bats, three bats flying.
Four bats, five bats, six bats soaring.
Seven bats, eight bats, nine bats landing.
Ten bats hang upside down!

ANIMAL HOMES WORLDWIDE
(Poem)

To add extra interest to this poem that classifies animals by the kind of habitat they live in, cut out pictures of jungle animals, Australian animals, desert animals, forest animals, and arctic animals. Mount the animal pictures on craft sticks so children can hold the pictures up like stick puppets. Each group of children speaks the various verses or they simply hold up the appropriate animal puppets as the animals are mentioned in the poem.

These words can also be sung to the tune of "On Top of Old Smokey."

We live in the jungle
In grasslands and swamps.
It's hot and it's humid
Wherever we romp!

We live in the outback
Australia's our land.
Our home is a wild,
Untamed wonderland!

We live in the desert
It's hot and it's dry.
Under the cactus
We sizzle and fry!

We live in the forest
In trees or the ground
In daytime or nighttime
Just look all around!

We live in the arctic
In ice and in snow
We hibernate sometimes
Or move very slow.

All kinds of places
We can call home
The world is a wonder
Wherever you roam.

TEN IN THE NEST
(Tune: "Ten Bears in the Bed")

Ten birds in the nest
Just taking their rest
Move over! Fly out now!
So they all moved over and one flew out!

Nine birds in the nest
Just taking their rest
Move over! Fly out now!
So they all moved over and one flew out!

Eight birds in the nest
Just taking their rest
Move over! Fly out now!
So they all moved over and one flew out!

Seven birds in the nest
Just taking their rest
Move over! Fly out now!
So they all moved over and one flew out!

Six birds in the nest
Just taking their rest
Move over! Fly out now!
So they all moved over and one flew out!

Five birds in the nest
Just taking their rest
Move over! Fly out now!
So they all moved over and one flew out!

Four birds in the nest
Just taking their rest
Move over! Fly out now!
So they all moved over and one flew out!

Three birds in the nest
Just taking their rest
Move over! Fly out now!
So they all moved over and one flew out!

Two birds in the nest
Just taking their rest
Move over! Fly out now!
So they all moved over and one flew out!

One bird in the nest
Just taking her rest
Stretch out now! Stretch out now!
(*spoken*) Good night!

DOWN BY THE OLD MUDHOLE
(Tune: "Old Mill Stream")

For a humorous presentation make paper-plate frog puppets (see illustration and directions in the craft section) to croak this song.

Down by the old mudhole
Where there's slime and goo
It was there I knew
Frogs and tadpoles, too.
There dragonflies all flew
And you loved me, too.
Mudpuppies brown
Newts run around
Down by the old mudhole.

Down by the old (not the new but the old) mudhole
    (*not the donut but the hole*)

Where there's slime (not sludge but slime) and goo
    (*not goop but goo*)

It was there (not here but there) I knew
    (*not thought but knew*)

Frogs (*not toads but frogs*) and tadpoles, too.
    (*not three but too*)
There dragonflies all flew
    (*not walked but flew*)
And I loved (*not liked but loved*) you, too.
    (*not three but too*)
Mudpuppies brown (*not orange but brown*)
Newts run around (*not a square but around*)
Down by the old (*not the new but the old*) mudhole
    (*not the donut but the hole.*)

ANT HILL ANTICS
(Fingerplay)

Here is the ant hill with ants hidden away	(*Touch fingertips to form small hill.*)
Count them as they come out to play.	
One little ant sees sky of blue	(*Hold up one finger.*)
Gets another	(*Put hand behind back.*)
Now there are two.	(*Hold up two fingers.*)
Two little ants climb up a tree	(*Hold up two fingers.*)
Get another	(*Put hand behind back.*)
Now there are three.	(*Hold up three fingers.*)
Three little ants—they need one more	(*Hold up three fingers.*)
Get another	(*Put hand behind back.*)
Now there are four.	(*Hold up four fingers.*)
Four little ants on a sunny day	(*Hold up four fingers.*)
Here's number five	(*Hold up all five fingers.*)
So they all run away.	(*Wiggle fingers as you hide them behind back.*)

POCKET HOME
(Action Rhyme)

Use this bouncy rhyme to invite children to form a line. The leader recites the poem and on the last line points to child to jump up and join the kangaroo line. The last line is repeated and another child joins the line until everyone is bouncing along.

Mama Kangaroo keeps her baby near,
Tucked right down in a pocket place.
Baby Joey rides in a bouncy home,
Peeking out—you can see his face.

Wouldn't you like to move right in
Snug with Joey Kangaroo?
Riding in a bouncing mobile home,
Mama Kangaroo has a place for you.

HOME IN THE BOTTOM OF THE SEA
(Tune: "Hole in the Bottom of the Sea")

There's a ship in the bottom of the sea,
It sunk to the bottom of the sea,
Now the fish call it home,
There's a ship in the bottom of the sea.

There's a whale in the ship in the bottom of the sea,
There's a whale in the ship in the bottom of the sea,
There's a whale, there's a whale,
There's a whale in the bottom of the sea.

There's a shark with the whale in the ship in the bottom of the sea,
There's a shark with the whale in the ship in the bottom of the sea,
There's a shark, there's a shark,
There's a shark in the bottom of the sea.

There's a crab with the shark with the whale in the ship in the bottom of the sea,
There's a crab with the shark with the whale in the ship in the bottom of the sea,
There's a crab, there's a crab,
There's a crab in the bottom of the sea.

There's a sponge with the crab with the shark with the whale in the ship in the bottom of the sea,
There's a sponge with the crab with the shark with the whale in the ship in the bottom of the sea,
There's a sponge, there's a sponge,
There's a sponge in the bottom of the sea.

They all live in the bottom of the sea,
In the ship at the bottom of the sea,
All the fish make their home
And they live there together happily.

COCOON TUNE
(Tune: "Mary Had a Little Lamb")

Caterpillar creeps along,   *(Wiggle fingers on arm.)*
Creeps along, creeps along,
Caterpillar creeps along
Time to build his home.

Spins his little round cocoon,   *(Touch fingertips to form hands into cocoon.)*
Round cocoon, round cocoon,
Spins his little round cocoon
Safe and snug inside.

Out will come a butterfly,   *(Hook thumbs and flap fingers.)*
Butterfly, butterfly,
Out will come a butterfly
Flies away from home.

Books for Barns and Birdhouses

Allamand, Pascale. **The Camel Who Left the Zoo**. Scribner, 1976.
A desert oasis becomes a haven for animals when a camel who longs for home leads an escape from the zoo.

Benchley, Nathaniel. **Walter the Homing Pigeon**. Illustrated by Whitney Darrow, Jr. Harper & Row, 1981.
A homing pigeon loses a race when he decides to stop for a snack.

Bond, Felicia. **Christmas in the Chicken Coop**. Crowell, 1983.
Two baby chicks want very badly to have a Christmas tree, but the grumpy hens refuse to leave the coop to get one.

Booth, Eugene. **At the Zoo**. Illustrated by Derek Collard. Raintree Children's Books, 1977.
Pictures of animals at the zoo are the starting point for prereading activities such as counting and identifying colors.

Brett, Jan. **The Mitten: A Ukrainian Folktale**. Putnam's, 1989.
Several animals sleep snugly in Nicki's lost mitten until the bear sneezes.

Brown, Margaret Wise. **Big Red Barn**. Illustrated by Rosella Hartman. Young Scott Books, 1956.
Among the animals that live in the big red barn are the bantam rooster, a little brown cow, an old black cat, and an old red dog.

Calhoun, Mary. **Mrs. Dog's Own House**. Illustrated by Janet McCaffrey. Morrow, 1972.
When Mrs. Dog tries to please all her friends by implementing their suggestions for improving her house, she realizes it is no longer a doghouse.

Calmenson, Stephanie. **Where Will the Animals Stay?** Illustrated by Ellen Appleby. Parents' Magazine Press, 1983.
Zoo animals needing a place to stay take up residence in an apartment house.

Cutler, Ivor. **The Animal House**. Morrow, 1976.
A family finds temporary shelter in a house built by their friends from the zoo.

Demarest, Chris. **Benedict Finds a Home**. Lothrop, 1982.
Tired of sharing his nest with noisy brothers and sisters, Benedict the bird sets off to find his own home.

Freeman, Lydia. **Pet of the Met**. Viking, 1953.
Maestro Petrini, a white mouse, and his family live in a harp case in the attic of the Metropolitan Opera House, where Petrini is page turner for the prompter. Their gracious life is momentarily disrupted by Mefisto the Cat during a performance until the two become friends and then have the run of the house.

Graham, Margaret Bloy. **Benjy's Dog House**. Harper & Row, 1973.
Unwilling to sleep in his new doghouse, Benjy looks for another nighttime home.

Harris, Dorothy. **The House Mouse**. Illustrated by Barbara Cooney. Warner, 1973.
Jonathan's new mouse friend moves into his sister's doll house for the winter.

Houston, John. **A Mouse in My House**. Illustrated by Winnie Fitch. Addison-Wesley, 1972.
Sometimes getting rid of a mouse in the house creates more problems than letting him stay.

Maris, Ron. **Is Anyone Home?** Greenwillow, 1985.
As he wanders about the garden looking for his grandparents, Ben greets everyone and everything he sees.

Palmer, Helen. **Why I Built the Boogle House**. Beginner Books, 1984.
A boy builds larger and larger houses for his pets and then finds himself with a pet house and no pet.

Pape, Donna. **Doghouse for Sale**. Illustrated by Tom Eaton. Garrard, 1979.
Freckles the dog fixes up his house to attract prospective buyers, but then changes his mind.

Parnall, Peter. **Winter Barn**. Macmillan, 1986.
An old barn in Maine is the shelter for many homeless animals in the winter, including snakes, cats, and a skunk.

Roffey, Maureen. **Home Sweet Home**. Coward-McCann, 1983.
Very simple text and peek-a-boo pages describe various animal homes.

Sattler, Helen Roney. **No Place for a Goat**. Illustrated by Bari Weissman. Elsevier Nelson, 1981.
Sam, Joey's pet goat, wasn't allowed inside the house, but he was curious about it anyway. After several attempts he butts his way inside. However, he soon gets into so much trouble that he agrees with Joey's mother: "A house is no place for a goat."

Schoenherr, John. **The Barn**. Little, Brown, 1968.
Owl and Skunk would both like to stay in the barn, but there is only space for one.

Schulz, Charles M. **Home Is on Top of a Doghouse**. Determined Productions, 1966.
All the familiar Schulz cartoon characters define home in such ways as "Home is where the supper dish is," "Home is a place to sulk," and "Home is a place with a warm, cozy attic."

Scruton, Clive. **Mary's Pets**. Lothrop, 1989.
Wanting someone to play with in the garden, Mary looks for each of her pets. The reader is an active part of finding them in the pages of the book.

Tressault, Alvin. **The Mitten, an Old Ukrainian Folktale**. Lothrop, 1964.
Various animals of all sizes try to squeeze into a lost mitten to stay warm.

Zimelman, Nathan. **Positively No Pets Allowed**. Illustrated by Pamela Johnson. Dutton, 1980.
Mrs. Goldberg refuses to let her son have a pet until she meets a gorilla named Irving.

Related Activities for Barns and Birdhouses

UNINVITED ATTIC GUESTS
(Tune: "Skip to My Lou")

Squirrels in the attic, what'll I do?	*(Hands on head in despair.)*
Squirrels in the attic, what'll I do?	
Squirrels in the attic, what'll I do?	
They should find a tree home.	*(Point finger to side.)*
Shoo, shoo, you squirrels, you.	*(Shooing motion with hands.)*
Out of my attic, shoo, shoo, shoo!	
Shoo, shoo, you squirrels, you.	
Go and find a tree home.	*(Point finger to side.)*

Set a trap to catch the two,	*(Clap on the word "catch.")*
Set a trap to catch the two,	
Set a trap to catch the two,	
Take them to a tree home.	*(Point finger to side.)*
Peanut butter just won't do,	*(Shake head.)*
Peanut butter just won't do,	
Peanut butter just won't do,	
To get them to a tree home.	*(Point finger to side.)*
Have to be the best cashews,	*(Rub stomach.)*
Have to be the best cashews,	
Have to be the best cashews,	
To get them to a tree home.	*(Point finger to side.)*
Shoo, shoo, you squirrels, you!	*(Shooing motion with hands.)*
Out of my attic, shoo, shoo, shoo!	
Shoo, shoo, you squirrels, you.	
Go and find a tree home—	*(Point finger to side.)*
NOW!	*(Hands on hips.)*

HOUSE FLY
(Prop Story)

In preparation for this story, cut out the pictures of the foods shown in the illustration on page 168: fettucini, chocolate cake, pizza, mud pie. Glue these to four paper plates. On top of each picture glue a small piece of Velcro. Cut out the picture of the fly and attach Velcro to it.

Select five children to hold the paper plates of food (two children hold the pizza) and move the fly as indicated in the story.

You will also need an empty jar to catch the fly at the end of the story.

Once there was a fly who had lived all of his life outside. But one day he flew by the Ortmans' house. Everyone in the Ortman household loved to cook. Mr. Ortman was a chef. His specialty was fettucini. *(Give child plate of fettucini.)* Mrs. Ortman was a baker. Her specialty was chocolate layer cake. *(Give child plate of cake.)* The Ortman twins liked to make pizza for snacks. *(Give two children the plate of pizza.)* Even Baby Ortman liked to make mud pies. *(Give last child plate of mud pie.)* Everyone liked to cook, but no one liked to clean up afterward. So the Ortman kitchen was a smelly mess.

When the fly flew by the Ortman house, he smelled the smelly mess. So he waited until Baby Ortman crawled out the back door for more mud, and the fly flew inside.

First the fly landed on Mr. Ortman's fettucini. *(Attach fly to Velcro on fettucini.)* Mr. Ortman swatted at the fly. *(Everyone claps as if trying to swat the fly.)* He tried and he tried, but he couldn't catch the fly. *(Remove fly from fettucini.)*

Next the fly landed on Mrs. Ortman's chocolate layer cake. *(Attach fly to Velcro on cake.)* Mrs. Ortman swatted at the fly. *(Everyone claps as if trying to swat the fly.)* She tried and she tried, but she couldn't catch the fly. *(Remove fly from cake.)*

Next the fly landed on the Ortman twins' pizza snacks. *(Attach fly to Velcro on pizza.)* The twins swatted at the fly. *(Everyone claps as if trying to swat the fly.)* They tried and they tried, but they couldn't catch the fly. *(Remove fly from pizza.)*

Finally the fly landed on Baby Ortman's mud pie. *(Attach fly to Velcro on mud pie.)* The fly got one foot stuck. He got a second foot stuck. He got a third foot stuck. He got a fourth foot

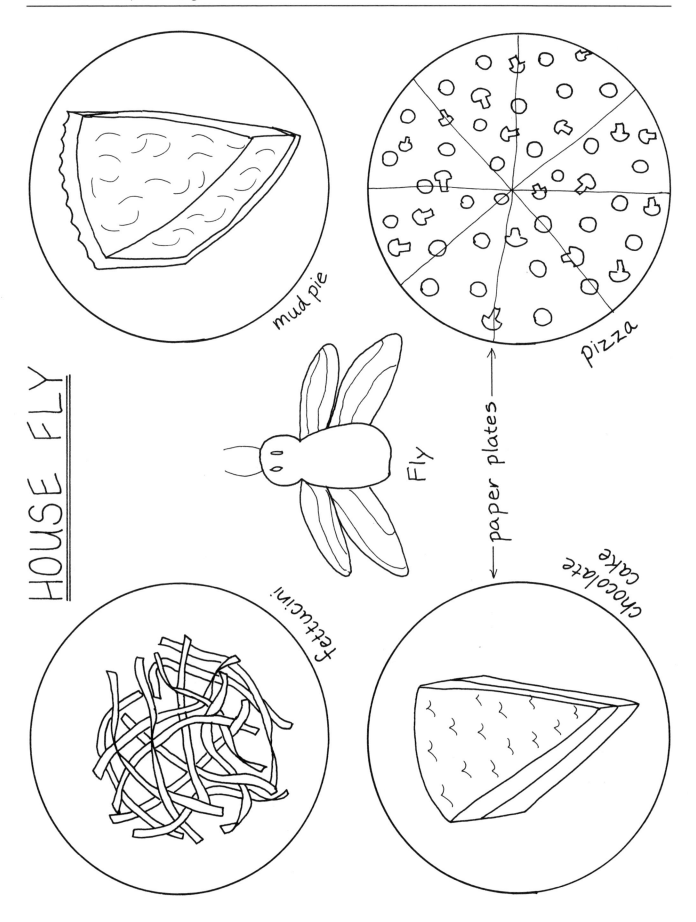

mud pie

pizza

HOUSE FLY

Fly

paper plates

fettucini

chocolate cake

stuck. He got a fifth foot stuck. And he got a sixth foot stuck. Baby Ortman started to swat the fly. (*Everyone claps as if trying to swat the fly.*)

"Wait," said one of the Ortman twins. "I have a better idea." And he ran to get a jar and popped it over the fly. The other twin put on the lid. (*Remove fly from pie and place in jar.*)

So the fly no longer spent his life outside. He became a regular everyday house fly. The Ortmans started cleaning up the smelly mess in their kitchen. But they saved the very smelliest leftovers for their pet house fly.

BIRDHOUSE SONG
(Tune: "Have You Seen the Muffin Man?")

To add extra interest to this song, make flannel-board houses and birds (see p. 170) to use as the song progresses. Or, make birdhouses out of shoeboxes and give them to three children. Three other children are given red, blue, and black birds cut from construction paper. These children place the birds in the appropriate houses as each verse is sung.

Who will buy this red birdhouse,
Red birdhouse, red birdhouse?
Who will buy this red birdhouse?
I'll sell it for a song.

Who will buy this blue birdhouse,
Blue birdhouse, blue birdhouse?
Who will buy this blue birdhouse?
I'll sell it for a song.

Who will buy this black birdhouse,
Black birdhouse, black birdhouse?
Who will buy this black birdhouse?
I'll sell it for a song.

BIRDHOUSE SONG

red birdhouse

red bird

blue bird

blue birdhouse

SILLY HOMES FOR SILLY PETS
(Response Poem)

Recite the first stanza, then prompt kids to respond "No, that's silly!" to each suggestion. At the end children will be given an opportunity to come up with their own ideas.

> Silly homes
> For silly pets
> Isn't this
> The silliest one yet?
>
> Would your pet giraffe
> Be at home in a skyscraper?
> (*No, that's silly!*)
>
> Would your pet jellyfish
> Be at home in a jar of grape jelly?
> (*No, that's silly!*)
>
> Would your pet polar bear
> Be at home in the refrigerator?
> (*No, that's silly!*)

Ask children to come up with other unlikely or likely houses for pet animals. Draw pictures of the houses with the animals inside for another fun activity!

WELCOME HOME, ARTHUR
(Flannel-board Story)

Use the patterns on page 172, cut the following shapes from felt: doghouse, box, bed, doll bed, laundry basket, window, sofa, welcome mat. Place on the flannel-board as the objects are mentioned in the story. You may wish to use a dog puppet or stuffed dog to be Arthur.

Everyone in the Hillson family was excited. They were getting a brand new puppy. They talked about what they would feed it. They talked about what they would name it. They talked about where it would sleep.

Finally they decided to feed it puppy food. They decided to call it Arthur. But they could not decide where Arthur would sleep.

Mr. Hillson said, "The dog sleeps in the doghouse. That way he can bark if anyone tries to break into the house."

Mrs. Hillson said, "But he might get cold out there. Arthur should have a box of his own in the kitchen by the stove."

Jack said, "The kitchen is too far away. Arthur will get lonely. He can sleep in my room, right on my bed."

Jill said, "But Arthur is not house-broken yet. He can't sleep with you. Arthur can sleep in my doll bed—the one with the ruffled canopy!"

"Yuk!" said Jack. "He can't sleep there!"

They talked and they talked, but they could not decide where Arthur would sleep.

WELCOME HOME, ARTHUR

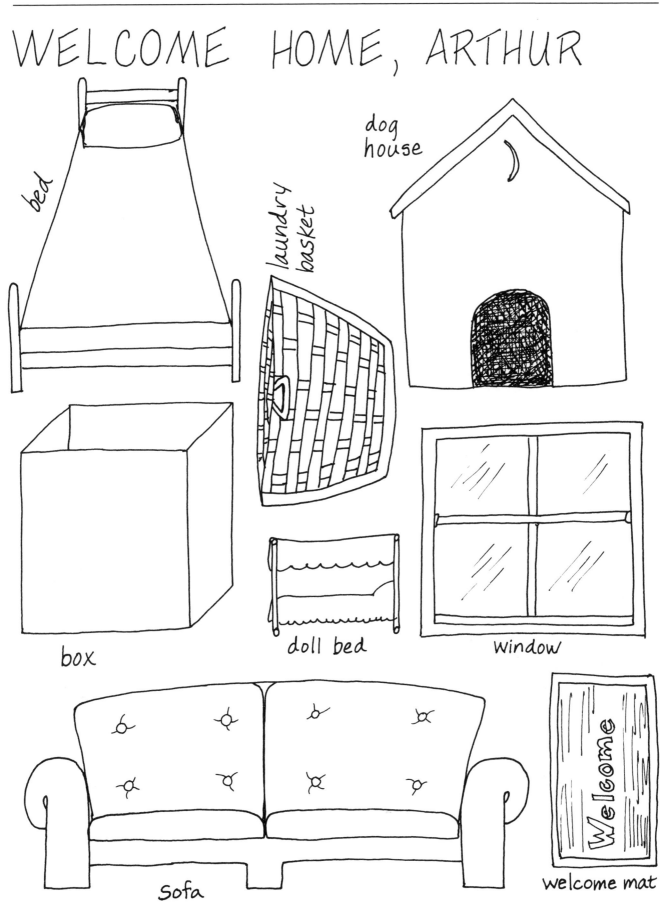

bed

laundry basket

dog house

box

doll bed

window

Sofa

welcome mat

Finally Arthur arrived. He liked his puppy food. He seemed to like the name Arthur. But when it was bedtime, the family still did not know where to put him for bed. So they decided to let Arthur choose.

First they showed Arthur the doghouse. Arthur shivered. It was too cold.

Then they showed him the box in the kitchen by the stove. But Arthur cried because he was lonely.

Then they showed Arthur Jack's bed. But the bed was so high that Arthur could not get up on it.

Then they showed Arthur Jill's doll bed. Arthur said, "Arf."

Jack said, "That means 'Yuk!'"

Mrs. Hillson said, "Well, where will Arthur sleep?"

Mr. Hillson said, "Let's follow Arthur and see where he decides to sleep."

Arthur sniffed the laundry basket, but he did not sleep there.

Arthur rubbed his paw on the window sill, but he did not sleep there.

Arthur looked under the sofa, but he did not sleep there.

Finally Arthur saw the rug at the front door. He sniffed it. He rubbed it with his paw. He looked at it. On the rug was the word "Welcome." Arthur couldn't read, but he knew it was a good place. So he curled up on the welcome mat and went right to sleep.

NEW AT THE ZOO
(Circle Story)

Prepare two circles (as shown in the illustrations on pages 174 and 175). The top circle has a picture of Maggie and the zoo keeper. A wedge is cut opposite these pictures. The bottom circle has pictures of the following animals: a penguin, a snake, a seal, a lion, and a bunch of monkeys. Fasten these circles together with a brad fastener in the center. To tell the story, turn the bottom wheel as Maggie Monkey visits the different zoo homes.

Maggie Monkey was new at the zoo. The zoo keeper said, "Welcome to the zoo, Maggie Monkey. Let me show you your new home."

So Maggie took the zoo keeper's hand and they walked through the zoo.

First they came to the penguin house. "Would you like to live here?" asked the zoo keeper.

The penguins dressed well, but their house was cold and full of ice. Maggie Monkey shook her head. This home was not quite right.

Then they came to the snake house. "Would you like to live here?" asked the zoo keeper.

The snakes didn't look friendly and their house was full of old snakeskins—most untidy. Maggie Monkey shook her head. This home was not quite right.

Then they came to the seal tank. "Would you like to live here?" asked the zoo keeper.

The seals clapped and were having a ball, but their tank was full of water and much too damp. Maggie Monkey shook her head. This home was not quite right.

Then they came to lion cage. "Would you like to live here?" asked the zoo keeper.

The lions roared so loudly that Maggie covered her ears. Too much noise in this home. Maggie Monkey shook her head. This home was not quite right.

Finally the zoo keeper brought Maggie to a brand new house. Inside were tall trees to climb, ropes to swing on, and lots of other monkeys to play with. "Would you like to live here?" asked the zoo keeper.

Maggie Monkey clapped her hands. This home was not too cold. It was not too wet. It was not too noisy. And the monkeys were friendly and lots of fun. Maggie jumped up in a tall tree. This home was just right.

(Text continues on page 176.)

NEW AT THE ZOO

cut out wedge

top circle
fasten to bottom circle
at center with brad

NEW AT THE ZOO

bottom circle

FARM HOMES
(Tune: "Farmer in the Dell")

Cows live in the barn,
Cows live in the barn,
Moo, moo, they like their home,
Cows live in the barn.

Chicks live in the coop,
Chicks live in the coop,
Cluck, cluck, they like their home,
Chicks live in the coop.

Pigs live in the pen,
Pigs live in the pen,
Oink, oink, they like their home,
Pigs live in the pen.

Sheep live in the fold,
Sheep live in the fold,
Baa, baa, they like their home,
Sheep live in the fold.

Goats live in the shed,
Goats live in the shed,
Naa, naa, they like their home,
Goats live in the shed.

GAMES FOR CAVES, COOPS, AND CAGES

HOME HATCHING

Arrange children in a circle with hands joined. Choose three children to be in the middle. Sing these words to the tune of "Skip to My Lou." The children in the center squat low during the first verse when they are "eggs" and hop up as they "hatch" in the second verse. Each "new baby bird" can choose a child to replace him or her as an egg and the game continues.

Nest of eggs up in a tree,
Nest of eggs up in a tree,
Count the eggs now: one, two, three.
When will they start hatching?

Pecking, pecking, what's inside?
Cracking, cracking, open wide.
Hatching, hatching, they arrive.
Nest of newborn birdies.

ZOO CAGE CAPER

For this creative dramatics activity the leader acts as zoo keeper and guides children through different actions. The following directions serve as a springboard for your own capers.

"Welcome to the zoo! I am George (or Georgine) the zoo keeper. I have many cages in my zoo for all sizes and shapes of animals. When I tell you what kind of cage I am opening, you pretend to be the animal that goes inside that cage. Are you all ready?

"First, I am opening a tall, tall cage. It's tall enough for a giraffe. Can you stretch your necks really tall and pretend to be giraffes striding into my cage? Good!

"Now, I'm opening the gate to a wide open cage. It has a big pool of water for a fat hippopotamus. Can you all pretend to be hippopotamuses wallowing into a pool of water? Good!

"Now, I'm opening a cage with big heavy bars. Inside are rocks and ledges for a lion. Can you all stride into the cage like lions and make one ferocious roar? Good!

"Now it is time to close the zoo cages for the night. I will open one last cage. It's the cage for the baby sloths. Can you all pretend to be baby sloths who amble into the cage and then fall asleep? Good night!"

FARMER SAYS

Play this game in the manner of "Simon Says" by directing children to move into the different kinds of houses or habitats found on a farm. Children pretend to be the different kinds of animals by making a sound or moving like the animal. Remember that no one moves unless the direction is preceded by the words "farmer says."

Farmer says all cows move out to the pasture.

Farmer says all cows graze in the pasture.

All cows go home.

Oops! Not yet! Now, farmer says all cows go home.

All cows go into the barn.

Not yet.

Farmer says all cows go into the barn.

Farmer says all pigs go to the pigpen.

Farmer says all pigs move two spaces to the pig trough.

Farmer says all goats butt their heads against the wall of the goat shed.

Farmer says all goats take one big jump into the goat shed.

All chickens fly into the chicken coop.

Oops! Not yet!

Farmer says all chickens fly into the chicken coop.

Farmer says all chickens sit down and lay your eggs!

I'M THINKING OF AN ANIMAL

Children have played this game in the car on family vacations for many years. Play it with the children in your classroom or library whenever you want to focus on classification skills or just enjoy a quiet game together. The leader begins by saying, "I'm thinking of an animal who lives in ..." (the forest, the ocean, the desert, or some other habitat). Children ask questions that can be answered by yes or no to discover the animal the leader is thinking of.

CRAFTS FOR CAVES, COOPS, AND CAGES

WHO'S LIVING IN THE DOGHOUSE?

Everyone knows that dogs aren't the only ones that live in doghouses. Anyone in disfavor is said to be "in the doghouse." But you can turn this little activity into a fun project by picturing people you know inside the doghouse.

Cut out little doghouses using the pattern shown on page 179 and paste pictures of your friends or family on the strip of paper, which can be slid through the slots in the house. Be certain to include a picture of your family dog to live in the house, too.

FROG PUPPET

Use two paper plates to make this big-mouth frog. Cut one plate in half. Staple the halves onto the whole plate around the edges so there are openings for your hand. Cut out the frog face from bright green construction paper and the eyes out of yellow and green circles using the pattern on page 180. Fold two strips of paper accordion fashion as in the illustration and attach to the plate for the two hind legs.

WELCOME TO OUR TREE HOME

Using the pattern on page 181, have children draw their favorite woodland animals peeking out of the holes in the tree.

WHERE'S MY HOME?

Use the circle patterns on page 182 to make the four homes mentioned in the "Initiating Activity" (nest, bowl, cave, mouse hole). Cut out the patterns of the four animals that live in these homes and paste on squares of paper. The children can use this game to match animals with their homes.

UNDERWATER HOME

Use underwater world books by Eric Carle and Leo Lionni as inspiration and invite children to fingerpaint backgrounds and add tissue-paper shapes of underwater plant life and construction-paper seashells and fish.

(Text continues on page 183.)

WHO'S LIVING IN THE DOGHOUSE?

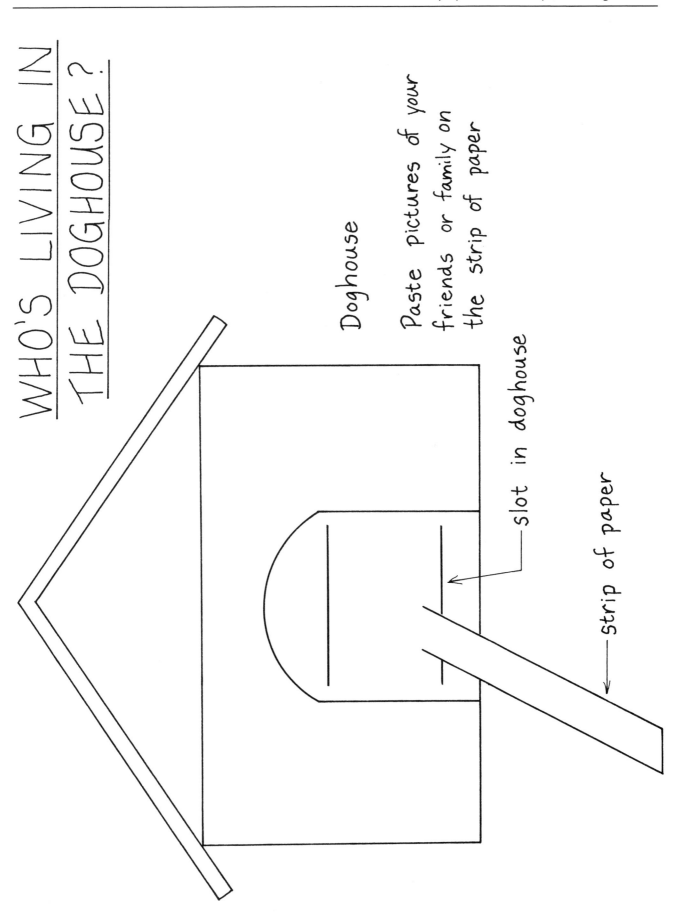

Doghouse

Paste pictures of your friends or family on the strip of paper

slot in doghouse

strip of paper

FROG PUPPET

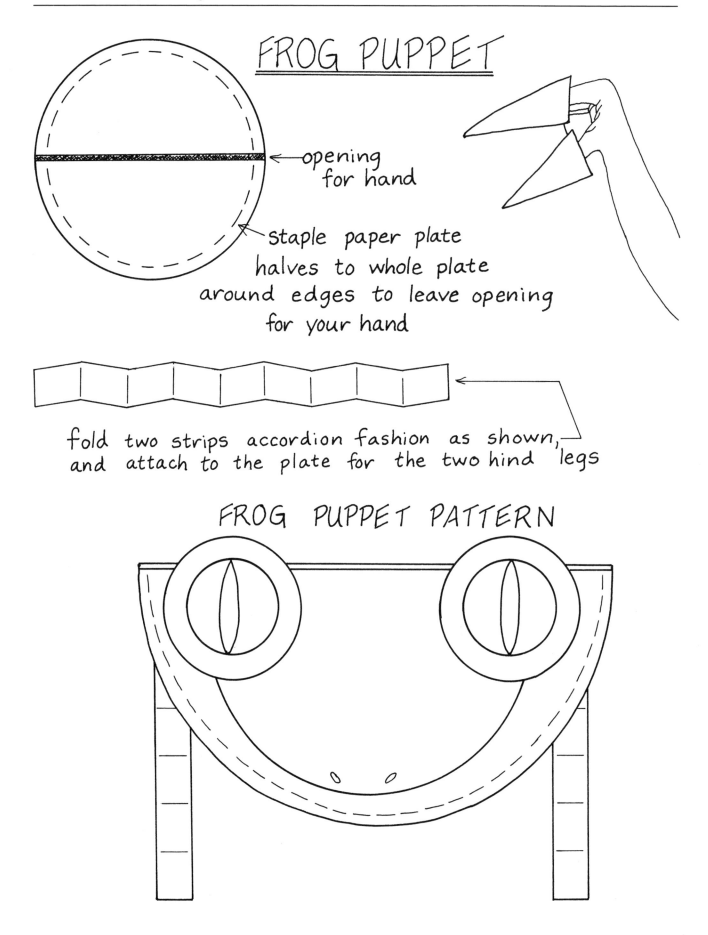

opening for hand

staple paper plate halves to whole plate around edges to leave opening for your hand

fold two strips accordion fashion as shown, and attach to the plate for the two hind legs

FROG PUPPET PATTERN

WELCOME TO OUR TREE HOME

WHERE'S MY HOME?

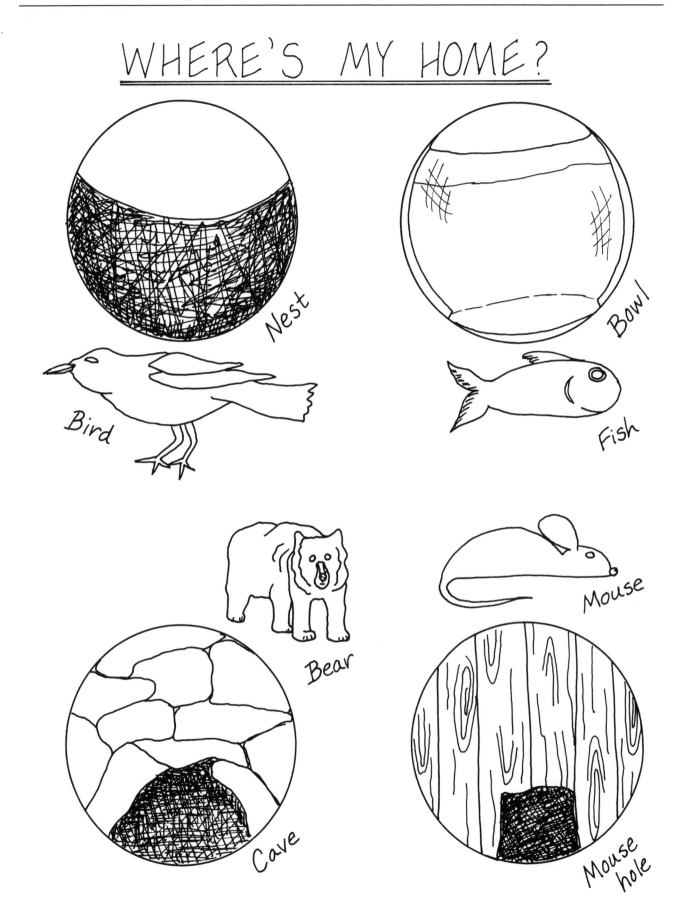

Nest

Bird

Bowl

Fish

Bear

Mouse

Cave

Mouse hole

FLOOR PLANS FOR CAVES, COOPS, AND CAGES

Focus Book: *Make Way for Ducklings* by Robert McCloskey

Reading Activities

The pictures in the book are authentic drawings of sights in the Boston area. Help children identify and locate places such as Beacon Hill and Louisburg Square. Finding other pictures of Boston will heighten their awareness and appreciation for this book. You may wish to point out the duck boat the mallards encounter since children will be delighted that they can see it is a boat and the ducks can't.

McCloskey kept pet ducks to study so the illustrations would be authentic. Have the children compare these drawings with photographs of mallards.

Words like "molt" are defined within the text of the story. Read the page where that word is used and help the children define exactly how ducks molt.

Speaking Activities

Use the words written in the illustrations themselves to help the children get involved with the story. Words like "weebk," "honk," and "queep" are fun to say and encourage children to use other sound words.

Use the pattern the Mallards used to name the ducklings to help the children learn the names. There are eight ducklings, the first one's name beginning with "J" and the last beginning with "Q."

Turn the group into a family of ducklings. Encourage waddling and quacking as one child assumes the role of mother duck and leads the ducklings to different places. Some children may prefer to play the part of Michael the police officer or the people driving cars that do stop to make way for the ducklings.

Writing Activities

Retell the story as a group by recording the sequence of events on the board or paper from the time the Mallards arrive in Boston until the ducklings bed down on the island. What is the most exciting part of the story? The happiest moment?

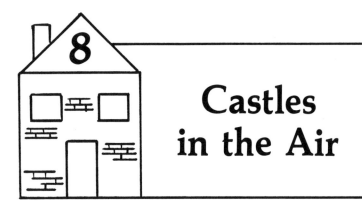

Castles
in the Air

INTRODUCTION

We've saved some of our favorite houses for the last chapter of this book—haunted houses, ginger-bread houses, and houses that come from fairy tales and dreamland. And these topics are so popular with children that the ideas suggested here will generate other programs and projects in your own classroom or library.

The first subtheme, "Mystery Mansions," invites children to enter the world of creaky doors and cobweb-covered rooms to confront their own fears of the unknown. By participating in the interactive stories and songs we have created, children can enjoy scary experiences in a controlled setting. Addressing fears in this way serves as a healthy release of feelings. We were surprised to discover a slim selection of picture books on haunted houses per se, although Halloween stories picture the abandoned mansion and spooky location without giving the haunted house prime importance. The books and activities in this section have been developed for year-round use, so don't wait until October to enjoy them.

The second subtheme, "Gingerbread and Sugarplums," opens the door to the three bears' house, introduces a gingerbread girl who runs along the path to make-believe houses, and retells "The Three Little Pigs" in a modern setting. Our stories and activities extend the use of the many picture book versions of folk tales listed in the bibliography. Several versions of the same folk tales have been included because we have found so many excellent retellings of these stories. "The Three Little Pigs," for example, has been retold and re-illustrated by such authors and author-illustrators as James Marshall, Margot Zemach, William Hooks, and Jon Scieszka. Each version offers a new wrinkle that encourages children to think of their own possibilities. Classroom teachers can use these folk tales as models for student writing projects. Older children will see the tales as familiar friends that can be enjoyed even more with each new rendition.

"Magic Castles and Cottages," the third subtheme, covers a broad spectrum of places from sand castles to doll houses and all the imaginary houses you might dream up. Secret hiding places and real-life castles are included in other chapters, but here you will discover pure fantasy. The focus book of this chapter, *A House Is a House for Me*, captures the imaginative play that characterizes this subtheme.

INITIATING ACTIVITY

MAGIC DOOR

Invite the children to the world of make-believe homes with this poem.

Follow the yellow brick road.
Nibble a gingerbread wall.
Enter the castle—a princess sleeps there,
Travel a dark, dark hall.
Climb up a beanstalk that's magic,
Go through a door in a tree.
Lower the drawbridge—come on inside
On a magic adventure with me.

LITERATURE-SHARING EXPERIENCES

Books for Mystery Mansions

Bright, Robert. **Georgie**. Doubleday Doran, 1944.
    Georgie the ghost leaves the house he has been haunting, but comes back in time to save his family from robbers.

Brown, Ruth A. **Dark Dark Tale**. Dial, 1981.
    Journeying through a dark, dark house, a black cat finds the only inhabitant of the abandoned residence. The book has a surprise ending!

Bunting, Eve. **In a Haunted House**. Illustrated by Susan Meddaugh. Clarion, 1990.
    A little girl and her father explore all the spooky parts of a haunted house that ends up to be a fun Halloween house for the girl.

dePaola, Tomie. **Tomie dePaola's Kitten Kids and the Haunted House**. Golden Books, 1988.
    The kids visit a haunted house for a big surprise.

Patterson, Lillie. **Haunted Houses on Halloween**. Illustrated by Doug Cushman. Garrard, 1979.
    Retells two folk tales in which a young man becomes involved with a ghost and a clever hunter meets a mysterious cat.

Pienkowski, Jan. **Haunted House**. Dutton, 1979.
    Strange happenings occur in this pop-up haunted house.

Ross, Pat. **M and M and the Haunted House Game**. Illustrated by Marylin Hafner. Pantheon, 1980.
    When Mimi and Mandy try to scare someone as part of a game, they are the ones who are frightened.

Schulman, Janet. **Jack the Bum and the Haunted House**. Illustrated by James Stevenson. Greenwillow, 1977.
    Jack the bum decides to settle down and takes up residence in a haunted house, which he finds isn't haunted by ghosts.

Ziefert, Harriet, and Mavis Smith. **In a Scary Old House**. Puffin, 1989.
   A simple tale of what lives in a scary old house unravels as the reader lifts flaps in the book.

Zimmer, Dirk. **The Trick or Treat Trap**. Harper & Row, 1982.
   Three trick-or-treaters go to a haunted house where they undergo adventures in flying pumpkins and walk through a cave with dancing skeletons. As they return to the real world, the witches and the ghosts invite them back next Halloween.

Related Activities for Mystery Mansions

GHOST HUNT
(Action Story)

We're going on a ghost hunt, but I'm not afraid.

Walk, walk, walk, (*Tap hands on legs.*)
Up the hill to the haunted house.
Open the squeaky gate. (*Swing arm as if on hinge.*)
Eeeeeek!
We're going on a ghost hunt, but I'm not afraid. (*Point to self.*)

Up the steps. (*Tap hands on knees.*)
tap,
tap,
tap,
squeek!
Oh, a squeaky stair! (*Hands to head.*)
We're going on a ghost hunt, but I'm not afraid. (*Point to self.*)

Open the door. (*Swing arm as if on hinge.*)
Shhhhh. (*Finger to lips.*)
Let's get through these cobwebs. (*Wave arms in front of face.*)
Turn on the flashlight.
Click. (*Click tongue.*)
There's something in the corner—(*Point to corner.*)
Meow!
It's only a cat! (*Wipe forehead.*)
We're going on a ghost hunt, but I'm not afraid. (*Point to self.*)

What's that in the hall?
It's big. (*Arms over head.*)
It's spooky. (*Form hands like claws.*)
It's a ...
a ...
a ...
Coat tree!
Whew! (*Wipe forehead.*)
We're going on a ghost hunt, but I'm not afraid. (*Point to self.*)

Down the hall on tiptoe. (*Tap hands quietly on knees.*)
tip,
toe,
tip,
toe.
Open the last door ...
Look inside. (*Circle eyes with fingers.*)
and it's a
Halloween party! (*Clap.*)

Have some cider.
Bob for an apple.
Yell "Trick-or-treat!"

Time to go home—
Close the party door. (*Swing arm as if on hinge.*)
Down the hall. (*Tap hands on knees.*)
Past the coat tree. (*Wave to the corner.*)
Pat the cat in the corner. (*Bend down to pat cat.*)
Nice kitty.
Back through the cobwebs. (*Wave arms in front of face.*)
Out the door. (*Swing arm as if on hinge.*)
Down the stairs. (*Tap hands on knees.*)
tap,
tap,
tap,
tap,
squeak!
There's that stair again! (*Point to floor.*)
Out the gate. (*Swing arm as if on hinge.*)
Eeeeeek!
And head for home. (*Tap hands on knees.*)
We went on a ghost hunt, and I wasn't afraid! (*Point to self.*)
Were you? (*Point to kids.*)

ARE YOU SURE YOU WANT TO GO IN?
(Participatory Story)

You can set up this story ahead of time by assigning the different parts to children in the room. Give the children their lines written out on big pieces of cardboard so they can read the words easily. Four children become Amy, Bobby, Corey, and Dan, who go to the haunted house. Other children become objects or animals found in the haunted house—the front steps, the front door, the bat, the cat, the ghost in the closet. Note that the children's lines change at the end of the story, so you will have to give out a second set of lines for that part. The leader tells or reads the story with children adding the parts as they are mentioned in the story.

Amy and Bobby and Corey and Dan first saw the haunted house on the hill the night they went trick-or-treating.

"I'm not afraid," said Amy.
"I want to go back," said Bobby.
"I want to go in," said Corey.
"Then let's go!" said Dan.

So the next day Amy and Bobby and Corey and Dan climbed to the top of the hill. It was a long way. It was getting dark when they got to the front walk of the house.

> "I'm not afraid," said Amy.
> "I want to go back," said Bobby.
> "I want to go in," said Corey.
> "Then let's go!" said Dan.

There were big cracks in the front walk. Amy and Bobby and Corey and Dan walked up the front walk. Then they walked up the front steps. The steps were really creaky. CREEEEAK! CREEEEAK! CREEEEEAK!

> "I'm not afraid," said Amy.
> "I want to go back," said Bobby.
> "I want to go in," said Corey.
> "Then let's go!" said Dan.

So they walked up the stairs and up to the front door. Should they knock first? Or should they open it slowly and go in? Dan turned the handle slooooowly. Squeeeeeeeeeeeak!

> "I'm not afraid," said Amy.
> "I want to go back," said Bobby.
> "I want to go in," said Corey.
> "Then let's go!" said Dan.

The door opened and they all walked in. The front hall was dark, but they could see a mirror with cobwebs all over it in the hall. They walked three steps ahead when a big brown bat flew by. Zooooooom!

> "I'm not afraid," said Amy.
> "I want to go back," said Bobby.
> "I want to go in," said Corey.
> "Then let's go!" said Dan.

They walked through the hall and into the parlor. There was a rocking chair and a sofa and an old piano. Should they touch anything? Corey sat down on the piano bench to play when— Meeeeooooooow! A black cat chased them out of the parlor and into another long hall.

> "I'm not afraid," said Amy.
> "I want to go back," said Bobby.
> "I want to go in," said Corey.
> "Then let's go!" said Dan.

So they walked down the long hall. Down at the end of the hall was a room. They pushed the door open.

> "I'm not afraid," said Amy.
> "I want to go back," said Bobby.
> "I want to go in," said Corey.
> "Then let's go!" said Dan.

They walked into the room. There was nothing in the room. It was dark. But they could still see that there was a closet in one corner of the room. Should they open the door to the closet?

"I'm not afraid," said Amy.
"I want to go back," said Bobby.
"I want to go in," said Corey.
"Then let's go!" said Dan.

They opened the door of the closet. It was really dark. It was deep. Should they step inside?

"I'm not afraid," said Amy.
"I want to go back," said Bobby.
"I want to go in," said Corey.
"Then let's go!" said Dan.

So they stepped into the deep, dark closet. Then a deep, dark voice called "Oooooooooo!"

"I'm afraid!" said Amy.
"I want to go back!" said Bobby.
"Me, too!" said Corey.
"Then let's go!" said Dan.

So out they ran—out of the closet—Oooooo—back down the hall and into the parlor—Meeeeoooooow—past the cat—three steps into the front hall—Zooooommm—past the bat—back to the front door—Squeeeak—out the door—creeeeaaak—down the front steps and down the front walk and all the way home.

"I wasn't afraid," said Amy.
"I don't want to go back," said Bobby.
"Me, either!" said Corey.
"Let's stay home!" said Dan.

And that's just what they did, too!

SPIDER'S OPEN HOUSE
(Tune: "Itsy-Bitsy Spider")

The big old furry spider	(*Crawl fingers across arm.*)
Lived in the haunted house	(*Touch fingertips over head to form roof.*)
There's a bat in the belfry	(*Flap arms.*)
In the basement lived a mouse.	(*Crawl fingers along ground.*)
Outside the window	(*Circle eyes with fingers.*)
A full moon can be seen	(*Touch fingertips overhead to form rounded moon.*)
Creak the door	(*Swing arm out.*)
And come on in	(*Gesture to come.*)
It's time for Halloween. Boo!	(*Hands up, fingers spread.*)

GHOST MACDONALD'S HAUNTED HOUSE
(Tune: "Old MacDonald Had a Farm")

Ghost MacDonald's haunted house
Makes a lot of noise
In this house are clanking chains
That make a lot of noise
With a clank, clank here
And a clank, clank there
Here a clank, there a clank
Everywhere a clank, clank
Ghost MacDonald's haunted house
Makes a lot of noise.

Ghost MacDonald's haunted house
Makes a lot of noise
In this house are rattling bones
That make a lot of noise
With a rattle, rattle here
And a rattle, rattle there
Here a rattle, there a rattle
Everywhere a rattle, rattle
Ghost MacDonald's haunted house
Makes a lot of noise.

Ghost MacDonald's haunted house
Makes a lot of noise
In this house are moaning ghosts
That make a lot of noise
With an oooooooooo here
And an oooooooooo there
Here an ooo, there an ooo
Everywhere an oooooooooo
Ghost MacDonald's haunted house
Makes a lot of noise.

Ghost MacDonald's haunted house
Makes a lot of noise
In this house are squeaking doors
That make a lot of noise
With a squeak, squeak here
And a squeak, squeak there
Here a squeak, there a squeak
Everywhere a squeak, squeak
Ghost MacDonald's haunted house
Makes a lot of noise.

Ghost MacDonald's haunted house
Makes a lot of noise
In this house are creaking stairs
That make a lot of noise
With a creak, creak here
And a creak, creak there
Here a creak, there a creak
Everywhere a creak, creak
Ghost MacDonald's haunted house
Makes a lot of noise.

Ghost MacDonald's haunted house
Makes a lot of noise
In this house are shrieking guests
That make a lot of noise
With an eeeeek, eeeeek here
And an eeeeek, eeeeek there
Here an eeeeek, there an eeeeek
Everywhere an eeeeek, eeeeek
Ghost MacDonald's haunted house
Makes a lot of noise.

Eeeeeeeeeek!

THIS HOUSE MUST BE HAUNTED
(Tune: "Skip to My Lou")

After you teach this song to children, try it again with children suggesting other animals they might find in other parts of a haunted house. For example, you might find a lizard in the hallway. Just be sure to fit the words to the rhythm of the song.

Bat in the attic
What'll I do?
Bat in the attic
What'll I do?
Bat in the attic
What'll I do?
This house must be haunted!

Ghost in the closet
What'll I do?
Ghost in the closet
What'll I do?
Ghost in the closet
What'll I do?
This house must be haunted!

Cat in the cellar
What'll I do?
Cat in the cellar
What'll I do?
Cat in the cellar
What'll I do?
This house must be haunted!

Bat in the attic
Shoo, bat, shoo!
Ghost in the closet
Shoo, ghost, shoo!
Cat in the cellar
Shoo, cat, shoo!
This house is not haunted!
(*spoken*) Boooooooo!

Gingerbread and Sugarplums

Woman and Red Pumpkin: A Bengali Folk Tale. Illustrated by Molly Bang. Mac-

n Indian folk tale in which a skinny old woman outwits the jackal, bear, and tiger who

Bryan. **Jack and the Beanstalk**. Putnam's, 1983.
des his cow for magic beans that grow into a giant beanstalk, Jack leaves his simple house to
beanstalk to the house of a giant, where he finds many treasures.

Cauley, Lorinda Bryan. **The Town Mouse and the Country Mouse**. Putnam's, 1984.
A town mouse and a country mouse exchange visits and discover that "there's no place like home."

Galdone, Paul. **The Three Bears**. Clarion, 1972.
The familiar tale of "Goldilocks and the Three Bears" is told with large, brightly colored illustrations in Galdone's humorously engaging style. The bears' house is a log cabin furnished in a primitive fashion.

Grimm, Jacob, and Wilhelm Grimm. **The Fisherman and His Wife**. Translated by Randall Jarrell. Illustrated by Margot Zemach. Farrar, Straus and Giroux, 1980.
An enchanted flounder grants wishes from the fisherman's wife for increasingly grander houses to suit her growing demands for powerful positions, until she oversteps her bounds.

Grimm, Jacob, and Wilhelm Grimm. **Hansel and Gretel**. Illustrated by Paul Galdone. McGraw-Hill, 1982.
The gingerbread house in this version is gaily decorated with lines of brightly colored cookies that invite the unsuspecting children into the witch's trap.

Grimm, Jacob, and Wilhelm Grimm. **Hansel and Gretel**. Illustrated by Susan Jeffers. Dial, 1980.
Fine colored-pencil and pen-and-ink drawings add to the classic text about Hansel and Gretel's journey through the forest to a tempting cake-and-candy house.

Grimm, Jacob, and Wilhelm Grimm. **Hansel and Gretel**. Illustrated by Anthony Braone. Julia MacRae, a division of Watts, 1981.
The classic text of Hansel and Gretel is set in modern times with scary illustrations. The bread-and-cake house is less tempting than in many versions.

Hague, Kathleen, and Michael Hague. **The Man Who Kept House**. Illustrated by Michael Hague. Harcourt Brace Jovanovich, 1981.
In this Norwegian folk tale a man, convinced he works harder in the fields than his wife does at home, trades places only to discover how difficult housekeeping is.

Haley, Gail. **Jack and the Bean Tree**. Crown, 1986.
In this Appalachian retelling of the Jack tale, the boy trades his cow for three magic beans and journeys to a giant's mansion in the sky by way of a magic bean tree. The giant's house in Haley's version looks like a Greek revival mansion, complete with scrolled columns and arches.

Heilbroner, Joan. **This Is the House Where Jack Lives**. Harper & Row, 1962.
Jack's house in this story is an apartment building full of city dwellers.

The House That Jack Built. Illustrated by Rodney Peppe. Delacorte Press, 1970.
This cumulative rhyme about Jack begins when he builds a house.

The House That Jack Built: A Mother Goose Rhyme. Illustrated by Janet Stevens. Holiday House, 1985.
What a series of events befalls Jack after he builds a house!

Hyman, Trina Schart. **The Sleeping Beauty**. Little, Brown, 1977.
Because she is not invited to Briar Rose's christening party, the thirteenth fairy casts a death spell on the princess, but the twelfth fairy softens the spell so a deep sleep falls on the castle and its inhabitants. The illustrations frame the text in the castle's many arches, emphasizing the overriding image of the stone castles choked in briar vines just as life is drained from the kingdom.

Jacobs, Joseph. **The Story of the Three Little Pigs**. Illustrated by Lorinda Bryan Cauley. Putnam's, 1980.
In this classic tale the three pigs build houses of straw, furze, and bricks. The wolf demolishes the first two houses. The owner of the brick house not only keeps his house intact but also devours the wolf at the end.

Marshall, James. **Goldilocks and the Three Bears**. Dial, 1988.
In this version of the traditional tale we meet a bratty Goldilocks who disobeys her mother's warning, takes a short cut (marked with danger signs) through the forest, and breaks into the charming cottage of the Bear family.

Marshall, James. **The Three Little Pigs**. Dial, 1989.
Marshall adds his droll touches to the traditional folk tale of the wolf and the three little pigs. The first two pigs are warned against using straw and sticks for their houses, but they proceed anyway. The third pig's brick house is not only solidly built but also is attractively decorated inside and out.

Rogasky, Barbara. **Rapunzel**. From the Brothers Grimm. Illustrated by Trina Schart Hyman. Holiday House, 1982.
Illustrations and text set in decorated frames tell the haunting fairy tale of the ill-fated Rapunzel, who is locked away in a tower by a witch.

Scieszka, Jon. **The True Story of the Three Little Pigs**. Illustrated by Lane Smith. Viking Kestrel, 1989.

This hilarious version tells the three pigs' story from the wolf's point of view. A. Wolf says he has been victimized by the press and claims he "accidentally" killed the pigs when their flimsy houses fell down during one of his sneezing fits.

Small, Ernest. **Baba Yaga**. Illustrated by Blair Lent. Houghton Mifflin, 1966.

The famous Russian witch lives in a hut that travels on chicken-leg feet and is surrounded by a fence of bones and skulls. Lent's goulish woodcut illustrations are a perfect accompaniment to the text.

Turkle, Brinton. **Deep in the Forest**. Dutton, 1976.

In this wordless book, a bear cub breaks into the log cabin of Goldilocks's family and makes innocent mischief in a reverse on the traditional tale.

Zemach, Margot. **The Three Little Pigs**. Farrar, Straus and Giroux, 1988.

In this faithful retelling of the story, three pigs set out to build houses of straw, sticks, and bricks. The first two houses are blown down by the wolf, who also eats the homeowners, but the third little pig builds a brick house and outsmarts the villain.

Related Activities for Gingerbread and Sugarplums

ONLY IN FAIRYLAND
(Tune: "Sing a Song of Sixpence")

Here's Rapunzel's tower
Can you find the stair?
Climb up to the window
On her golden hair.
Here is Peter's pumpkin
Who can live inside?
He has built a cozy cottage
For his pretty bride.

Here's a witch's cottage
Gingerbread and treats.
Little children found it
Good enough to eat.
Woman and her children
What is she to do?
Tucked them down inside a house
Made of a high-topped shoe.

THE GINGERBREAD GIRL
(A Draw-and-Tell Story)

This variant of the traditional gingerbread boy story is set in the land of make-believe with the main character, a gingerbread girl, visiting the houses of several well-known fantasy characters.

Children will be delighted to see the shape of a house emerge as you draw and tell this story.

Once upon a time in the land of make-believe there lived a gingerbread girl. She was unhappy in her plain, ordinary cottage with the little old woman who had made her out of gingerbread. The gingerbread girl wanted to see castles and fairyland. She wanted to see sights beyond her wildest dreams. So—

> The gingerbread girl
> Set out to explore
> Places beyond
> Her own front door.

She ran and she ran and she came to the house of Red Riding Hood's grandmother. (*Draw vertical line as shown.*)

She peeped in the window. Grandma was not in her bed. A great big wolf was in the bed instead. The gingerbread girl was afraid, so she ran on.

> Run, run
> I'm on my way
> I know it's not
> Safe to stay.

She ran and she ran and she came to the castle of Sleeping Beauty. (*Continue drawing line at an upward slant as shown.*)

Everyone and everything in the castle were sound asleep. She could not awaken them. Maybe an awful spell had been put on the castle. The gingerbread girl was afraid, so she ran on.

> Run, run
> I'm on my way
> I know it's not
> Safe to stay.

She ran and she ran and she came to the bridge of the Three Billy Goats Gruff. (*Continue drawing line at a downward slant as shown.*) Under the bridge she saw a great, big, ugly troll sound asleep. She didn't want to awaken him, So she quietly tiptoed over the bridge.

> Run, run
> I'm on my way
> I know it's not
> Safe to stay.

She ran and she ran and she came to the lily pond where the Frog Prince lived. (*Continued drawing line straight down as shown.*)

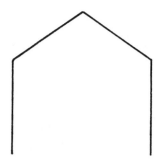

The gingerbread girl knew that a strong magic had turned the prince of the castle into a frog. She took one look at the frog and decided she didn't want to end up as ugly as that, so she ran on.

> Run, run
> I'm on my way
> I know it's not
> Safe to stay.

She ran and she ran and she came back to where she had started from. (*Continue drawing line back to the original point.*)

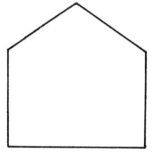

She had seen castles and fairyland. She had seen sights beyond her wildest dreams. But now she decided that she liked her own little cottage after all. So she went inside and stayed safe and sound behind her own front door. (*Draw front door to house as shown.*)

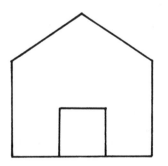

And there she lived happily ever after.

GINGERBREAD HOUSE MADE TO ORDER
(Chant)

Use the beginning stanza to start building your own gingerbread house just the way you like it. The sweets that we have added are only suggestions. Let your children come up with their own creations. This chant builds in a cumulative fashion, as you will see from our examples. When everything has been added, conclude with the final line.

Let's make a house of gingerbread
Warm and brown and sweet
Now add the trimmings all around
It's good enough to eat.

Let's start with (candy canes)
On the house that's good enough to eat.

Now add (gum drops)
To go with the (candy canes)
On the house that's good enough to eat.

Now add (lollipops)
To go with the (gum drops)
To go with the (candy canes)
On the house that's good enough to eat.

Now go on adding other sweets to suit yourself. When you've added everything you like, conclude with the line, "Now that's a gingerbread house made to order!"

KNOCK, KNOCK, WHO'S THERE?
(A Goldilocks Chant Story)

Retell the story of the three bears with chants and interaction with children. The asterisks indicate when you motion to children for them to repeat the line you have spoken.

Now here's a little story*
Of three ol' bears*
Papa Bear*
Mama Bear*
Baby Bear—three!*

They lived in the forest
By the big pine tree*
Papa Bear, Mama Bear, Baby Bear—three.*

They lived in a house
Snug as can be*
Papa Bear, Mama Bear, Baby Bear—three.*

Mama made porridge
Too hot to eat
So they went on a walk
On their ol' bear feet*

Food too hot
So they went on a spree
Papa Bear, Mama Bear, Baby Bear—three.*

'Long came Goldilocks
Set to explore
Knock, knock, knock,
Who's behind that door?*

Nobody's home
She went in—swish!
Ate all the porridge
In the Baby Bear's dish.*

Out to the living room
In a flash
Plopped in the baby's chair
Fell down—crash!*

Right up the stairs
To the three bears' beds
The little one's right
For a sleepy head.*

Back home again
Came the Bear family
Papa Bear, Mama Bear, Baby Bear—three.*

Porridge all gone
Boo, hoo, hoo,*
Chair's all broken
What'll we do?*
Up the stairs
Creeping quietly
Papa Bear, Mama Bear, Baby Bear—three.*

Knock, knock, knock,
Who's in this bed?*
It's only me
Little Goldilocks said.

Next time you come
Be good like a bear
Go knock, knock, knock,
Who's sittin' in there?

But don't break in
If no one's there
'Cause this is the house
Of the three ol' bears.*

Now let's go down
You stay to tea
With Papa Bear, Mama Bear, Baby Bear—three.*

THIS IS THE HOUSE WHERE JILL SLEPT

This is the house where Jill slept.

Here is the wind that blew on the house where Jill
slept.

Here is the branch that scraped the window
where the wind blew
on the house where Jill slept.

This is the squirrel that ran out on the branch
that scraped the window
where the wind blew
on the house where Jill slept.

This is the cat that chased the squirrel
that ran out on the branch
that scraped the window
where the wind blew
on the house where Jill slept.

This is the dog that chased the cat
that chased the squirrel
that ran out on the branch
that scraped the window
where the wind blew
on the house where Jill slept.

This is the wasp that stung the dog
that chased the cat
that chased the squirrel
that ran out on the branch
that scraped the window
where the wind blew
on the house where Jill slept.

Then Jill woke up!

Jill swatted the wasp,
who stopped stinging the dog,
who stopped chasing the cat,
who stopped chasing the squirrel,
who stopped running out on the branch,
which stopped scraping the window,
so there was nothing left
but the wind blowing
softly
on the house where Jill went back to sleep.

THREE PIGS IN A BLANKET
(Mask Story)

This story is told with masks shaped like the houses of the three pigs. The first house is decorated with drinking straws. The second house is decorated with pretzel sticks. The third house is decorated with bread slices and sprayed with decoupage glue to preserve it. (See illustration on page 200.) The house masks are next mounted on craft sticks so they can be held up to children's faces. Now, here's the fun part. Place pink paper circles on the noses of three children so they can become the pigs who live in the houses. Children hold up the houses and poke their noses through the window holes in the masks. The leader uses a wolf hand-puppet for the villain of the story.

Once upon a time there were three little pigs. They lived in a cozy apartment just above their papa's supermarket. Now when they got old enough to leave home and build their own houses, Papa Pig wanted to help them get started.

Papa Pig said to his three little pigs, "Help yourselves to anything you can find in my supermarket to build your houses."

The first little pig chose drinking straws because they were light and easy to carry. And so he built his house out of straws. (*Give first house to the first pig child.*)

The second little pig chose pretzel sticks because they also were light and easy to carry. And besides, they were good to snack on. And so he built his house out of pretzel sticks. (*Give second house to the second pig child.*)

The third little pig chose bread because he wanted a house of strength. It was day-old bread, so it was not light and easy to carry. It was hard as a brick. So the third little pig built his house of bread that was hard as a brick. (*Give third house to the third pig child.*)

Now on the edge of the neighborhood lived Long Tooth the wolf. (*Leader brings out the wolf puppet now.*) He saw the construction going on and decided to make some mischief once the houses were built.

One morning he went to the house of the first little pig. It was made of drinking straws. (*Move wolf puppet as if he is speaking.*) Long Tooth said,

"Here is the house of the first little pig.

It's made out of straws and it's not very big." (*Leader points to first pig child, who is peeking through the window hole of the first house.*)

The first little pig said, "It's my home and the very best straw house in town."

(*Move wolf puppet as if he is speaking.*) Long Tooth said, "I bet I can blow it right down!"

And with one blow, two blows, three blows, the house fell right down! The first little pig ran as quick as his little trotters could take him straight to the house of the second little pig. (*Take down the house-of-straws mask. The first pig child then runs over to hide behind the house-of-sticks mask with the second pig child. The wolf puppet moves on to the second house.*)

Now the wolf went over to the house of the second little pig. It was made of pretzel sticks. (*Move wolf puppet as if he is speaking.*) Long Tooth said,

"Here is the house of the second wee pig.

It's made out of sticks and it's not very big." (*Leader points to second pig child, who is peeking through the window hole of the second house. The first pig child is peeking through another window hole.*)

The second little pig said, "It's my home and the very best stick house in town."

Long Tooth said, "I bet I can blow it right down!"

And with one blow, two blows, three blows, the house fell right down! The first and second little pigs ran as quick as they could on their little trotters to the house of the third little pig. (*These two children put down the stick-house mask and run over to the bread-house mask with the third child. The wolf puppet also moves over to this house.*)

Now the wolf went over to the house of the third little pig. It was made of bread as hard as bricks. Long Tooth said,

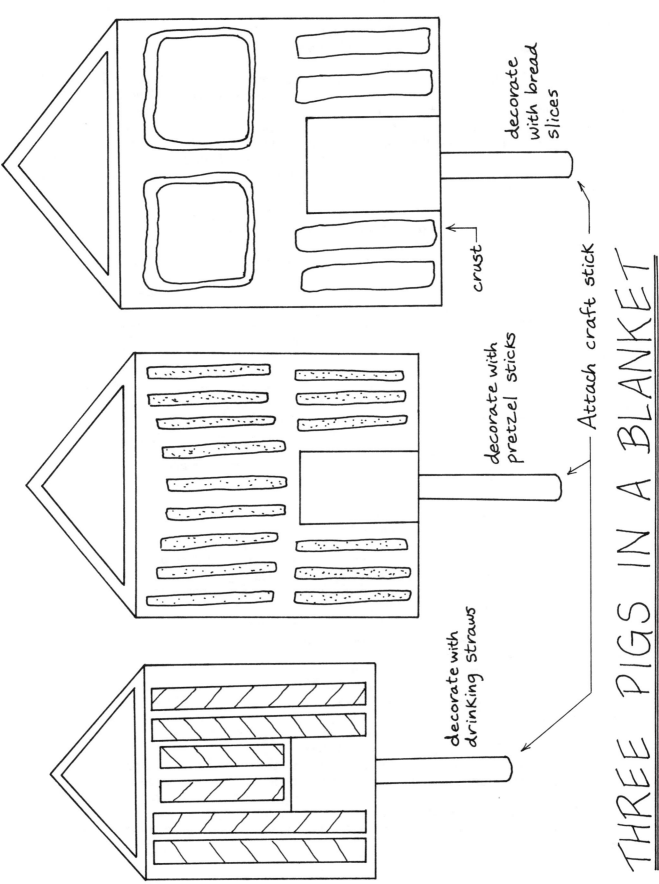

decorate with bread slices

crust

decorate with pretzel sticks

Attach craft stick

decorate with drinking straws

THREE PIGS IN A BLANKET

"Here is the house of the third little pig.

It's made out of bricks and it's not very big." (*Leader points to house of third pig with the three pig children peeking through the window holes.*)

The third little pig said, "It's my home and the very best brick house in town."

Long Tooth said, "I bet I can blow it right down!"

He gave one blow, two blows, three blows, but the house did not fall down!

Let's see if everyone here can help the wolf. One blow, two blows, three blows. But the house still did not fall down!

Okay. Let's try one more time. One blow. Two blows. Three blows.

Wait a minute. The wolf took a closer look at the house. The bricks were made of bread. But they were still hard as bricks.

"Well," said the wolf. "If I can't blow your house down, I'll eat you out of house and home."

And Long Tooth the wolf opened his mouth wide to take a big chomp out of the house made out of bread as hard as bricks. Chomp! Crack! Ooooowwwww!

Long Tooth broke off his great long chompers on the hard house. (*The wolf puppet exits.*) The pigs never saw him again, but they heard that he spent a long time at the dentist's office getting false teeth. And, as for the pigs, they liked the house made of bread as hard as bricks so well that they all settled in together. They ate at one table. They sat on one sofa. And when they went to bed, they all snuggled up under the same cover. (*Wrap big blanket loosely around the shoulders of three pig children.*) They were three pigs in a blanket.

THE FISHERMAN AND HIS WIFE RETOLD
(Tube Story)

Retell this favorite folk tale with a cardboard tube and cutout pictures of the different houses that the wife wishes for. Mount each house on a cardboard ring that slips over the tube. (See illustrations on pages 202 and 203.) As each new house appears, flip it up. You could use stick puppets for the fish, the fisherman, and his wife if you wish, or you could simply focus on the houses on the tube for the new visual prop to tell this story.

Once upon a time there was a poor fisherman who lived with his wife in a miserable shack by the sea. (*Flip up the shack and point to it, then go on with the story.*) The fisherman went down to the sea every day to catch fish. Usually he caught just one fish for his wife to cook for dinner plus one extra fish to sell.

But one day, the fisherman caught a third fish. It was a rainbow-colored fish. And it spoke. "Please, dear fisherman, do not take me home. I am a magic fish and I am not good to eat. Just throw me back in the water."

Well, the fisherman had no intention of eating a talking fish. So he did just as the fish asked. He threw it back in the water and he went home with the other two fish he had caught. That night he told his wife about the rainbow-colored fish that talked.

"What? You mean you didn't ask the fish for something?" she said.

"Well, I didn't think of that," said the fisherman.

"You didn't think of that! Well, I think you should go back and ask the fish for a nice little white cottage with blue shutters and a red chimney," said the wife.

"Oh, I really don't think I should," said the husband.

"Well, I do," said the wife. And she kicked the poor man out the door.

So the poor fisherman went down to the water and he said to the fish,

> "Fishy, fishy in the sea
> Listen now to poor old me.
> My wife kicked me out the door
> Because she wants to have some more!"

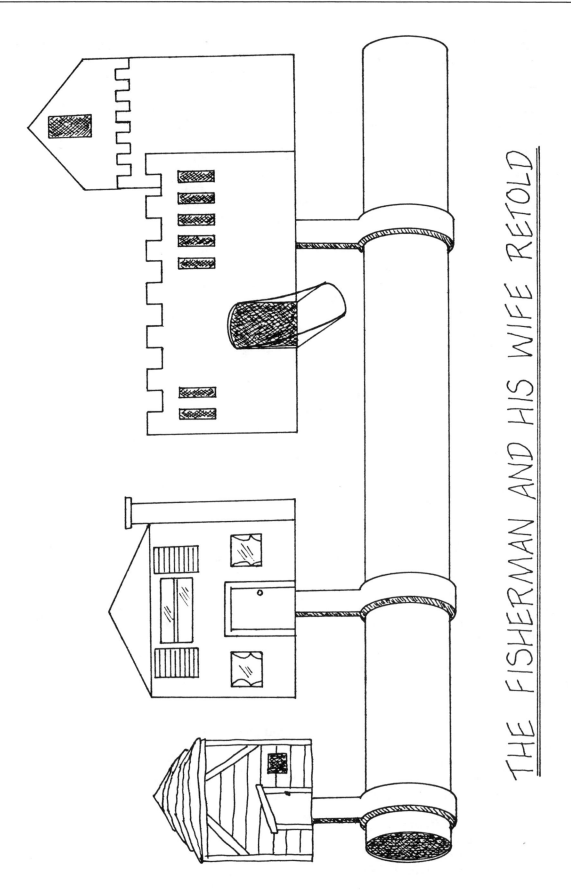

THE FISHERMAN AND HIS WIFE RETOLD

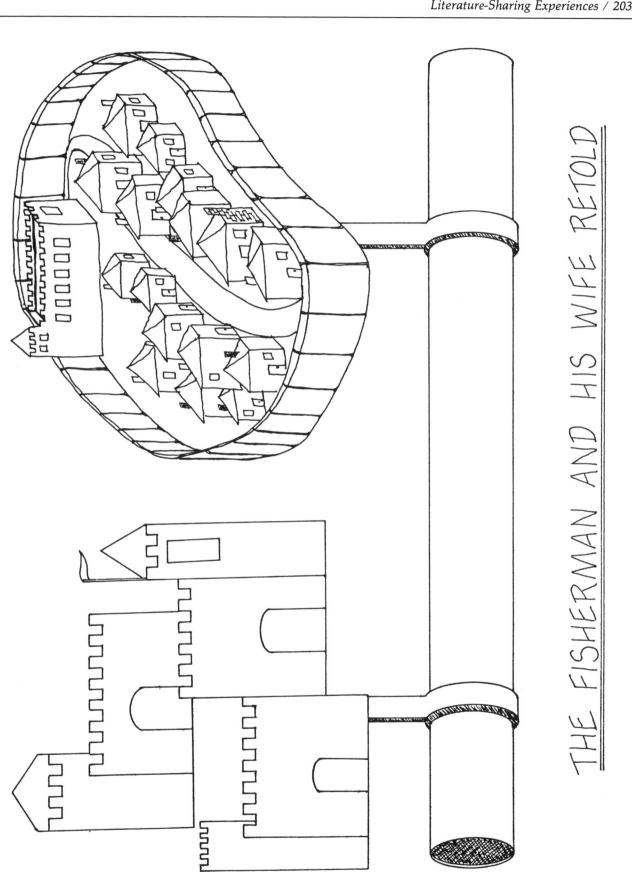

THE FISHERMAN AND HIS WIFE RETOLD

("The Fisherman and His Wife Retold" continues on page 204.)

The fish swam up and said, "Well, what does she want?"

"She wants a nice little white cottage with blue shutters and a red chimney," said the fisherman.

"Well, go home to your cottage," said the fish. (*Flip down the shack, and flip up the cottage.*)

The fisherman was amazed when he saw the cottage with the shutters and the chimney. His wife was waiting for him by the door. They lived in the cottage for many months. Finally, one day the wife said to her husband, "Husband, this cottage is way too small. Go back to the fish and ask him for a castle."

"Oh, I don't think I should do that," said the fisherman.

"Well, I do," said the wife. "I want a big stone castle with a tower and a drawbridge." And the wife kicked him out the door.

So the poor fisherman went down to the water and he said to the fish,

> "Fishy, fishy in the sea
> Listen now to poor old me.
> My wife kicked me out the door
> Because she wants to have some more!"

The fish swam up and said, "Well, what does she want?"

And the fisherman said, "She wants a big stone castle with a tower and a drawbridge."

"Well, go home to your castle," said the fish. (*Flip down cottage, and flip up castle.*)

The husband was amazed when he saw the castle with the tower and the drawbridge. His wife was waiting inside. So there they lived for many weeks. Finally the wife said, "Husband, I'm getting tired of this old castle. Go back and tell the fish that I want three castles—one for morning, one for midday, and one for night."

"Oh, I don't think I should do that," said the fisherman.

"Well, I do," said the wife. "I want three castles—one for morning, one for midday, and one for night." And the wife kicked him out the door.

So the poor fisherman went down to the water and he said to the fish,

> "Fishy, fishy in the sea
> Listen now to poor old me.
> My wife kicked me out the door
> Because she wants to have some more!"

The fish swam up and said, "Well, what does she want?"

And the fisherman said, "She wants three castles—one for morning, one for midday, and one for night."

"Well, go home to your three castles," said the fish. (*Flip down the castle, and flip up three other castles.*)

The fisherman went home. He was amazed to find three castles in place of the one castle. He looked through all three castles and finally found his wife. She was sitting out in the courtyard and she was stamping her foot.

"Husband," she said, "this isn't good enough."

"What do you mean?" he said. "You've got your three castles. Aren't you content now?"

"No. Now I need a whole kingdom to go with my castles. Go back and ask the fish for a whole kingdom with a wall around the outside."

"Oh, I don't think I should do that," said the fisherman.

"Well, I do," said the wife. "I want a whole kingdom to go with my castles. Go back and ask the fish for a whole kingdom with a wall around the outside." And the wife kicked him out the door.

So the poor fisherman went down to the water and he said to the fish,

> "Fishy, fishy in the sea
> Listen now to poor old me.
> My wife kicked me out the door
> Because she wants to have some more!"

The fish swam up and said, "Well, what does she want?"

And the fisherman said, "She wants a whole kingdom to go with her castles."

"Well, go home to your kingdom," said the fish. (*Flip down three castles, and flip up kingdom.*)

Well, the husband was astounded when he saw the whole kingdom for his home. He searched everywhere. Finally, at the end of the kingdom on a throne sat his wife.

"Now, husband, I am ruler of all the kingdom, so I order you to go back to the fish and tell him I want to own all the houses in all of the kingdoms in all of the world."

"Oh, I don't think I should do that," said the fisherman.

"Well, I do," said the wife. "I want to own all the houses in all of the kingdoms in all of the world. Go back and ask the fish for all of the houses in all of the kingdoms in all of the world." And the wife kicked him out the door.

So the poor fisherman went down to the water and he said to the fish,

> "Fishy, fishy in the sea
> Listen now to poor old me.
> My wife kicked me out the door
> Because she wants to have some more!"

The fish swam up and said, "Well, what does she want?"

And the fisherman said, "She wants to own all the houses in all of the kingdoms in all of the world."

And the fish said, "That is too much. Go back and find her in your old shack." (*Flip down the kingdom, and flip up the first shack.*)

So the poor old fisherman went home. There he found his wife in their first house—the old shack. And that's where you'll find them living to this very day.

But I don't think you'll find them living happily ever after.

Books for Magic Castles and Cottages

Bider, Djemma. **The Biggest Little House in the Forest**. Illustrated by John Sandford, Caedmon, 1986.

Bernice the butterfly finds a pretty little house in the forest, so she moves in and so do a mouse, a frog, a rooster, and a rabbit. But when a bear tries to join them the little house collapses, so they rebuild it to become the biggest little house in the forest.

Boegehold, Betty. **In the Castle of Cats**. Illustrated by Jan Brett. Dutton, 1981.

Miou the younger cat in the castle of cats looks through the magic telescope in the tower and sees the scary things that happen to cats who leave the sanctuary of the castle. She decides she is not old enough to go out on her own.

Bottner, Barbara. **Fun House**. Prentice-Hall, 1974.

This book has nonsense poems and suggestions for fun activities around the house.

Brown, Marcia. **The Neighbors**. Scribner, 1967.

When Fox steals Rabbit's house, only Rooster can help Rabbit get the house back.

Brunhoff, Laurent de. **Babar Visits Another Planet**. Random House, 1972.
　　Babar and his family are kidnapped and taken to a planet with kinds of houses they have never seen before.

Buchanan, Heather S. **George and Matilda Mouse and the Doll's House**. Simon & Schuster, 1988.
　　After George and Matilda Mouse get married, they set off to find a perfect home in an abandoned doll house. Jewel-like illustrations carefully detail the rooms and furnishings of the house, modeled after Ms. Buchanan's doll house, which was bought by her great-grandmother.

Faunce-Brown, Daphne. **Snuffle's House**. Illustrated by Frances Thatcher. Children's Press International, 1980.
　　When Snuffle the hedgehog's square house burns down, he experiments with other shapes of houses—round, oval, triangular—until he settles on a rectangular one.

Friedman, Aileen. **The Castles of the Two Brothers**. Illustrated by Steven Kellogg. Holt, Rinehart and Winston, 1972.
　　Klaus tries to escape from his brother, but only gets himself into more trouble.

Gedin, Birgitta. **The Little House from the Sea**. Illustrated by Petter Pettersson. Translated by Elisabeth Dyssegaard. R & S Books, distributed by Farrar, Straus and Giroux, 1988.
　　In this fanciful tale from Sweden a little house made from the timber of a boat longs to return to the sea until the north wind raises a threatening storm.

Godden, Rumer. **The Old Woman Who Lived in a Vinegar Bottle**. Illustrated by Mairi Hedderwick. Viking, 1970.
　　A little old woman who lives in a stone vinegar-bottle house finds a coin, with which she buys a fish that she throws back in the water. The fish is magic and grants her wishes until she becomes so greedy that her fine cottage and servants are taken away. The woman does salvage one small favor: a Sunday dinner each week. This is an English variation of "The Fisherman and His Wife."

Hayward, Linda. **Hello, House**. Illustrated by Lynn Munsinger. Random House, 1988.
　　In this beginning reader, the Uncle Remus character Brer Wolf hides in Brer Rabbit's house to capture him, but the clever rabbit outsmarts the wolf again.

Heide, Florence Parry. **My Castle**. Illustrated by Symeon Shimin. McGraw-Hill, 1972.
　　A child alone on the fire escape of his city apartment imagines his place as a castle on a summer day.

Hoberman, Mary Ann. **A House Is a House for Me**. Illustrated by Betty Fraser. Viking, 1978.
　　Rhythmical text and carefully detailed illustrations explore houses from beehives and mouse holes to igloos, pueblos, and even far-fetched kinds of houses—barrels for pickles, cartons for crackers, a shoe for a foot.

Hutchins, Pat. **King Henry's Palace**. Greenwillow, 1983.
　　In three little stories, King Henry lives happily in his palace with a devoted staff. The king's staff fool a jealous army ready to take over the palace, prepare a feast, and make presents for the king.

Ichikawa, Satomi. **Nora's Castle**. Philomel Books, 1984.
　　Nora sets off with her teddy bear, doll, and dog to explore the rooms in an old castle. They invite the owl in the tower and various woodland animals to join them for a party in the castle. That night they sleep in the tower before returning home.

Krahn, Fernando. **Arthur's Adventure in the Abandoned House**. Dutton, 1981.
　　In this wordless adventure, Arthur explores an abandoned house, meets up with bandits, is nailed inside a room, sends a note for help, is rescued, and watches the house be bulldozed as the bandits are captured.

Krahn, Fernando. **The Secret in the Dungeon**. Houghton Mifflin, 1983.

Touring a medieval castle with her parents, a little girl slips away from the group and explores various passages before she is flung into the dungeon, where the dragon still lives. This wordless adventure offers excellent opportunities for creative writing and storytelling.

Krauss, Ruth. **A Very Special House**. Illustrated by Maurice Sendak. Harper & Row, 1953.

A young boy romps through this book that proclaims the pleasures of his house. Part of the fun is bringing home a variety of animals to dance on the ceiling, eat the door, and sing, but mostly the fun is just in the "moodle of my head." Word play adds to the whimsical tone of this book.

Lenski, Lois. **Let's Play House**. Walck, 1944.

Three children pretend to play house with dress-up clothes, dolls, and stuffed animals.

Lobel, Arnold. **The Man Who Took the Indoors Out**. Harper & Row, 1974.

A man invites all his house furnishings to go on a parade and journey outside and around the far reaches of the land. When he returns to his house, he is lonely for them and winter has come—soon followed by the return of the furniture.

Logan, Dick. **Thunder Makes a Sand Castle**. Illustrated by Judy Coldren. Creative Education, 1977.

Thunder the dinosaur saves the day at the beach by building a prize-winning sand castle.

McAllister, Angela. **The King Who Sneezed**. Illustrated by Simon Henwood. Morrow, 1988.

While King Parsimonious does not care about the comfort of his subjects, his own drafty castle teaches him a lesson.

McGovern, Ann. **Mr. Skinner's Skinny House**. Illustrated by Mort Gergerg. Four Winds Press, 1980.

A lonely, thin man searches for just the right companion to share the narrowest house in the city.

Sharmat, Mitchell. **Come Home, Wilma**. Illustrated by Rosekrans Hoffman. Whitman, 1980.

Punished by being sent to her room for a while, an angry child imagines she is running away from home.

Stevenson, Robert Louis. **Block City**. Dutton, 1988.

A child creates a world of his own with mountains and a city from toy blocks.

Related Activities for Magic Castles and Cottages

CASTLE, CASTLE, IN THE AIR
(Tune: "Twinkle, Twinkle, Little Star")

Castle, castle, in the air,

Let me climb your crystal stair.

Let me crawl up in the tower,

Filled with fragrant springtime flowers.

Castle, castle

In my mind,

Magic places

That are mine.

SAND CASTLES
(Poem)

Down at the beach,
Here in the sand,
I build a castle
With my two hands.

I'll add a tower
And a hall.
A moat surrounds
The fortress walls.

But when the waves
Come in to play
My castle of sand
Just melts away!

For castles of sand
Will never stay,
But there's always another
Sand-building day.

HIGH-TOP HIGHRISE
(Object Story)

To tell this story, use a bootie, ballet slipper, penny loafer, swim fin, and high-top sneaker. Show each as it is mentioned in the story. For more fun use toy figures of a woman, bird, cat, dog, pig, and children, and put them in the shoes. The children can all say the magic words "shoe-zam" with you.

There was once an old woman who lived all alone. She didn't live in a cottage or a little house, however, she lived in a bootie. It was just a little bootie, but she was just a little woman. Every morning she swept and cleaned her house and wished she had a little pet to live with her.

One morning as she was cleaning she found a silver button. It did not look like it came from any of her dresses, but she rubbed it on her apron to shine it up. Suddenly, with a puff of smoke a wizard appeared. The woman was amazed, but she remembered that wizards were often good at granting wishes, and she did so want a little pet. So she politely asked, "Wizard, could you give me a little pet—maybe a bird to live with me in my bootie?"

The wizard looked around and said, "This bootie is so small you couldn't even get a bird's foot in here. I'll give you a bird—and a ballet slipper for you both to live in."

And that's just what he did. SHOE-ZAM!

The woman and her new bird were very happy in the ballet slipper, but the woman kept the silver button, and one day she rubbed it again. When the wizard appeared she asked, "Wizard, could you give me another little pet—maybe a kitten to live with me and my bird in my ballet slipper?"

The wizard looked around and said, "This ballet slipper is so small you couldn't even get a kitten's whisker in here. I'll give you a kitten—and a penny loafer for you all to live in."

And that's just what he did. SHOE-ZAM!

The woman and her bird and her new kitten were very happy in the penny loafer, but the woman kept the silver button, and one day she rubbed it again. When the wizard appeared she asked, "Wizard, could you give me another little pet—maybe a puppy to live with me and my bird and my kitten in my penny loafer?"

The wizard looked around and said, "This penny loafer is so small you couldn't even get a puppy's tail in here. I'll give you a puppy—and a swim fin for you all to live in."

And that's just what he did. SHOE-ZAM!

The woman and her bird and her new kitten and her new puppy were very happy in the swim fin, but the woman kept the silver button, and one day she rubbed it again. When the wizard appeared she asked, "Wizard, could you give me another little pet—maybe a pig to live with me and my bird and my kitten and my puppy in my swim fin?"

The wizard looked around and said, "This swim fin is so small you couldn't even get a pig's squeal in here. I'll give you a pig—and a high-top sneaker for you all to live in."

And that's just what he did. SHOE-ZAM!

The woman and all her new pets were very happy, but the woman kept the silver button. Once in a while she thought about rubbing it to ask for a goat or some chickens, but the truth was that all her new pets were so much fun that children had come to live with her, too. The high-top sneaker was really a highrise high-top hotel, with kids and pets at every window.

And that is the true story of how there came to be an old woman who lived in a shoe with so many children she didn't know what to do!

A HOUSE FOR EVERYONE
(Circle Story)

Cut two circles of posterboard. Cut a wedge from one, place it on top of the other, and fasten at the center with a paper fastener. (See illustration on page 210.) On the top circle draw or paste cutout pictures of a frog, spider, lizard, cricket, and ladybug. On the bottom circle show a pond with a lily pad, a barn with a spider web, a sandy desert with a rock, a forest at nighttime, and a doll house. Space these on the bottom circle so they are seen one at a time through the cutout wedge. As you tell the story, turn the bottom circle to show the type of house you are talking about.

There were once five friends who were tired of living under rocks and leaves and decided to look together for a good place to live. They all sat by the edge of the forest and tried to agree on what kind of house to look for.

Frog said, "It must be very damp and have a lily pad for a rug. There should be an open window to let in bugs and gnats."

"That will never do," said Spider. "The house must be large and airy and have lace curtains I will spin myself."

"Nonsense," said Lizard. "The house must be dry and very warm and have a sand floor for sunbathing."

"Absurd," said Cricket. "The house should be cool and have a big door to let in the moonlight. Then we can make music there all night."

Ladybug didn't say anything.

The friends could not agree on what the house should have, but they began to look around at houses anyway. Frog found the first one on the banks of the pond.

"Perfect," he said. "Damp and green and plenty of bugs and ants. We'll take it."

"Oh, no," said Spider. "My weaving would be ruined by all this water. We can't live here."

Ladybug didn't say anything.

So Spider picked the next house. She found the corner of an old barn.

"Perfect," she said. "This house is shaded all day from the sun. And look at all the open space for weaving webs. We'll take it."

"Oh, no," said Lizard. "I must have plenty of light and warmth so I can sunbathe. We can't live here."

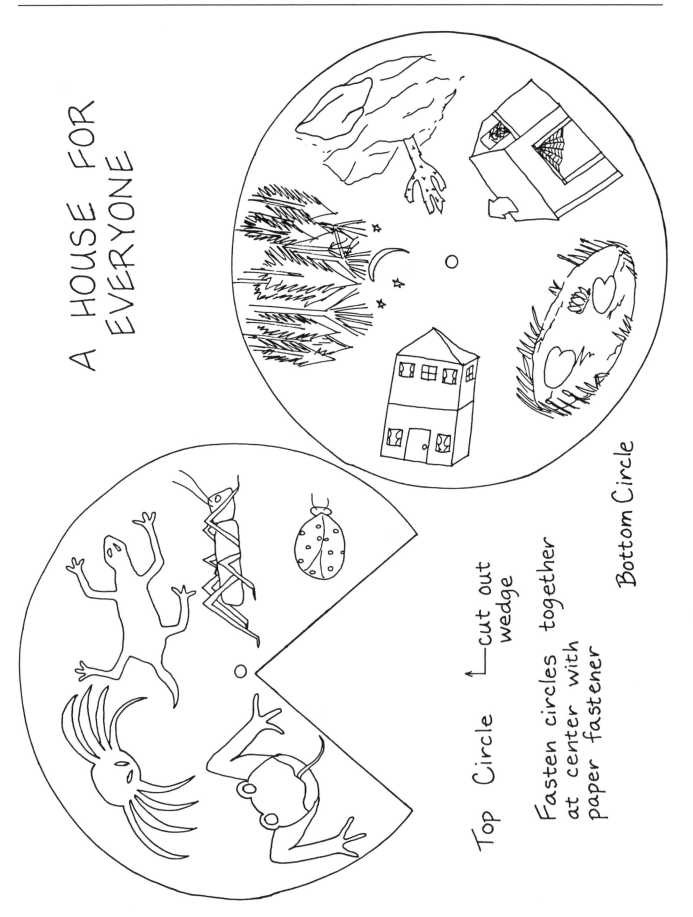

A HOUSE FOR EVERYONE

Bottom Circle

Top Circle ⌐ cut out wedge

Fasten circles together at center with paper fastener

Ladybug didn't say anything.

So Lizard picked the next house. He found a sandy spot near a rock.

"Perfect," he said. "This house is sunny and far from anything else. I can sleep on this rock without being disturbed. We'll take it."

"Oh, no," said Cricket. "I must have a place with moonlight nights near enough that my friends can come make music. We can't live here."

Ladybug didn't say anything.

Cricket found the next house. It was deep in the forest.

"Perfect," said Cricket. "The moonlight comes through the trees and all my friends live nearby. We'll make music all night long. We'll take it."

"Oh, no," said Frog. "It is miles to the nearest pond. I'd be all day just getting there for a swim. We can't live here."

Ladybug didn't say anything. Instead she led the friends to a house she knew of. There was a bathroom with a tub so Frog could have water nearby. There was a parlor with shade so Spider could spin webs. There was a sunroom with windows so Lizard could sunbathe. There was a music room so Cricket could make music all night. Ladybug had found an old doll house that suited everyone just fine.

So all the friends moved in and were very happy. But happiest of all was Ladybug, because she lived in the library where it was always very quiet, and she didn't have to say anything at all.

GAMES FOR CASTLES IN THE AIR

COBWEB TANGLE GAME

Cobwebs can be found in any haunted house or in Sleeping Beauty's castle. Form some human cobwebs by playing this cooperative cobweb tangle game.

Have all children stand in a line and join hands. The leader weaves the line around the room with children ducking under the joined hands of other children and the line doubling back upon itself so that everyone becomes one giant cobweb tangle.

When the tangle becomes a hopeless mess, the leader yells "Clean up!" All drop hands and reform the straight line to begin again.

TRACK THE TREATS GAME

This game will remind the children of Hansel and Gretel leaving a trail of bread crumbs so they can find their way back home. In this game we suggest you use wrapped mints.

Repeat the stanza as you lead children into corners of the room, down halls, into closets, or outside. After each stanza direct a different child to drop his or her candy. When all candies have been dropped, follow the trail back with each child picking up the candy he or she dropped. When you return to the starting place, repeat the second stanza, which is the signal to enjoy the treats.

> Deep in the forest
> You'll want to get back
> Mark your way
> With a candy track.
>
> Deep in the forest
> We left our track
> Home, sweet home—
> Now we're all back.

CRAFTS FOR CASTLES IN THE AIR

RAPUNZEL IN HER TOWER CRAFT

Give each child a Rapunzel figure made from the pattern shown below. Children may color the gown with markers and glue long strands of yellow yarn to the head for her hair. The figure is next glued to a craft stick.

Cut the top edge of a plain paper cup to simulate the crenellated wall of the tower. Ivy can be drawn on the tower if desired. Now poke a hole in the bottom of the cup so that the Rapunzel figure can be placed inside the tower.

RAPUNZEL IN HER TOWER CRAFT

Rapunzel

←— Attach to craft stick

HAUNTED HOUSE PEEK-A-BOO CRAFT

Cut out two house shapes from black construction paper using the pattern on page 214. Cut along the solid window lines on one house and fold on the dotted lines. Place the two house shapes on top of one another and glue around the outer edges only. Fold back the windows and doors and place spooky objects behind. You may use cutouts of the objects shown here or encourage children to make their own spooky things.

DOLL HOUSE DREAM HOUSE

Cover the inside of a standard-sized shoebox with blue wrapping paper or construction paper. Cover the "ceiling" of the room with gummed stars and cloud shapes using the pattern on page 215. Now make a bed for the room (pattern shown) and decorate the bedspread with more stars and clouds if you wish. Add cutouts of teddy bears or any other object you might take to bed with you for sweet dreams. Since this is intended to be a doll house, children may bring in small dolls of their own to complete the playhouse.

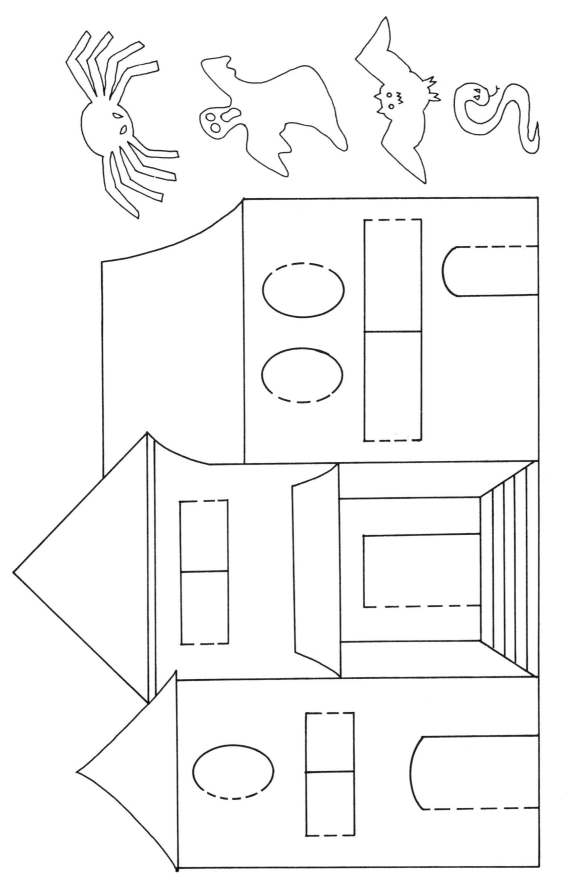

HAUNTED HOUSE
PEEK-A-BOO CRAFT

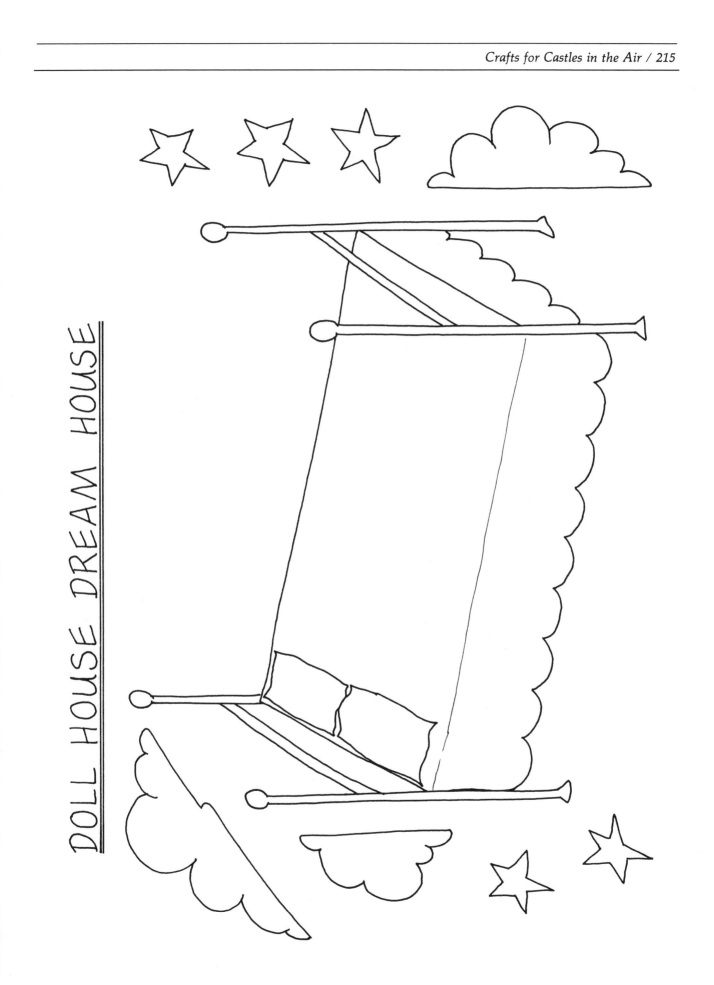

DOLL HOUSE DREAM HOUSE

FLOOR PLANS FOR CASTLES IN THE AIR

Focus Book: *A House Is a House for Me* by Mary Ann Hoberman

Reading Activities

Since the line "A house is a house for me" is repeated throughout this book, this will be a natural sentence for children to learn to read on their own. Write each word on a separate card and back the paper with sandpaper so the cards can be stuck to a flannel-board. You might write other nouns naming animals and their houses to make other sentences. For example: A nest is a house for a bird. A cave is a house for a bear. An ocean is a house for a whale.

Speaking Activities

Turn to the double-page spread in the book that shows the girl in the hammock (the only pages where the text does not describe the individual houses). Ask children to identify the "house" and its resident (a baseball glove is a house for a baseball, a jack-o-lantern is a house for a candle, a bowl is a house for a salad, etc.).

Writing Activities

Write the name for a room of the house on the board. Then list places or "houses" found in that room. For example, a toaster, a cupboard, a can, and an eggshell would all be "houses" found in the kitchen. Then ask each student to write down inhabitants or things that live in those places—bread, plates, peas, an egg. More advanced students might like to name both places and inhabitants for another room of the house.

Students can make house-shaped books with the objects that live inside that house illustrated on the inside pages. The house shape might be a tree with all the things that live in it.

Resource Bibliography

Adkins, Jan. **How a House Happens**. Walker and Co., 1972.
A family builds a new house. The text and illustrations explain floor plans and the financial arrangements, as well as the actual building from digging the foundation to the finishing carpentry and painting.

The American Girls Theater. Pleasant Company, 1989.
This collection of plays with scripts and directions for staging and costumes includes a story of Kirsten's life in pioneer America entitled "Home Is Where the Heart Is."

D'Alelio, Jane. **I Know That Building!** Preservation Press, 1989.
Children will learn about historical buildings through drawings and photographs, games, models to construct, gargoyle masks to cut out, and so much fun that everyone will want to become an architect or, at least, a historical preservationist.

Fisher, Leonard Everett. **Monticello**. Holiday House, 1988.
Describes the planning, construction, and occupancy of Thomas Jefferson's dream home.

Fisher, Leonard Everett. **The White House**. Holiday House, 1989.
The history of the president's residence and its inhabitants from 1790 are outlined in this book.

Fisher, Timothy. **Huts, Hovels, and Houses**. Illustrated by Kathleen Kolb. Addison-Wesley, 1977.
Directions are given for making dwellings such as a house of cans, milk-carton house, newspaper log cabin, sod house, and double-decker snow house. Extra features include windmills, greenhouses, and solar heating.

Giblin, James Cross. **Let There Be Light: A Book about Windows**. Crowell, 1988.
Surveys the development of windows from prehistory to the modern era.

Horwitz, Eleanor Lander. **How to Wreck a Building**. Photographs by Joshua Horwitz. Pantheon, 1982.
Photographs and brief text describe people's feelings and the physical steps involved in the demolition of an old school building.

Huntington, Lee Pennock. **Simple Shelters**. Illustrated by Stefen Bernath. Coward-McCann, 1979.
Eighteen simple shelters around the world—from North American Indian longhouses, tepees, and Pueblo Indian villages to Masai and Bushman huts in Africa—are described briefly and illustrated with clear line drawings.

Isaacson, Philip. **Round Buildings, Square Buildings, and Buildings That Wiggle Like a Fish**. Knopf, 1988.
Most of the buildings in this book are public buildings rather than private houses, but the text and photographs inform the reader about such architectural details as doors and windows and ideas such as harmony and use of space that apply to all kinds of buildings.

James, Alan. **Homes in Hot Places**. Lerner, 1989.

Part of the "Houses and Homes" series that describes how homes are designed, built, and used throughout the world. Other titles by James include *Castles and Mansions*, *Homes in Cold Places*, and *Homes on Water*. Other titles in the series: *Homes in the Future* by Mark Lambert and *Building Homes*, *Homes in Space*, and *Mobile Homes* by Graham Rickard.

Macaulay, David. **Castle**. Houghton Mifflin, 1977.

Text and detailed drawings follow the planning and construction of a castle in Wales. A video recording of this story is also available.

Macaulay, David. **Pyramid**. Houghton Mifflin, 1975.

Step by step the ancient pyramid is constructed. This labor-intensive marvel is detailed with wonderful black-and-white drawings.

Paul, Sherry. **Ancient Skyscrapers: The Native American Pueblos**. Contemporary Perspectives, 1978.

This history of the Pueblo Indians includes color photographs and brief discussion of the pueblos on the mesas with ancient ruins of the kivas.

Shachtman, Tom. **The President Builds a House**. Simon & Schuster, 1989.

This photo essay shows the work of Habitat for Humanity, a volunteer organization with people like Jimmy and Rosalynn Carter who build houses for the needy.

Simon, Nancy, and Evelyn Wolfson. **American Indian Habitats**. Illustrated by Nancy Poydar. David McKay, 1978.

The major tribes of North America are listed, then the book describes the kinds of homes built in each of six general regions of the country (California-Northwest, Great Basin-Plateau, Southwest, Plains, Southeast, and Northeast). Directions are provided for making such typical homes as a wigwam.

Smith, Beth. **Castles**. Illustrated by Anne Canevari Green. Watts, 1988.

European castles from A.D. 500 and castle life are described through detailed text accompanied by drawings and photographs.

Sobol, Harriet Langsam. **Pete's House**. Photographs by Patricia Agre. Macmillan, 1978.

In this photo story, Pete tells his friend about the step-by-step process of his house being built—from the architect's plans and the ground being cleared to the completion as the family moves in.

Tunis, Edwin. **Colonial Living**. Crowell, 1957.

This book about sixteenth-, seventeenth-, and eighteenth-century living includes pictures and descriptions of New England, New Netherland, Pennsylvania German houses, southern mansions, and log cabins. This is a valuable teacher resource that older children will also enjoy.

Tunis, Edwin. **Frontier Living**. World Publishing, 1960.

Line drawings and accompanying text explore different aspects of frontier living with information on log cabins, farms of the northwest, and sod houses. This is a useful teacher resource or a good book for older children.

Walker, Les. **Housebuilding for Children**. Overlook Press, 1977.

Photographs show six different houses with the tools and equipment necessary to construct them.

Weiss, Harvey. **Shelters, From Teepee to Igloo**. Crowell, 1988.

Particular houses such as igloos, tepee, yurts, and log cabins are described as well as houses grouped by building materials (e.g., stone) and by location (e.g., underground).

Williams, Vera B. **It's a Gingerbread House**. Greenwillow, 1978.

Within the framework of a story about three children who receive a gingerbread house in the mail from their grandpa is a step-by-step recipe for making and decorating a gingerbread house. Patterns are also given.

Yue, David, and Charlotte Yue. **The Tipi**. Knopf, 1984.

Information about tepee (tipi) construction and a description of the Plains Indians who built them, as well as an examination of their way of life gives a comprehensive look at this complex kind of dwelling.

Skills List

Skill	Code
Self-Awareness	SA
Gross Motor	GM
Color Recognition	CR
Counting	CO
Size and Shape	SS
Following Directions	FD
Group Cooperation	GC
Role Playing/Creative Dramatics	RP
Sequencing	S
Classification	CL
Musical	M
Artistic	A
Language Play/Rhyme and Rhythm	RR
Word Recognition	WR
Cause and Effect	CE
Predictable Language/Outcome	L
Finger Plays	FP

Breakdown of Activities by Skills Area

Refer to Alphabetical Index of Activities for page numbers.

Self-Awareness Skills

Anywhere You Hang Your Hat Is Home
Are We Home Yet?
At My House
Budding Architects
Clean Up
Hidey Hole Hello
If You Could Choose Your Neighbors
My House Is Your House
New Neighbors
Open House
Picture My House
Place for My Face, A
Talk of the Town
Welcome Song

Gross Motor Skills

At My House
Birthday Party Streamer Game
Breakfast Symphony
Build a House—Quick
Building Our Dream House
Camp Misfortune
Cat and Mouse Game
Chair for Me, A
City Life Has Its Ups and Downs
Cobweb Tangle Game
Fix It Up
Household Ballet
Mummy Hunt
No Exit
Out the Window
Pocket Home
Quiet in the Country
Rain House
Rock Around the Room

Spooky Decorations
This Is the Castle
Town or Country
Under the Bed
Welcome Song
Where Do They Live?

Color Recognition Skills

Bedtime for Baby Bear
Birdhouse Song
Blanket Full of Love
Getting Your House in Shape
Home Run
More Blankets
Mouse House
Paint the Town Red
Perfect Match
This Place Is for the Birds
Very Height of Fashion
Where's the Last Egg?

Counting Skills

Ant Hill Antics
Anywhere You Hang Your Hat Is Home
At My House
Backyard Sleepover
Bats in the Belfry
Big Move, The
Blankets for My Bed
Decorating for Owl's Party
Easy as Pie
Five Little Boxes
Happy Birthday, Roberta Rhino
Home in a Trunk
Home on the Farm

Pup Tent
Scrubby Tub Bubbles
Simple Bath, A
Ten in the Nest
Tent Tenants
This Place Is for the Birds
Under the Bed
What Is Making the Noise and Why
What's in the Bed?
Where's the Last Egg?

Size and Shape Skills

Farm House Keys
Finding the Right House
Getting Your House in Shape
Gingerbread Girl, The
Happy Birthday, Roberta Rhino
Hightop Highrise
Home Is Where the Heart Is
Inside Penelope's Closet
Just Exactly Alike
Lend Me a Hand Craft
Mouse House
No Place Like Home
Open House Place Card
Talk of the Town
What's That Noise?
Your Very Own Home

Following Directions Skills

Adobe or Egyptian Mud House
Animal House
Apartment Noise
Birthday Party Streamer Game
Camp Misfortune
Castle Simplified
Cat and Mouse Game
City Life Has Its Ups and Downs
Cobweb Tangle Game
English Cottage
Everything-You-Ever-Wanted-in-a-
    Cleaning-Machine
Farmer Says
Frog Puppet
Good, Clean Fun
Haunted House Peek-a-boo Craft
Hidey Hole Hide-and-Seek
Home Hatching
In Tents
Keep the Home Fires Burning
Knock, Knock Craft

Log Cabin Pretzel House
More Blankets
Moving In and Out
Mummy Hunt
My Own House
Not-Just-Like-Everybody's House Craft
Packing Game
Perfect Match
Plains Indian Tepee
Puppy's Pup Tent
Roll Out the Red Carpet
Tent Time
Tour of Homes Worldwide
Town or Country
Track the Treats Game
Trunk Collage Craft
What's in the Bed?
Where Does This Go?
Zoo Cage Caper

Group Cooperation Skills

Cobweb Tangle Game
Everything-You-Ever-Wanted-in-a-
    Cleaning-Machine
Good, Clean Fun
Hidey Hole Hide-and-Seek
Keep the Home Fires Burning
More Blankets
Moving In and Out
Perfect Match
Tent Time
Town or Country
Track the Treats Game
Who Will Hide with You?
Zoo Cage Caper

Role Playing/Creative Dramatics

Apartment Noise
Decorating for Owl's Party
Everything-You-Ever-Wanted-in-a-
    Cleaning-Machine
Farmer Says
Ghost Hunt
Gypsy the Moth and the Bright Lights
House Fly
If You Could Choose Your Neighbors
Lazy Luke and the Clean Genies
My Very Own Hiding Place
Pup Tent
Rock Around the Room
Tent Tenants

Three Pigs in a Blanket
Tour of Homes Down through the Ages, A
Wreck Room
Zoo Cage Caper

Sequencing Skills
Animal Squatters
Apartment Noise
Are You Sure You Want to Go In?
Big Farmhouse, The
Blanket Full of Love
Blankets for My Bed
Build a House—Quick
Cocoon Tune
Easy as Pie
Eat You Out of House and Home
Fisherman and His Wife Retold, The
Fixing the House Song
Ghost Hunt
Gingerbread Girl, The
Gingerbread House Made to Order
Hightop Highrise
Home Hatching
Home in the Bottom of the Sea
Home Run
House Fly
Inside Penelope's Closet
Lazy Luke and the Clean Genies
More Blankets
Mouse House
Mummy Hunt
New at the Zoo
New House
No Exit
No Place Like Home
Pup Tent
Quiet as a Mouse
Room Service
Save Everything
Spring Cleaning
This Place Is for the Birds
This the House Where Jill Slept
Tour of Homes Down through the Ages, A
Very Height of Fashion
Welcome Home, Arthur
What's in the Bed?
What's Under the Bed?
Where Does It Go?
Where's the Last Egg?
Wreck Room

Classification Skills
Animal Homes Worldwide
Are We Home Yet
Budding Architects
Chair for Me
City and Country Homes
City Lights
Farm Homes
Farmer Says
Finding the Right House
Fisherman and His Wife Retold, The
Four Cities of the World
Gypsy the Moth and the Bright Lights
Heads in the Cloud and Feet on the Ground
Home in the Bottom of the Sea
Home Is Where the Heart Is
Home Run
Hot Houses and Cold Storage
House for Everyone, The
I'm Thinking of an Animal
Just the Right Place
My House Is Your House
Room Service
Rooms of the House Chant
Three Pigs in a Blanket
Tour of Homes Worldwide
Town House, Country House
Tree Full of Houses
Welcome to Our Tree Home
Where Do They Live?
Where Does It Go?
Where Does This Go?
Where's My Home?

Musical Skills
Animal Homes Worldwide
Apartment Noise
Big Farmhouse, The
Birdhouse Song
Birthday Party Streamer Game
Blankets for My Bed
Bugs in the Basement
Camp Kitchen
Castle, Castle in the Air
Cave Homes
City and Country Homes
City Life Has Its Ups and Downs
City Lights
Cocoon Tune
Decked Out for the Holidays

Decorate with Hearts and Lace
Down by the Old Mud Hole
Farm Homes
Fix It Up
Fixing the House Song
Floating Homes Everywhere
Gazebo Home
Ghost MacDonald's Haunted House
Home Cooking
Home Hatching
Home in the Bottom of the Sea
Home on the Farm
Home Spun
Hot Houses and Cold Storage
Kitchen Sounds Song
More Blankets
Motel Fun
Moving In and Out
Mud Room
New House
New Neighbors
Only in Fairy Land
Open House
Out the Window
Pocket Homes
Quiet in the Country
Raise the Roof
Scrubby Tub Bubbles
Secret Places I Like to Hide
Simple Bath, A
Spider's Open House
Spring Cleaning
Ten in the Nest
Tent Time
This House Must Be Haunted
Time to Clean
Tour of Homes Down through the Ages, A
Tour of Homes Worldwide
Tree Full of Houses
Uninvited Attic Guests
Welcome Song
Wet Towel Monster Your Mother Told You About
Whole Kitten and Kaboodle, The

Artistic Skills

Adobe or Egyptian Mud House
Budding Architects
Carpenter Ant Toolbox
Castle Simplified
City Night
Clean Up Your Act Craft
Closet Craft

Dollhouse Dream House
English Cottage
Frog Puppet
Getting Your House in Shape
Haunted House Peek-a-boo Craft
Hideaway Mask
If You Could Choose Your Neighbors
In Tents
Knock, Knock Craft
Lend Me a Hand Craft
Log Cabin Pretzel House
My Own Floor Plan
My Own House
Not-Just-Like-Everybody's House Craft
Open House Place Card
Paint the Town Red Craft
Picture My House
Plains Indian Tepee
Puppy's Pup Tent
Rapunzel in Her Tower Craft
Roll Out the Red Carpet
Room of Your Own Craft
Shoebox Highrise
Talk of the Town
Trunk Collage Craft
Underwater Home
Welcome to Our Tree Home
Where's My Home?
Who's Living in the Doghouse?
Your Very Own Home

Language Play/Rhyme and Rhythm Skills

Animal Homes Worldwide
Animal House
Animal Squatters
Ant Hill Antics
Anywhere You Hang Your Hat Is Home
Apartment Noise
Are We Home Yet?
Backyard Sleepover
Bedroom Pets
Big Farmhouse, The
Blankets for My Bed
Breakfast Symphony
Bugs in the Basement
Building Our Dream House
Bunk Full of Monkeys
Cabin Fever
Camp Kitchen
Castle, Castle in the Air
Cave Homes
Celebrate the Fourth

Chair for Me, A
Christmas Cheer
City and Country Homes
City Life Has Its Ups and Downs
City Lights
Clean Up
Cleaning Crew
Decked Out for the Holidays
Decorate with Hearts and Lace
Decorating for Owl's Party
Down by the Old Mud Hole
Five Little Boxes
Floating Homes Everywhere
Garden Jungle
Gazebo Home
Gingerbread Girl, The
Gingerbread House Made to Order
Gypsy the Moth and the Bright Lights
Head in the Clouds, Feet on the Ground
Here Is the House
Hidey Hole Hello
Home Cooking
Home in a Trunk
Home Is Where the Heart Is
Home on the Farm
Home Spun
Hot Houses and Cold Storage
Household Ballet
Keep It in My Room
Knock, Knock, Who's There?
Magic Door
More Room! More Room!
My House Is Your House
No Exit
Only in Fairy Land
Packing Chant
Packing Game
Perfect Match
Place for My Face, A
Pocket Home
Quiet as a Mouse
Rain House
Raise the Roof
Rock Around the Room
Rooms of the House Chant
Sand Castles
Save Everything
Secret Hiding Places
Spider's Open House
Spooky Decorations
Spring Cleaning
Ten in the Nest
Tent Tenants

This Is the Castle
This Place Is for the Birds
Three Pigs in a Blanket
Time to Clean
Tour of Homes Down through the Ages, A
Town House, Country House
Track the Treats Game
What's in the Bed?
What's That Noise?
Where Do They Live?
Whole Kitten and Kaboodle, The
Wreck Room
Yuri and the Yurt

Word Recognition Skills

Lend Me a Hand Craft
My Own Floor Plan
My Own House
Open House Place Card

Cause and Effect Skills

Backyard Sleepover
Bedtime for Baby Bear
Blankets for My Bed
Bugs in the Basement
Bunk Full of Monkeys
Cabin Fever
Decorating for Owl's Party
Eat You Out of House and Home
Fisherman and His Wife Retold, The
Garage Sale Junkie
Just the Right Place
Lazy Luke and the Clean Genies
More Room! More Room!
Out the Window
Paint the Town Red
Scrubby Tub Bubbles
Tent Tenants
Tour of Homes Down through the Ages, A
Town Mouse and Country Mouse
Uninvited Attic Guests
Wet Towel Monster Your Mother Told You About
What's That Noise?
Where's the Last Egg?
Yuri and the Yurt

Predictable Language Skills

Animal Squatters
Are You Sure You Want to Go In?

At My House
Bedroom Pets
Big Move, The
Easy as Pie
Garden Jungle
Knock, Knock, Who's There?
New at the Zoo
Pocket Homes
Sand Castles
Scrubby Tub Bubbles
Silly Homes for Silly Pets
Simple Bath, A
Tent Tenants
This House Must Be Haunted
This the House Where Jill Slept
Three Pigs in a Blanket
Tree Full of Houses

Wet Towel Monster Your Mother Told You About
What Is Making the Noise and Why
Where Does It Go?
Where's the Last Egg?

Finger Plays

Ant Hill Antics
At My House
Backyard Sleepover
Breakfast Symphony
Cleaning Crew
Five Little Boxes
Here Is the House
Place for My Face, A
This Is the Castle

Alphabetical Index
of Activities Showing
Associated Skills

This index is designed so that it can be used in two ways: All the activities in the book—games, songs, crafts, projects, etc.—are listed alphabetically, each with its page number. Thus we have an activities index. In addition, the skills enriched by the activities in *Raising the Roof* are listed across the top of each column (see Skills List on p. 221 for code key), and for each activity *X*'s mark the associated skills. Thus we have a chart for immediate skill identification.

Activity	SA	GM	CR	CO	SS	FD	GC	RP	S	CL	M	A	RR	WR	CE	PL	FP
Adobe or Egyptian Mud House (p. 78)						X					X						
Animal Homes Worldwide (p. 161)									X	X		X					
Animal House (p. 24)						X					X						
Animal Squatters (p. 102, 112, 125)								X			X				X		
Ant Hill Antics (p. 163)				X							X						X
Anywhere You Hang Your Hat Is Home (p. 2)	X			X							X						
Apartment Noise (p. 40)						X	X	X	X		X						
Are We Home Yet? (p. 30)	X								X		X						
Are You Sure You Want to Go In? (p. 187)								X							X		
At My House (p. 4)	X	X		X										X			X
Backyard Sleepover (p. 51)				X									X	X			X
Bats in the Belfry (p. 161)				X													
Bedroom Pets (p. 13)													X		X		
Bedtime for Baby Bear (p. 160)			X											X			
Big Farmhouse, The (p. 44)					X				X		X	X					
Big Move, The (p. 112, 131)				X											X		
Birdhouse Song (p. 169)			X							X							
Birthday Party Streamer Game (p. 107)		X				X				X							
Blanket Full of Love (p. 95)			X					X									
Blankets for My Bed (p. 95)			X					X			X		X		X		
Breakfast Symphony (p. 5)		X									X						X
Budding Architects (p. 53)	X									X		X					
Bugs in the Basement (p. 141)											X		X		X		
Build a House—Quick (p. 122)		X						X									
Building Our Dream House (p. 118)		X									X						
Bunk Full of Monkeys (p. 21)											X		X				
Cabin Fever (p. 66)											X		X				
Camp Kitchen (p. 50)										X	X						
Camp Misfortune (p. 50)		X				X											
Carpenter Ant Toolbox (p. 133)												X					
Castle Simplified (p. 78)						X					X						
Castle, Castle in the Air (p. 207)											X	X					
Cat and Mouse Game (p. 51)		X				X											
Cave Homes (p. 65)											X	X					
Celebrate the Fourth (p. 103)												X					
Chair for Me, A (p. 23)		X							X			X					
Christmas Cheer (p. 103)												X					
City and Country Homes (p. 33)										X	X	X					
City Life Has Its Ups and Downs (p. 38)		X				X					X	X					
City Lights (p. 37)										X	X	X					
City Night (p. 54)											X						

Activity	SA	GM	CR	CO	SS	FD	GC	RP	S	CL	M	A	RR	WR	CE	PL	FP
My Very Own Hiding Place (p. 154)								X									
New at the Zoo (p. 173)									X						X		
New House (p. 118)									X	X							
New Neighbors (p. 125)	X									X							
No Exit (p. 72)		X							X				X				
No Place Like Home (p. 144)						X			X								
Not-Just-Like-Everybody's House Craft (p. 108)						X					X						
Only in Fairy Land (p. xiv, 193)									X	X							
Open House (p. 113)	X								X								
Open House Place Card (p. 25)					X						X		X				
Out the Window (p. 89)		X								X				X			
Packing Chant (p. 126)													X				
Packing Game (p. 132)						X							X				
Paint the Town Red (p. 101)			X											X			
Paint the Town Red Craft (p. 108)											X						
Perfect Match (p. 25)			X			X	X						X				
Picture My House (p. 54)	X										X						
Place for My Face, A (p. 3)	X												X				X
Plains Indian Tepee (p. 78)						X					X						
Pocket Home (p. 163)		X											X				
Pocket Homes (p. 138)											X				X		
Pup Tent (p. 142)				X			X	X									
Puppy's Pup Tent (p. 154)						X					X						
Quiet as a Mouse (p. 146)									X				X				
Quiet in the Country (p. 45)		X								X							
Rain House (p. 142)		X											X				
Raise the Roof (p. 118)											X		X				
Rapunzel in Her Tower Craft (p. 212)											X						
Rock Around the Room (p. 24)		X					X						X				
Roll Out the Red Carpet (p. 25)						X					X						
Room of Your Own Craft (p. 108)											X						
Room Service (p. 48)								X	X								
Rooms of the House Chant (p. 4)										X			X				
Sand Castles (p. 208)													X		X	X	
Save Everything (p. 139)									X				X				
Scrubby Tub Bubbles (p. 16)				X						X					X	X	
Secret Hiding Places (xiii, 152)													X				
Secret Places I Like to Hide (p. xiii, 143)										X							
Shoebox Highrise (p. 52)											X						
Silly Homes for Silly Pets (p. 171)																X	
Simple Bath, A (p. 17)				X						X						X	

Activity	SA	GM	CR	CO	SS	FD	GC	RP	S	CL	M	A	RR	WR	CE	PL	FP
Who's Living in the Doghouse? (p. 178)												X					
Whole Kitten and Kaboodle, The (p. 112, 126)										X		X					
Wreck Room (p. 90)							X	X				X					
Your Very Own Home (p. 53)					X						X						
Yuri and the Yurt (p. 56, 67)													X		X		
Zoo Cage Caper (p. 177)						X		X	X								

Literature Index

About the Authors

JAN IRVING

Jan Irving has been a teacher, a children's librarian, and a visiting professor of children's library services at the University of Iowa's School of Library and Information Science. She was a 1984 recipient of the Putnam Publishing Award sponsored by the Association for Library Service to Children of the American Library Association. In addition to the three other resource books (*Mudluscious*, *Glad Rags*, and *Full Speed Ahead*) with Robin Currie, Jan has authored *Fanfares: Programs for Classrooms and Libraries* for Libraries Unlimited and coordinated the state summer library program for the State Library of Iowa. She currently presents workshops and teacher inservices and lectures nationally in addition to her writing and storytelling.

Jan lives in Iowa with her husband, two teenage children, and two dogs. She loves to travel and enjoys all kinds of ethnic food.

ROBIN CURRIE

Robin Currie received her master of library science degree from the University of Iowa in 1983. She is currently Grade School Liaison for the Palatine Public Library District and School District 15 in Palatine, Illinois. She has been library director in a rural Iowa community, consultant for an Illinois library system, and a curriculum editor. She wrote *Mudluscious*, *Glad Rags*, and *Full Speed Ahead* with Jan Irving, for Libraries Unlimited. She is also the author of *Rainbows and Ice Cream: Storytimes about Things Kids Like* and *Double Rainbows: More Storytimes about Things Kids Like*, both for the Iowa State Library.